# Practical
# reference
# work

*Second edition*

# Practical reference work

## Second edition

Denis Grogan

*Senior Lecturer, Department of Information
and Library Studies, University
College of Wales, Aberystwyth*

LIBRARY ASSOCIATION PUBLISHING
LONDON
A CLIVE BINGLEY BOOK

© Denis Joseph Grogan 1979, 1991

Published by
Library Association Publishing Ltd
7 Ridgmount Street
London WC1E 7AE

First published 1979
This second edition 1992


British Library Cataloguing in Publication Data

Grogan, Denis
    Practical reference work. — 2nd ed.
    I. Title
    025.5

    ISBN 0 85157 409 2

Typeset from author's disks in 10/12pt Baskerville by Library Association Publishing Ltd.
Printed in Great Britain by Bookcraft Ltd., Midsomer Norton, Avon.

# Contents

# Introduction

There is only one satisfactory way to learn the art of reference work, and that is to do it. Samuel Butler once said that 'An art can only be learned in the workshop of those who are winning their bread by it', and reference librarians acknowledged this very early. Over the last century each generation of reference librarians has confirmed it afresh. The very first published article to use the term 'reference work' included a paper read exactly a hundred years ago in May 1891 by William B. Child, who succeeded Melvil Dewey as Librarian of Columbia College (soon to become Columbia University). He gave as his considered opinion that 'the first three qualifications indispensable to a reference librarian are: 1st, experience; 2d, experience; 3d, experience'. In 1937 in his widely read column 'Reference libraries' in the *Library Association record* Herbert Woodbine wrote that 'experience does, time after time, show the way to the solution of a problem'. In 1985 the assessment of Fred Batt, head of a university reference department in the United States, was that 'One truism that I find for reference services is that there is no substitute for experience'.

But this is not to imply that there is no profit in taking time to study and to think and even to read about the subject. Of course books cannot furnish a substitute for practice, but they can prepare the mind for a more rapid assimilation of experience, and they can develop and broaden understanding of even the most practical arts, from building bridges to playing the violin. And where the art is based on a body of theory it can be studied as a discipline as well as practised as an art. Alfred North Whitehead draws a distinction between a craft, 'based on customary activities and modified by the trial and error of individual practice', and a profession, 'whose activities are subject to theoretical analysis, and are modified by theoretical conclusions derived from that analysis'. Learning the theoretical basis of a professional discipline by relying on unstructured experience alone is haphazard and time-

1

consuming. As Minna Antrim put it, 'Experience is a good teacher but she sends in terrific bills'. In the case of reference work, resting as it does on a basis of systematic bibliography, close theoretical study of the reference process is necessary if the art is to be more than mere mental gymnastics.

As important as the bibliographical component in reference work is the human element, its intrinsic one-to-one, and usually face-to-face, nature, comprising all that is encompassed by the term 'reference interview'. This too is an art, and though it can quite usefully be studied as a special branch of the well-established discipline of human interpersonal communication, Peter McNally informed an audience of reference librarians in 1977: 'I have no hesitation in saying that the reference interview must ultimately be learned, not taught'.

The student should note that this volume deals only with reference work in the strict sense, defined by Samuel Rothstein as 'the personal assistance given by the librarian to individual readers in pursuit of information'. It does not discuss reference service in general, which Robert E. Balay has concluded 'consists of whatever it is that reference departments do'. Though reference work is the backbone of their task, reference librarians do lots of things that are not reference work: in a 1974 PhD thesis C. B. Duncan identified 118 different tasks being performed in reference departments in college and university libraries; and a 1977 listing at the University of Kentucky library reference department, based on interviews with the staff themselves, comprised 93 activities.

There is therefore nothing here on the study, evaluation, and selection of reference materials, or on bibliographical compilation, or on current awareness services and the dissemination of information. Similarly, user education, community information (or information and referral) service, and interlibrary loans, which are sometimes regarded as reference services, are not treated here. Readers' advisory service, or guidance in the choice of books to read – that most delicate form of personal assistance to readers, sadly neglected in the West for a generation or more – is not reference work either, strictly speaking, and has also been omitted. The student will probably know already that the term 'reference service' is frequently used in the literature and in libraries when the narrower term 'reference work' would strictly be more accurate.

The first edition of this book in 1979 appeared as one of a series of 'Outlines', and although when inviting me to prepare this second edition the publisher was able to offer somewhat more space, the work retains the same character – that is to say, only the framework of the subject is sketched in. This means, to take one example, that although the computer features largely in most chapters, no attempt is made to teach the specifics of online searching, a topic on which there are many excellent and detailed textbooks. It is hoped, nevertheless, that the whole area of reference work has been comprehensively mapped and that the salient points thus marked will allow the student exploring the terrain to chart an individual route without difficulty. For the beginner the intention has been to offer an immediate plunge into the world of *practical* reference work, though necessarily at one remove from actual enquirers with their real problems.

The intensely personal character of reference work, ministering to so basic a need as the desire to know, means that its underlying principles have changed little, if at all, over the century or so since they were first established, as will become plain to the alert reader of this text. Nevertheless, this revision attempts to use the extra space provided by the publisher to reflect the more important developments in the field over the last dozen years or so. Notably, these include the ever-advancing front of the new technology (as exemplified by online public access catalogues (OPACs), databases in compact disc read-only memory (CD-ROM) form, expert systems, etc.); the greatly increased attention paid to the human factor in reference work, specifically the reference interview; recent illuminating work on question analysis and taxonomy; new perceptions from cognitive research into the roots of information-seeking behaviour; some sharp new insights into the search process, reaping the fruits of 20 years' experience with online databases; and the spread of direct and specific methods of evaluating reference work with their less than flattering findings.

More has been published on reference work in the dozen years since the first edition than in any comparable earlier period. On every point that I have touched I am aware that there is much more that could have been said, and I am even more conscious of issues not even mentioned, such as the role of non-professionals in reference work, the charging of fees to users, and attempts at cost-benefit analysis in the reference field.

I have not tried to be original and I have drawn constantly on the findings and opinions of others. Like Montaigne, the 16th-century French essayist, 'I have gathered a posie of other men's [more commonly women's] flowers and nothing but the thread that binds them is my own'. Furthermore I have to admit that this does not pretend to be a work of scholarship: the reader will not find my borrowings supported by the academic apparatus of footnote and bibliographical citation. The literature of reference work, even strictly defined, extends over a century and amounts to thousands of papers and dozens of books in the English language alone, and to cite all my sources would add unnecessary bulk to an outline text designed to be affordable by the student. Where I feel I owe a particular debt to the writings of a specific individual for an illuminating idea or a penetrating insight, I mention the author by name (and include the name in the index), but I confess I have drawn on most of my colleagues' work without acknowledgement.

The 268 examples of reference queries used to illustrate points that I wish to make are in every instance actual genuine questions that have been asked in libraries by real enquirers.

In my other books on reference work I have been at pains to explain that they were not written as 'how-to-do-it' manuals. This volume *is*. Of course, I do not claim that my way is the only way, and in any case much of the advice I offer is culled from the experience and writings of others; but it is based on many years' front-line experience of enquirers' problems, followed by even more years of study and observation and teaching about reference work. This then is confessedly a prescriptive work: it really does set out to advise novice reference librarians of the best way to practise their art. In this I am merely the latest follower in a distinct tradition in reference work reaching back over a hundred years. The very first published paper on the subject in 1876 was openly didactic in tone: 'In such a case, of course, the librarian must get the books which contain the desired information, and hand them to the reader open at the proper pages'.

To forestall one inevitable criticism I had better explain that I have thought it right in a textbook for students to take the perhaps idealistic view that where library users have questions to which they require answers, the responsible library authorities have provided the resources, including enough appropriately trained staff, to answer them. The fact that this is increasingly not the case is plain to see. As Donald Davinson so characteristically put it in his 1980 text, 'Reality is often too few staff chasing too much work and never quite catching up with it ... the actuality for most reference librarians is a desperate plugging of the more obvious holes in the library dyke to hold back the flood-tide of enquiries which threaten to swamp them.'

There are also indications that a combination of diminishing real resources with a growing burden of demand for new services – what

William Miller has called 'reference sprawl' – has reduced morale and even provoked symptoms in some reference librarians of 'burnout', defined in its briefest form by Christina Maslach as 'a syndrome of emotional exhaustion and cynicism that occurs frequently among individuals who do "people-work" '. The evidence is not conclusive, and many would echo George R. Bauer's view: 'I confess a certain amount of impatience with the concept'. Stress does not inevitably lead to burnout; indeed for some it provides a needed stimulus. Some studies seeking to investigate stress and burnout among reference librarians have failed to find any. Julie E. Hodges noted wryly that 'The stress level of librarians rose dramatically when Professor Cary Cooper [an occupational psychologist at the University of Manchester Institute of Science and Technology] ranked them bottom in an occupational stress "league table" in 1984. The Professor was besieged by letters from outraged librarians.' The conclusion reached in 1990 by David P. Fisher after a thorough survey of the literature was that 'it is not possible to state that the questions posed . . . have been satisfactorily answered; librarians may or may not be burning out'.

It has been my intention to produce a work of equal use to those wishing to be academic, special, or public reference librarians. As Margaret Hutchins pointed out in her 1944 textbook, 'The actual techniques used in answering reference questions are fundamentally the same in all types of libraries'. A generation later Gerald Jahoda and Judith Schiek Braunagel confirmed in their 1980 text that this was still the case: 'While reference services may differ from library to library, the process of satisfying specific information needs probably remains essentially the same'. This book may also help prepare those entering what some have called 'alternative librarianship', who do not practice their profession within a library or information unit at all, but serve as specialists in answering questions, locating information, and assisting in the process of synthesizing knowledge, plying their trade on the open market, for fees. Variously described as freelance or itinerant librarians, librarians-without-a-library, private researchers, information consultants, independent information specialists, and so on, and more usually now as information brokers, they form an ever-growing corps within the profession. Perhaps too, since their information skills are identical, the advice given here might benefit a similar group of search intermediaries, intelligence officers, in-house strategists, interface specialists, resource persons, and the like, increasingly to be found functioning as the house reference librarian for planning units, research groups, clinical teams, think-tanks, and so on, working as an integral member of a small user group.

And finally I would wish once again to express my gratitude to the successive generations of my own students at the University College of Wales Department of Information and Library Studies (formerly the College of Librarianship Wales), without whom this book would never have been written.

*D. J. Grogan*
*Aberystwyth*
*May 1991*

# — 1 —

## Reference work

There is a university library in the United States which has carved over its front door this aphorism: 'The half of knowledge is knowing where to find it'. This is a reference to the oft-quoted saying by the great Dr Samuel Johnson over 200 years ago, 'Knowledge is of two kinds. We know a subject ourselves, or we know where we can find information upon it.' This in its turn has frequently been taken as a text by reference librarians, for it gives recognition to the sources of information as a branch of knowledge – what Louis Shores has called the *where* of scholarship as opposed to the *what*. More recently it has been adopted by online searchers, heading a chapter in a 1982 textbook on search strategies, and appearing in a 1987 brochure advertising the services of an online search broker.

We have left far behind us the day (if ever there was such) when a single human mind could encompass all knowledge: we are told that it was possible in ancient times, but by the late Middle Ages it was already slipping beyond reach. The Renaissance Man was probably an impossible ideal, with perhaps Leonardo da Vinci approaching closest. Leibniz (1646 – 1716) was said to be the last man to know everything; this was a pardonable exaggeration, for he was a universal genius, renowned as a lawyer, mathematician, philosopher, scientist, historian, linguist, theologian, politician, and man of affairs. He was, moreover, 'the greatest librarian of his age', according to the *Encyclopaedia Britannica*, serving for many years as Court Librarian to the Dukes of Brunswick; and though a Lutheran, he was offered the post of head of the Vatican Library, which he declined. When he died, the young Johnson was just about to enter Lichfield Grammar School.

It was, however, still possible in particular subject areas to master all that was known – in astronomy, for example, or anatomy; and this remained true for some while. But by the time the mature Johnson uttered his famous dictum in 1775, even this limited goal was receding over the horizon. A hundred years later, the ancillary skill of knowing where to find information had in its turn begun to elude the grasp of those who needed it for their study and research. In Ranganathan's words, 'It was no longer possible for the scholar to be his own reference librarian'.

**The profession of reference work**
Thus was born the art of reference work as a professional accomplishment of the librarian. Then, as now, it had only one justification: library users, helped by the reference librarian, are able to get better value from a library's collections than they would on their own. This 'maximization of resources' is the principle lying at the heart of the very concept of the library, which is the collective sharing and use of graphic records for the benefit of society as a whole and of the individuals making up that society. After all, Ranganathan's First Law of Library Science is that 'Books are for use'.

In the case of reference work, however, this task of exploiting the store of accumulated wisdom has been entrusted to human agents, who supplement and reinforce the help afforded by the library's cataloguing and classification systems by providing personal assistance to individual users in search of information. This 'living link between the text and the reader' is necessary because, as James I. Wyer explained in 1930 in the first textbook ever written on reference work, 'it is not possible to organize books so mechanically, so perfectly, as to dispense with personal service in their use'. Donald Davinson further explained in his textbook, just 50 years later, that the role of the reference librarian is 'to comprehend the structures of recorded knowledge where they exist and to assist in the structuring process where they do not'.

But reference work is more than a contrivance for the convenience of the user. One of the facts of library life is that much of the material in the collections requires deliberate exploitation if it is to be of benefit. As Kenneth Whittaker has pointed out, 'The purpose of reference and information service is to allow information to flow efficiently from information sources to those who need information. Without the librarian bringing source and seeker together, the flow would either never take place at all, or only take place inefficiently.' Mary Francillon used an illuminating analogy: 'There is a sort of equation by which each question eventually meets the proper answer, but in every case, someone must write the equation, must put in the equivalent sign – indeed in a sense, must be the equivalent sign'.

Reference librarians know this well enough: they see examples every day. Approaches that would be second nature to even the most inexperienced librarian often come as a revelation to many users. Nonplussed to discover from the catalogue that the library has no books on urban bicycle routes, for example, they are amazed to learn of the existence of *Current technology index* and *Applied science and technology index* and gratified to discover that each lists several periodical articles on the topic.

Unfortunately, many library users have been led to believe that in a properly organized collection they can find their own answers without help. Yet a whole generation of research into catalogue use has demonstrated conclusively that with known-item searches (i.e., for a specific author and/or title as distinct from a subject) up to a quarter of users fail to find what they are looking for in the library catalogue, even where the materials are owned by the library and represented in the catalogue. User studies also show that most searchers then give up, with only about a fifth asking the librarian for help. And so far as subject searches are concerned, Mary Robinson Sive has reminded us recently that 'Despite what is frequently taught and what is widely believed by the public, the card catalog is not the place to start a subject search'. Marcia J. Bates tells us that 'between two-thirds and three-quarters of catalog subject searches involve only one lookup ... most library catalog users do not revise their original search and try again'.

The coming of the online public access catalogue (OPAC), and more recently similar catalogues in compact disc read-only memory (CD-ROM) format, has transformed the scene in many ways, notably by increasing the apparent ease of subject searching by means of keywords, and users have certainly taken to OPACs 'like ducks to water', as one writer put it. But failure at the catalogue is still a major issue, with OPACs bringing in their train a new set of problems.

It is common knowledge that a proportion of known-item searches in the card catalogue fail because the user comes with inaccurate or defective bibliographical information, usually a garbled title or a misspelt author. This proportion tends to increase in an OPAC search, as the unforgiving computer does not permit the 'fumble and stumble' method that can sometimes hit on what is wanted by browsing through an alphabetical sequence of cards, and research has revealed that OPAC users are weak at spelling. Surveys also show that they have particular difficulties in devising strategies for coping when an unmanageably large number of items are retrieved, or at the opposite extreme, when no matches are found.

At present most OPACs supplement existing card (or microfiche) catalogues, requiring both to be consulted for a comprehensive search. Some users appear unaware of this, but in any case they have always resisted looking in more than one place, and this reluctance is reinforced by the presence of an OPAC, perceived as so much more user-friendly than the card or fiche format. And even though there is already evidence to show that searchers actually perform more successfully and speedily at the unpopular card catalogue than at the fashionable OPAC, this is not sufficient to persuade them: at least one is on record as admitting 'I know I do better in the card catalog, but I still prefer online'.

Reference librarians therefore have always had to devote a substantial part of their time to interpreting the catalogue for users. In 1971 after survey visits to 13 major United States university libraries, Florence Blakely was reporting that 'Reference librarians simply accept the fact of life that the card catalog is almost totally nonself-explanatory to the majority of library users'. Similarly, Gillian M. McCombs, herself a university cataloguer, felt obliged to conclude in 1985 that 'readers are quite incapable of using a library catalog without help of some sort, written or oral'.

As with the catalogue, so too with the other sources comprising the information store, whether in printed or electronic form: bibliographies, reference materials, and the literature in the field. As William Miller has explained, 'Finding information in a library, and particularly a large research library, is difficult ... We try to make libraries seem easy and enjoyable. But the real world is a complex place, and application of even simple principles of library use is difficult and frustrating for the inexperienced.' Unfortunately, the increased provision of bibliographic instruction has tended to strengthen rather than dispel the myth of user self-sufficiency. Constance McCarthy is obviously right when she says that 'people have been allowed to think that they have enough instruction to use libraries without help ... Their idea of library research, if they can be said to have one, is extremely naive, and they have no conception at all of the complexity of the bibliographic universe.' Indeed she believes that many reference users feel guilt and anger when they discover their skills are inadequate. Alexander Pope's warning that 'A little learning is a dangerous thing' was never more appropriate. As Frederick Holler claims, 'Information retrieval is nothing less than a full-fledged discipline and not simply a minor skill acquirable as a byproduct of other studies'.

There really is no room for doubt on this score. As Stephen Stoan

10

has reminded us about the results of library skills tests, 'almost everyone but professional librarians routinely fail'. It would nowadays be perverse to deny that the mastery of the bibliographical and reference tools necessary to exploit a library's potential is beyond the reach of those without extensive training in systematic bibliography. The truth of this is recognized by some non-librarians also. Worried by his students' reluctance to consult the librarian as distinct from the library, Donald MacRae, professor of sociology at the London School of Economics, once told a conference 'Where official papers, statistical sources, documentary and/or local sources are involved it can be a severe handicap not just to the political scientist, but to all library users'.

The view of Eve Johansson, Head of Reading Room Information at the British Library and formerly in the Official Publications Library, was that 'The approach of the old British Museum assumed that, given a general library catalogue and the provision of necessary reference works, a reader would be able to find out for himself the information he wanted with a minimum of help from staff. This approach assumes a degree of knowledge about the material he is handling which is conspicuously lacking with most users of official publications: and it is the job of the staff doing reference work to supplement it.'

Like official publications, periodicals require for their exploitation the exercise of advanced reference skills. In 1990 Barbara P. Pinzelik published a flow chart for finding information in periodicals that has eight levels to negotiate, incorporating 38 decision points. She argued that 'Using periodicals [for a subject search] is more complex and bewildering than [even] librarians care to admit. The steps needed for a successful completion of an information need can weed out all but the most determined user. Reference assistance with periodicals is essential.'

### The reference librarian

Such claims might seem like arrogance to many library users, and perhaps even to some librarians. But they are not. They are the cool and perfectly proper expression of a confident professionalism, still only faintly discernible, sad to relate, in dealings with users, and largely absent from the image of the reference librarian conceived by the far more numerous non-users.

If to the general public the librarian is a 'fussy old woman of either sex, myopic and repressed', to use Penny Cowell's words, 'surrounded by an array of notices which forbid virtually every human activity', it is not unreasonable to assume that, as is the case with many such stereotypes, the image did once have a kernel of truth and nowadays owes its perpetuation to folk memory. As Steven Falk has explained, 'The status of any profession is determined by a host of factors that have evolved over the history of a profession. For librarianship, such factors include the fact that the profession is a female-dominated one, that the majority of people in a given community (including a campus community) do not need and do not use their library, that librarians are transmitters rather than creators of information, that most librarians are public employees, and that most libraries are nonprofit institutions in a profit-oriented society.'

It is regularly urged in the professional literature that 'there is a need in some way to change the image'. This is a mammoth task, but it can be achieved. It is not done, however, by fabricating a counter-image, or indeed by any form of 'public relations', such as altering the occupational label, or 'position designation', as has been frequently proposed. John Galsworthy said that 'the blowing of one's own trumpet is the insidious beginning of the inferiority complex'. The secret is to change the reality behind the image and let the image take care of itself. This is not accomplished overnight: it took the barber-surgeons several generations.

As Norma J. Shosid urged some years ago, one important step along this road would be the firming up or even redefining of librarians' own concepts of their role. It is at least arguable that the discreditable public image is to some extent a reflection of the librarian's own self-image. Laurence Clark Powell has pointed out that because 'librarians are stereotyped as prim, austere, timid, nondescript, dull, superficial, petty, and tyrannical technicians ... this popular conception ... has come to be believed of themselves by many librarians'. The results of a 1974 British opinion survey showed clearly that 'librarians are certainly seen as introverted [and] even serving librarians saw the profession as significantly so'. David P. Fisher too, a sociologist-turned-librarian, has remarked that 'Librarians seem to want to make things worse for themselves and confirm their stereotypes', even though his own examination of the psychological data led him to conclude in 1988 that 'no matter what conventional stereotypes assert, we have not found any evidence to support the argument that the majority of librarians have a distinct personality type'. In her remarkable analysis of 1,221 comments on the stereotype made by United States librarians in their own writings between 1921 and 1978, Pauline Wilson found that '62 percent of the sentences analyzed constituted acceptance of the stereotype'. The sad irony is that some of the public too have now come to take librarians at their own valuation.

Even those who are regular library users know little of what librarians do, and non-users inevitably know less. The activities they see and the staff they encounter are mainly clerical or manual. But of the professional activities they do observe or make use of, direct personal assistance by the reference librarian is the most visible, and as Carl M. White pointed out, 'if we may judge from the prefaces of books, the one *consciously* most appreciated'. But those who are aware of the existence of reference service still make up only a small minority of the general public. It was in fact a library school student who confessed in an examination script, 'I admit that before I started this course I was unaware of the fact that the library did provide a reference [i.e., enquiry answering] service'. And even among this enlightened minority, as Wilson has pointed out, 'the librarian's knowledge is sometimes assumed to be general knowledge of the contents of the books and journals in the library's collection rather than specialized knowledge of bibliographical apparatus and library processes'. There is a long line of research investigations that shows, to use Samuel Rothstein's words, that 'reference is indeed the secret service'.

It is tempting to blame the populace for their ignorance, but this would be to dodge the real issue. If librarians *as a group* would calmly and publicly and increasingly lay claim to this area as their professional domain and, more to the point, guarantee willing and efficient service to all would-be users who take them at their word, they would gradually bring about that change in public attitudes that many desire to see.

## Reference policy and reference philosophy
But what lies in the way is what Sandra M. Naiman has called the 'agonized, organized self-doubt of librarianship'. The melancholy truth of the matter is that for at least three generations reference librarians have been unable to reach agreement on what to the average intelligent bystander is the blindingly obvious proposition, so clearly stated by William A. Katz in the most widely used textbook on the subject: 'the first duty of the reference librarian, quite simply, is to answer questions'. In their profound and perceptive essay on professionalism Mary Lee Bundy and Paul Wasserman wrote at some length on this extraordinary phenomenon, 'the essential timidity of practitioners, clearly reflected in the widespread, deep-seated, and trained incapacity or high degree

of reluctance to assume responsibility for solving informational problems and providing unequivocal answers'.

Such apparently self-evident objectives need only be stated in some quarters for immediate reservations to be voiced and qualifications made and caveats entered. To take some common examples, many academic libraries will not answer telephone enquiries from students, or any questions at all from people unconnected with the university or college; the policy of a number of public libraries is not to accept puzzle or quiz questions, or enquiries from people trying to trace their ancestors.

This of course is their privilege, and doubtless they have good reasons for adopting such policies. Confusingly for the user, however, other libraries – public and academic, and apparently identical in character – place no such limitations on their service. And whatever the policy, only a minority have it stated in black and white and even fewer have made it known publicly, despite the availability since 1979 of a model from the American Library Association in the form of a 'Draft outline of information service policy manual'. Even within the individual institution the situation may well parallel that in one large university library in the United States which reported deadlock in its attempts to devise a policy statement because 'We found it difficult to come to a consensus of the professional staff on several key points'. In practice, what often happens is that several different unofficial policies are implemented at the same time by individual members of staff, or as Dorothy Broderick more bluntly put it, 'the individual librarian is given free rein to impose his or her own biases'. In any professional task this could be a potent source of friction between colleagues working side by side, but particularly so in this field because 'individual principles of conduct affect reference librarianship more than any other library activity', as Bernard Vavrek has pointed out.

To young librarians taking their first steps in reference work such a climate of opinion may well be bracing and challenging; perhaps more often its effect is to bewilder. A 1980 study in six Australian academic libraries found that 'many reference librarians are not certain as to the central purpose of reference work and that service attitudes are confused'. Even plainer to see is the effect of this library lottery on enquirers: in Naiman's words, 'patrons do not know what they can reasonably, legitimately expect', with the result that, as Katz has written, 'never knowing quite what to expect, the patron usually expects little or nothing'. There is no doubt that many users with questions to ask do not choose to negotiate this built-in hazard. Maurice Line's 1962

14

survey of undergraduate library users at Southampton found that 39% were disinclined to put their queries to library staff. More significant still were the reasons given: 70% of this reluctant group felt that their question was too elementary to bother the librarian with. A similar 1972 survey on the other side of the Atlantic found that 41% of Syracuse University library users had questions they wanted answering, but 65% of them said they 'would not ask a librarian for aid because they were not satisfied with the image or past service of a librarian, or because they felt the question was too simple, or they didn't want to bother the librarian'. To illustrate further the puzzle posed for users by differential policies, implicit or explicit, a good example was provided by the University of Chicago: a 1975 survey by Mollie Sandock showed that less than half the students knew that the reference library would help find the answer to a factual question or deal with questions on the telephone.

The major obstacle to the resolution of this perpetual dilemma is the presence in the profession of a strong lobby whose unwavering views were well expressed in 1984 by Ray Lester, librarian of the London Business School: 'the academic user should answer his own question rather than the librarian because: a. Only he really understands what he needs. b. Answering, with its refinement of the question, is an integral part of the research process. c. Only he can judge the value of the material he retrieves'. Many of those who support this argument establish their case on pragmatic policy grounds, but others are concerned at a deeper philosophical level. The ideal of 'self-help' has a respectable 19th-century pedigree: in 1876 Otis Hall Robinson, librarian of the University of Rochester, was arguing that 'No [college] librarian is fit for his place unless he holds himself to some degree responsible for the library education of his students ... if we send students out self-reliant in their investigations, we have accomplished very much.' Even some public librarians argued along similar lines: over a hundred years ago Andrea Crestadoro was proclaiming in Manchester that 'It is the duty of a librarian to make himself useless'. Another vigorous prophet of self-help was John Cotton Dana, for many years librarian of Newark Public Library. In a paper read in 1910, 'Misdirection of effort in reference work', he asserted that 'The prime duty of the library is not to answer the question, but to instruct the inquirer in the use of the material by which he may secure the answer for himself'.

For some the issue even has a moral dimension: there have always been librarians uneasy about giving too much help to enquirers. Like W. H. Auden's Oxford don who admitted 'I don't feel quite happy about pleasure', they are concerned that by answering enquirers' questions for them they are taking on work which users should be doing for themselves. This is the 'reference librarian as puritan' syndrome, to use Katz's trenchant phrase.

The role that the late-20th-century disciples of Robinson, Crestadoro, and Dana envisage for the reference librarian is primarily that of teacher. They would give first priority to library user education, or bibliographic instruction, as it is sometimes called, with the aim of providing, in the words of the American Library Association, 'guidance and direction in the pursuit of information, rather than providing the information itself'.

Of course, reference service in its broadest sense has generally included both the informational (i.e., reference work) and the instructional functions; but, as Anita Schiller pointed out in her 1965 study of this long-running dispute, 'these have often been at cross purposes to one another, because each has been associated with a conflicting view of the kind and amount of assistance to be offered'. In 1930 in his pioneer textbook Wyer characterized these opposing views as 'conservative' and 'liberal', with a 'moderate' school as a practical compromise. Thirty years later in a seminal paper Rothstein revived the controversy with his own version of the dispute and his own alliterative labels for the contending dogmas: 'minimum', 'maximum', and 'middling'.

No one denies that students should know how to use libraries, and if required should be taught, up to a certain level of competence. The tussle starts when it is argued that they should be trained to become independent 'so they will not remain forever dependent on the costly and inefficient services of the reference librarian', as Daniel Gore argued.

By 1980 Davinson was describing user education as 'one of the biggest growth industries in the library field', and in 1987 Katz reported in his text that 'A vast amount of time, energy, and money has been funneled into library instruction over the past 20 or 30 years'. It has been claimed that in the United States over 3,000 individuals are active in the field, and over 75% of advertisements for academic reference librarians stipulate bibliographic instruction as an integral part of the job. Not surprisingly, this 'library instruction juggernaut', as at least two observers have described it, has generated a whole shelf-full of literature and has added new spice to the debate. Its proponents have

16

pitched their camp on the highest possible policy ground, issuing a manifesto in 1981 in the form of 'Think Tank recommendations' from the Bibliographic Instruction Section of the Association of College and Research Libraries. Here they claimed that bibliographic instruction (BI) is 'the very heart of the reference process' and that BI librarians are 'coming to define themselves as a political movement within academic librarianship'.

They have been otherwise defined by their opponents: as 'self-righteous reformers and elitists' (David Isaacson, 1985), 'chasing moonbeams' (Davinson, 1984), with a 'head-in-the-clouds approach' (C. Paul Vincent, 1984). It has been noticed that not all of them have experience as reference librarians. Their motives too have been questioned. Librarians at a 1982 British conference wondered 'whether the growth in user education had been a reflection of the fact that during the 60s and 70s librarians were under-employed, over-qualified, and keen to improve their status'. This may or may not be true, but there has certainly been exhortation in the literature that 'Librarians must abandon the reference desk and heighten their profile within the academic community'.

Apart from what one critic has called 'strident rhetoric and ... dogmatic pronouncements' of this kind, the literature on user education generally, according to Neil A. Radford, writing in 1980 from the University of Sydney, 'is formidable in quantity, and is mostly appalling in quality ... boring, repetitive, self-serving, and frequently of trivial consequence'. Surveying the United Kingdom scene six years later, Hugh Fleming, himself a user education librarian, was obliged to admit that 'whereas there is an enormous weight of literature written at an anecdotal level, there are few publications which aim to develop a sound teaching base for user education'.

But the most telling criticism levelled at BI is that it does not work, inasmuch as it fails to produce the results it seeks, namely self-reliant users. This point has been made constantly in the literature by scores of practising reference librarians whose daily commerce with actual users leaves them unconvinced by the assertions of the 'BI missionaries', as they have been called. The only consistent and widely remarked effect of user education is an increase in the number of questions asked at the reference desk, sometimes doubling them. In the 1987 fifth edition of his standard text, Katz, who over the years has closely observed BI, had to conclude that 'Despite many informal courses on how to use a library, apparently the majority of people are not much better off at the end than at the beginning'. If he and those who agree with him are mistaken, the burden of proof must lie with the advocates of BI, but as he explained, 'few librarians have the time or the knowledge to follow up the instruction with evaluative studies'.

On this quite crucial issue the case for BI is not helped by the edict of the Think Tank that 'Bibliographic instruction needs no more justification than instruction in composition or any of the liberal arts, and evaluation studies aimed at justifying its existence are unnecessary'. It is not difficult to see why BI librarians have been tagged as 'The moral majority of the library profession'. They further argue that assistance given only to those who ask questions is service confined to the elite few, whereas instruction is praised as 'distributing reference service in as egalitarian a manner as possible'.

Of course for those who take this high moral tone the fact that it does not work is irrelevant. They would maintain that the effort must still be made to make students independent of the librarian, because 'the privacy of the reference transaction, combined with low user expectation, fosters superficial work and protects incompetence', as Frances L. Hopkins argued. The challenge is to devise a mode of instruction that is effective.

It is recognized that in the world of special libraries the issue of user self-sufficiency does not arise: as Davinson ironically remarked, 'Attempts to inveigle senior management and research staff into undertaking their own literature searches would not be well received'. But increasingly there are strong voices urging that the BI gospel should be preached in public libraries also. It is the policy of the American Library Association that 'all libraries [should] include instruction in the use of libraries as one of the primary goals of service', and a survey of 310 Canadian public librarians reported in 1989 that 'Most not only agreed that instruction is desirable, but that public librarians have an obligation to teach users about the correct use of library tools'. In a number of instances voluntary courses have been offered, and the response has been promising, but as Davinson has commented, 'What usually happens in such cases, however, is that the kinds of users who are encouraged to enrol on these programmes are the very people who are in least need of user education'.

But all this philosophizing as to what is desirable leaves untouched the pragmatic policy question of whether it is in fact possible to produce self-reliant users able to answer their own reference questions, as Lester would wish. The issue may not be susceptible of proof either way, but there is substantial evidence that the objective is now beyond our grasp. Though most of it rests on opinion, it is none the less genuine, deriving from the expert witness of many reference librarians: 'Most of this reservoir of experience [that reference librarians have] cannot be taught in the form of library instruction' (Jeremy W. Sayles, 1980); 'it has become unreasonable to presume that bibliographic education is going to produce an independent, self-reliant library user' (Vincent, 1984); 'Anyone who has worked as a reference librarian will acknowledge ... the futility ... of attempting to make all library users (students and faculty) experts in the intricacies of the library' (John Budd, 1984).

As the world of information grows daily more complex, the self-sufficient user appears more of a will-o'-the-wisp than ever. The advent of online, with its early rash promise to eliminate the intermediary (a term used by Wyer as long ago as 1930), has on the contrary reinforced the reference librarian's role. The overwhelming majority of online searches in libraries are still undertaken by library staff. CD-ROM, much more user-friendly, distinctly more popular, and free from connect charges and the psychological pressure of timed access to information, has still not brought the self-sufficient user. In the first place, the surveys by Ching-Chih Chen and David I. Raitt reported in 1990 that CD-ROMs are being used mainly by library staff as opposed to end-users, both in the United States and Western Europe. In the second place, while end-user CD-ROM searching is high compared to online (though mainly in the simpler databases), reference librarians have found themselves required to devote a great deal of their time to assisting such users, discussing their search strategies, helping them determine the most appropriate database for a particular topic, explaining database construction, and overseeing the actual search. The effect observed by Bill Coons and Linda Stewart in 1989 is typical: it was soon realized that 'everyone on the staff needs to learn more about CD-ROM than we previously thought'. Mary Pagliero Popp and A. F. M. Fazle Kabir reported in 1990 that at Indiana University Undergraduate Library 'The greatest impact seems to be the increased volume of business at the reference desk ... reference questions increased by more than 100%'.

Here too then genuine doubts can be found as to whether user education can deliver what it claims: 'sole reliance on bibliographic instruction and notions of training self-reliant users may no longer be feasible in a complex information-based society' (Robert M. Hayes, 1986); 'Traditional academic library reference notions of instructing users to be self-reliant must be reconsidered as the complexity of new information technologies engulfs the library' (Teresa L. Demo and Charles McClure, 1988); and even a coordinator of library instruction found it necessary to argue that 'So many new reference sources appear in both print and electronic formats that it is unfair and unrealistic to expect a user to keep track of even a few. This is the job of the librarian' (Elizabeth Bramm Dunn, 1988).

What online, and CD-ROM especially, have done in this area is to enhance the age-old informal one-to-one instructional role of reference librarians and their predecessors down the centuries, what Jane A. Reilly has called 'Library instruction through the reference query'. As Davinson noted, such 'Nonformalized, usually highly personalized instruction is second nature to many reference librarians'. Even Joanne R. Euster, the facilitator of the Think Tank, acknowledges as much: 'Bibliographic instruction at its most elemental level is simply one-on-one reference assistance'. At its best this teaching at the reference desk rather than in the classroom is an art in itself, as John C. Swan explains, giving students 'a genuine sense of the search, showing them a searcher in action, grappling with content as well as index terms, ideas as well as citations. The reference librarian in particular has the excellent opportunity to serve as the role model, the expert learner demonstrating for the novice learner.'

In this war of words one voice has been notably absent: that of the user. One central criticism of the Think Tank recommendations, as voiced by Budd, was that they are 'overwhelmingly slanted towards librarians and conspicuously ignore the recipients of library instruction'. So far as concerns library users' attitude to the catalogue, we know from research studies conveniently summarized for us in 1987 by David W. Lewis that 'People avoid using the catalog where they can'. Donna Senzig, also drawing on catalogue use studies, has reminded us that 'People ... do not really enjoy searching for the item or information they want. They do not want to be a Sherlock Holmes, following elusive clues through bibliographies, indexes and catalogs ... In spite of its usefulness, the catalog is still seen by many as a barrier to finding materials, or at the very least an unnecessary in-between step.'

As for being taught how to search for their own information, the view of Radford is that 'The great majority of the population has no interest in learning how to use a library effectively' and even if compelled to learn, 'most people are not greatly interested in practising and improving their library skills'. In any case a goodly proportion of enquirers ask for help by telephone – 35% in a 1982 survey of large city reference libraries in England and Scotland. What users want, in Pinzelik's words, is 'to get the information needed in a simple process that allows them to begin their real task, using information to write a paper or solve a problem'.

There is a moral case to be made here too, as explained by Tom Eadie, himself a former user education librarian: 'user education is a special service of questionable value that arose not because users asked for it, but because librarians thought it would be good for them'. Constance Miller and James Rettig argued that the role of the reference librarian has never been articulated more sublimely than in S. R. Ranganathan's Fourth Law of Library Science: '"Save the Time of the Reader"'. No activity common to academic libraries' reference departments violates this more flagrantly than their extensive bibliographic instruction programs.' Eadie commented that 'This is more important than the Principle of Cost Effectiveness: Save the Time of the Librarian'. And there are indications, as mentioned earlier, that BI can actually be harmful, leaving users with the distorted view that finding information in libraries is simple, and sowing the seeds of the frustration, guilt, and anger they may experience when they discover it is not. Students who have been misled by BI into thinking that they can be independent of the librarian do not in fact know how to use a library properly, because the reference librarian is one of its most important resources.

There may never be a resolution of this historic ambivalence in reference librarianship, but at least it should be possible to offer the library user a choice, as Katz has argued with increasing cogency over 20 years through five editions of his textbook: 'The user should have the option either (1) to learn how to use the library or any of its parts, or (2) not to learn how and still expect a full, complete, and total answer to his or her question(s) from the reference librarian'. Rettig has spelled out in detail what this means in practice: 'The type of service a librarian gives in response to a particular inquiry should be determined by the type of information the inquirer wants, not by the librarian's allegiance to a level of service. Thus the librarian must determine if the information a particular inquirer wants is (1) an information source, (2) instruction in the use of an information source, or (3) messages culled from an information source. In different situations the same inquirer may want a different one of these. Different inquirers with the same inquiry may want different ones. Furthermore, the level of service and type of information that satisfies a patron may not be what the patron imperfectly expresses a need for in the initial message.'

## The need to know
But reference work is far more than a skilled technique or a professional accomplishment. It is a profoundly human activity, ministering as it does to one of the most deeply rooted needs of the species, the desire to know and understand. This particular spring of human motivation starts with the simple curiosity also observed in the higher mammals: indeed organized activity directed to the satisfaction of curiosity about the natural world is one of the definitions of science. And, as Aristotle noted, 'All men possess by nature a craving for knowledge'. This need even encompasses our desire to systematize the universe. Jesse H. Shera has reminded us that 'man abhors chaos as nature is said to abhor a vacuum', and we seek constantly to impose a pattern on what we see. This is what led Sir Charles Sherrington to call the human brain 'the enchanted loom'. We can no more ignore such inner compulsions than we can the need for food. The psychologist Abraham H. Maslow has warned of 'true psycho-pathological effects when cognitive needs are frustrated'.

If reference librarians would make a point of constantly reminding themselves that what they are doing is not simply providing information but serving these cognitive needs, it might serve to counteract a tendency often commented on: they seem to take more interest in the question than the questioner. It does of course require bibliographical knowledge and searching skill to provide a technically competent answer to queries such as 'Have you anything on sandblast guns and their uses?', 'What was the Order of Battle at Minden in 1759?', 'I am looking for books dealing specifically with revenue or fiscal stamps', 'What is the inscription carved on the rock at the Pool of Siloam?', 'I would like a description of a typical day in a Benedictine monastery, for use in a novel'. Any good reference librarian would rightly feel a sense of professional accomplishment at mastering the intellectual challenge of such questions. But it is essential not to lose sight of the fact that to the enquirer the answer to the question is only incidentally a requirement, and at a deeper level the answer is needed to satisfy a basic cognitive need. Psychologists tell us that questions arise in people's minds because of a gap in their knowledge, or a failure to make sense of the world around them, or some inconsistency or conceptual conflict in what they already know. It is often asserted in the literature of library and information science (for example by William B. Rouse and Sandra H. Rouse) that 'Humans seldom seek information as an end in itself', but that they usually require it to help with problem-solving or decision-taking or resource allocation and so on. But a 1982 survey by Terry L. Weech and Herbert Goldhor of 463 public library enquirers in Illinois found that curiosity was the motive in 16% of the cases. Bertrand Russell has said that what people really want is not knowledge but certainty; whatever other value the information that librarians supply may have, it can scarcely help but reduce uncertainty. And there must be many occasions when library users ask questions simply to reduce subjective uncertainty.

As a human art, the second great contribution made by reference work is the supply of assistance on an individual basis. The concept of provision carefully and specifically matched to the needs of an individual is fundamental to librarianship. The importance of reference work in such a context is not only that it is done, but like Lord Hewart's imperative about justice, it is manifestly and undoubtedly seen to be done. It openly demonstrates, in its one-to-one character, Ranganathan's Second Law: 'Every reader his book'.

## Origins of reference work

It is chastening to be reminded that reference work has not always been an inherent part of librarianship. One of the many lessons taught by Rothstein is that it is a relatively 'new dimension' in librarianship, compared with the acquisition and cataloguing of books. Until the mid-19th century many scholars would only turn to the library when their own, often vast, private collections failed them. As library users they needed no help, familiar as they normally were with the bibliography of their own subjects, and content to rely on the author catalogue for the rest. Of course the subject-matter of the books was more limited then and library collections were much smaller; as Ranganathan admits, 'If the number of books in a library is very small there would be no need perhaps to provide any reference service'. No doubt on occasion, individual librarians, often scholars themselves and knowledgeable as many of them were about the contents of the collections in their care, would find themselves able to assist readers in their investigations; but all such activity remained for many years peripheral to their primary duties of acquisition, cataloguing, arrangement, and control.

It was the great upsurge in both publication and literacy that forced a change. Scholarship expanded, with books appearing on smaller and smaller topics, and libraries grew larger. The time came when scholars no longer knew even the names of those who wrote about the subjects that concerned them, and so they began to search for books by subject, and librarians responded with more subject catalogues, classification schemes, and personal help. The spread of popular education and the advance of literacy created a whole new reading public. It is in the assistance required by this new kind of reader in a new kind of library, the tax-supported public library, particularly in the great industrial cities of Britain and the United States, that can be traced the origins of what we now know as reference work. Such libraries were not established without opposition, though this was less in the United States than in Britain, and from their inception they were under pressure to justify the expenditure of public funds.

The first published paper on reference work was in 1876, though it was to be another 10 years before that term appeared in print. Its author was Samuel Swett Green, a Harvard divinity graduate and librarian of the public library of the city of Worcester, Massachusetts, one of the most important manufacturing cities of New England. It was Green's own first paper too, and was delivered on 5 October 1876 at the famous Centennial Conference of Librarians at Philadelphia which led to the establishment of the American Library Association. According to Rothstein, this was the 'first explicit proposal for a *program* of personal assistance to readers, as distinct from occasional aid'. Its title deserves giving in full: 'The desirableness of establishing personal intercourse between librarians and readers in popular libraries'. It was at this same meeting in direct response to Green's paper that Robinson made his plea, quoted above, for the library education of students. A year later, to the very day, Green was in London giving an address on the same topic, 'Access to librarians', as a delegate from the ALA to another pioneering Conference of Librarians at which the 'Library-Association of the United Kingdom' was founded.

There is no doubt that good sound reference work was already being done in a number of libraries at the time, as is evident from the discussions of Green's views at both conferences, though it was probably not widespread and was described variously as 'personal help', 'aid to readers', or 'assistance to readers'. Reuben A. Guild, the librarian of Brown University from 1848 to 1893, claimed that 'For the past thirty years during which I have been in charge, the public have not only been allowed free access to the library . . . but also consult the librarian, instead of the catalogue, inquiries being mostly for information rather than for certain works'. Robert Harrison of the London Library told how he was once asked by Thackeray for a book about General Wolfe: 'I do not want to know about his battles. I can learn all about those from the histories. I want something that will tell me the colour of the breeches he wore.'

Indeed in England Green had been anticipated to some extent by the remarkable Edward Edwards, the largely self-educated son of a Whitechapel bricklayer, who laid down as early as 1859 in his *Handbook of library economy* that 'the assistance of Readers in their researches' is one of the duties that 'have daily to be provided for' in ordinary public libraries. He was the first librarian of the public library of Manchester, the world's earliest example of an industrial city, regarded with a mixture of fear and awe as a portent of a new age by the eminent visitors from many countries curious to see for themselves what the future was going to be like. It served as one of the models for 'Coketown' in *Hard times* (1854) by Charles Dickens, who had seen it for himself when he spoke at the Reference Library opening ceremony in 1852. Two years later a visitor to the Reference Library wrote of 'a noble and chastely decorated hall, surrounded with shelves of books ... and three librarians, noiselessly dusting the books and attending to the wants of the readers'. From the outset Edwards proclaimed his intention of 'supplying information on points of serious and definitive enquiry' and in 1873 an article in the *Manchester Evening News* noted that in the Reference Library 'a general desire to assist earnest students is most courteously shown by the officers'. In 1871 Manchester became the first library in Britain to employ women, and in 1884 a reader in the Reference Library was so grateful for the help provided by one of them that he felt moved to write to the *Manchester Guardian*: 'I have always noticed that the attendants at this library are most attentive and anxious to help those searching for information'.

Interestingly enough, on his way to the 1877 London Conference, Green himself had paid a visit to the Manchester Reference Library where he was shown round by Crestadoro, one of Edwards' successors, now best remembered as the pioneer of permuted keyword indexes. He was astonished 'to see a great reading-room filled in the evening by readers all with their hats on'.

**Systematic bibliography**
Though it has been little commented on, it is a fact not without

significance that the beginnings of reference work as a profession coincided with the huge expansion of periodical literature in the mid- and late-19th century. For the scholar and the general reader alike this transformed the whole familiar terrain of knowledge. In their search for information among even the largest collections of books and pamphlets, they had until that time been able to pick their way by relying on the signposts furnished by the titles of the works themselves and the handlists or catalogues provided by the librarian.

Compared to this fairly ordered monographic literature, the multiple contents of a collection of periodicals seemed like a terrible jumble. Then as now the conglomerate of articles making up an issue of a periodical did not appear in the catalogue, and readers began asking librarians for assistance. So insistent and wide-ranging in subject scope were these requests for articles on particular topics that librarians found they could no longer depend on their own personal knowledge and so in a number of libraries lists of such articles were compiled by the librarian as an *aide-mémoire*. The manuscript index compiled at Yale by a young assistant librarian, William Frederick Poole, proved so popular that in 1848 it was published by George Putnam. As Poole's biographer explains, 'It was a new and unique instrument of bibliographical control, the general index to a number of different periodicals in one alphabet. It inaugurated a bibliographic form which became one of the basic cornerstones of library service.' By the time it reached its third edition in 1882 Poole had risen to become the first librarian of Chicago Public Library and his great *Index to periodical literature, 1802 – 1881* had grown to 230,000 entries covering 232 periodicals. It continues in regular use today, and is still in print.

Other major bibliographies founded about this time extended control over larger and larger sectors of the world of print and established systematic bibliography as the basic professional discipline of this new kind of librarian. Typical examples of many which could be cited are *Newspaper press directory* (commenced 1846), *English catalogue of books* (1864), *Index to 'The Times' newspaper* (1868), *Publishers' trade list annual* (1873), British Museum *Catalogue of printed books* (1881), S. Halkett and J. Laing *Dictionary of anonymous and pseudonymous English literature* (1882), W. S. Sonnenschein *The best books: a reader's guide* (1887). The advent of such powerful new tools also extended the bibliographical reach of the 'reference librarian' into the world of recorded knowledge beyond the walls of the local library with its limited holdings.

Increasing systematization in print of the field of substantive knowledge itself is seen in the battery of now indispensable reference tools also published for the first time in the mid- and late-19th century. Random examples still in daily use, with dates of foundation, are *Who's who* (1849), *Chambers's encyclopaedia* (1850), *Statistical abstract for the United Kingdom* (1854), *Bartlett's familiar quotations* (1855), *Crockford's clerical directory* (1858), *Statesman's year-book* (1864), *Wisden's cricketers' almanack* (1864), *Whitaker's almanack* (1868), *World almanac* (1868), *Grove's dictionary of music and musicians* (1878), *Statistical abstract of the United States* (1878), *Dictionary of national biography* (1885), *Oxford English dictionary* (1888), *Kelly's manufacturer's and merchant's directory* (1889), *Municipal year book* (1897).

## Growth of reference work

The delights of reference work were recognized very early: in his pioneering paper Green confessed that 'there are few pleasures comparable'; in 1882 Poole told the American Library Association Conference at Cincinnati that 'To aid inquirers . . . is one of the most pleasant duties of my position'. Inevitably there were those who had reservations. The same conference heard James W. Ward of Buffalo describe the librarian as 'The oftenest consulted book in the library. He is expected to know everything, in the library and out of it.' He made it clear that this was not entirely to his liking, though his audience was not slow to take up the challenge, led by Green himself roundly declaring 'I do not like the tone of the paper'.

By 1888 Melvil Dewey was using the term 'reference librarian', but specific provision of such assistance was not a universally accepted public library function until the early years of the 20th century. Academic libraries had expanded also, but naturally had not been subjected to the same scale of demand from their users. Progress in reference work in United States university and college libraries was steady though not spectacular, but it did receive a boost from the new trend in higher education towards 'learning by inquiry', with teachers encouraging students to read widely rather than depend on the lecture and the textbook. In British universities progress was invisible. Indeed, assistance to readers was scarcely to be found at all until the mid-20th century. A basic textbook for many years was G. Woledge and B. S. Page, *A manual of university and college library practice*, published by the Library Association in 1940: reference work was not mentioned at all; the matter of 'information and advice given to enquirers in the reading room' was covered in seven lines. As late as 1958 the distinguished librarian of University College London, seat of the oldest library school in the country, asserted in a standard work, also published by the Library Association, that 'there is ... little room in the university library for service to readers'. But as his 1986 obituary noted, 'He believed in traditional academic librarianship and could be intolerant of innovation'.

By way of contrast, the great majority of the libraries grouped together as 'special', many of them serving business or government, are very much 20th-century institutions, custom-built for the sole purpose of providing reference and information services. Finding information for enquirers is what they are there for and there has never been any question about it. Indeed, in industrial libraries, where some of the most intensive reference work is to be found, it is not unknown for management to warn those of their staff who need to use the library that they must call on the services of the librarians and not lapse into do-it-yourself habits. This does not mean that management is familiar with Wyer's theories of conservative and liberal reference service; they just know it is cheaper. The simple fact of industrial library life is that all the users are on the payroll, and Ranganathan's Fourth Law, 'Save the time of the reader', makes good sense in economic as well as professional terms. As Edwin M. Cortez has explained about such libraries, 'They must constantly justify themselves to their parent organizations by demonstrating that they contribute more than they cost'.

**Misconceptions**
Perhaps some day, in defining reference work, it will only be necessary to say what it is. At the present time the misunderstandings that still persist, even among those who should know better, oblige any apologist to take particular care to make clear what reference work is not.

To begin with, it is wrong simply to equate it with the skilful deployment of the contents of reference books (or their electronic equivalents). Let us hope too, in parentheses, that one error it is no longer necessary to extirpate is that a reference book is one 'whose use is restricted to the library building'. The alternative definition and the one appropriate here is a book that is 'designed by the arrangement and treatment of its subject matter to be consulted for definite items of information rather than to be read consecutively' (*The ALA glossary of library and information science*). It is plain for anyone to see that such works form only a proportion of the stock of libraries where reference work is done, and in general the larger the library the smaller the proportion of reference books. We have known for years that much

28

reference work is done with non-reference books, and an increasing amount does not depend on books at all. Dorothy Cole's pioneering survey of 1,026 reference questions in 13 United States libraries as long ago as 1941 showed that 45% of the sources used were not reference books: 10% were periodicals, 10% documents, 4% pamphlets, 3% newspapers, and 18% books other than reference books. Herbert Goldhor's smaller 1978 survey of 100 questions asked in Urbana (Illinois) Public Library found little changed. Sources other than reference books provided 41% of answers: 14% were from the vertical file or picture file, 11% from circulating books, 9% from periodicals, 3% from outside sources, 1% from the catalogue, and 3% unspecified.

It cannot be said often enough that between the reference librarian and the book there is no inevitable and eternal connection. The stuff of reference work is information, and not any particular physical artefact. Set against the span of human existence the half-millennium history of the printed book is but an instant. Sayles believed 'the concept *book*, as a unit of information, is habitual, misleading, restrictive, and detrimental to the reference process. ... Librarians are trapped by knowledge defined in book units and continue to search reflexively for book titles in response to reference inquiries.' He exaggerated, of course, but he went on to elaborate his point: 'it is the unique, opinionated, and factual information in many sources – expressed in chapters, sections, pages, paragraphs, illustrations, glossaries, tables, charts, graphs, appendixes, footnotes, references, bibliographies, tables of contents, indexes – that must be discovered, isolated, and formed into a new unity'. And of course there is a whole range of printed material besides books, as well as information in electronic format. But the written word itself, with a history 10 times as long as the printed book, has serious limitations as a medium of human communication: it cannot be used by those unable to read (a majority of the human race), and reading is a artificial, solitary, and static activity.

In the 1960s John Gloag was able to say: 'Since the nineteenth century we have depended almost exclusively on what used to be called book learning, so much so that we have become visually illiterate'. He could scarcely say the same about the multi-media world of today, inevitably reflected in libraries on an ever-increasing scale. All formats, book and non-book, printed and electronic, audio and visual, are now grist to the reference librarian's mill. Furthermore, the measure dispensed now is the item of information, not the bibliographical unit.

Once, however, that ritual point has been made, it is time to remind the student – to proclaim, indeed – that the written word is one of the three greatest practical achievements of the human mind, comparable only to the invention of agriculture and the discovery of steam power. In the form of the printed book it is still by far the most common means of storing information, after the human brain, and it can still perform a score of tasks that are beyond the machine. And even the electronic database relies very largely for its input and output on alphanumeric characters mainly in the form of words.

Apart from the special case of mathematics, no one has found a better way of dealing with abstract ideas than the use of words (and even mathematical concepts can often be verbalized). Much of the ingenuity that has been expended on attempts at visualization has been wasted effort, inasmuch as they are frequently more difficult to follow than the original words and almost always ambiguous. It is difficult to see how any of the following not untypical queries could ever be answered in any way other than by the use of words; and it is not really possible at the moment to imagine a satisfactory answer being supplied without the consultation of a printed text at least somewhere along the line: 'I would like something on incentive schemes in industry', 'Can you find me the legend of John O'Groats?', 'What are the duties of a godfather?', 'I am interested in the present position on Sunday observance', 'What have you got on the early history of opinion polls?'.

And as Archie G. Rugh has so compellingly reminded us, very many people do in fact come to a library specifically seeking a book rather than information. Sometimes it is a particular book, whose author or title they may or may not know, or it may simply be a book of poetry, for example, or even a book 'to read'.

Another lingering misconception is that reference work is restricted to reference libraries. For a start, most special libraries and many academic libraries do not have a separate reference department or even reference section or area (though certain reference books may be shelved together). Yet clearly reference work is practised there; indeed, as has been said already, in many special libraries it is the main justification for the library's existence.

But even in public libraries, with a traditional though no longer universal separate reference library, it is a serious mistake to assume that reference work is confined to reference departments. The philosophy behind D. J. Foskett's 1952 work *Assistance to readers in lending libraries* was that in an average town it is the lending library that is the focus of requests for information. In 1956 research from the United States confirmed this: 'Reference in the small library is evidently centered in the circulation department. Sixty-eight percent have reference service done at this point.' William Warner Bishop had been aware of this in 1908: 'Most readers will ask questions at the loan desk. We might as well make up our minds to that fact.' Robert Pierson has further pointed out that in many small libraries the circulation desk is the only desk, in others it is the 'main' desk, and at certain times, even in multi-desk libraries, it is the only one staffed.

There is an increasing amount of reference work undertaken outside the library altogether, working directly with clients. While it is scarcely possible to conceive of a reference librarian solving people's problems without access to an information store, there is no rule that says the whole of the reference process must take place within the same four walls. In 1977 Susan Klement proclaimed 'It is time to separate the concept of librarian from the concept of libraries', and many entrepreneurial librarians have heeded this call and set up shop as independent consultants, private researchers, or, to use the term now most commonly applied, information brokers. Providing a convenient boost at just the right time was the availability of information online, accessible anywhere there was a telephone line. Currently, it is estimated that half of the work of such brokers is online searching.

But they still practise reference work. As Kathleen Voigt said, 'What are they? They are very much like a reference librarian.' We have been told by one of the best-known pioneers in the field, Alice Sizer Warner, that 'when you are working with a client, it's almost as if you were a reference librarian'. Certainly at least some of the queries that they deal with are no different to those asked in libraries. Indeed they continue to draw heavily on library resources, including the services of reference librarians, and this has worried a minority who are perturbed by the thought that these brokers then make their clients pay for the information provided. The brokers argue that they do not sell information, which is in the public domain. As Anne K. Beaubien explained, 'it is the *service* to gather the information for which we charge: the expertise to know where to look for information efficiently and effectively, the staff time necessary to retrieve the information, and the direct, calculable expenses incurred while doing so (photocopies, postage, long distance telephone, online time, etc.)'.

Yet to some of their common or garden reference librarian colleagues they still appear exotic creatures, 'entrepreneurs doing much the same work as librarians but apparently being paid royally and working with much more independence'. In 1987 they held their first international conference at Milwaukee, and an estimate at the time was that in the United States and Canada there were between 500 and 1,000. The 1990 *Directory of fee-based information services* included over 800 listings from 30 countries, though not all of them were independent (several were actually libraries). Many of them had several staff, and librarians appeared among them in large numbers.

It also has to be pointed out that reference work is not the whole of librarianship. It is not even the most important part of librarianship in every circumstance. Acknowledging this truth does not compromise the well-nigh universal conviction among those who do reference work that therein is to be found the very essence of library service. After all, by definition they do provide direct personal assistance to an enquirer with an expressed need for information: one could scarcely find a service more central than that. But there are many instances of people in need of what libraries can provide where it falls to colleagues to help: children who are not seeking information, for example, but who would benefit from having their imaginative horizons extended; or the manager in industry needing to keep abreast of technical advance day by day; or the countless thousands, even millions, for whom, though functionally literate, reading is an alien experience and the library as remote as the North Pole. Reaching out to serve these, and the many other individuals and groups that libraries can benefit, is a task deserving high priority. But it is not reference work as defined here.

Acceptance of what is the essentially passive nature of reference work is unwelcome to some: such a role is derided as supportive or ancillary and thus intrinsically inferior to virtually any kind of active stance. Similarly asserted in the controversy over information versus instruction discussed earlier, this common view shows confusion of thought. Preventive medicine in the community, for example, is obviously vital, but this is no reason for hospital doctors and nurses to feel conscience-stricken because they wait for patients to come to them. Like medicine, librarianship must certainly have its Marthas, but it needs its Marys too. As Milton explained over 300 years ago, 'They also serve who only stand and wait'. Receptivity is a virtue, and repose is a quality for which those whose profession is personal service should strive. It is worth remembering what we are told by the Evangelist: 'The part that Mary has chosen is best'. To think that everyone should be doing everything is a sign of immaturity in a profession, which depends for its success on a harmony between its dynamic and static elements. Those who urge the former at the expense of the latter not only misunderstand their profession, they also betray their ignorance of elementary mechanics.

## The heart of library service

There is no doubt that its practitioners see reference work as the keystone of professional practice. They describe it as the *raison d'être* of the whole of librarianship. As early as 1904 we find Mary Eileen Ahern proclaiming that 'The reference work of the library gives the institution its greatest value and may be called the heart of the work'. For John Ballinger in 1908 it was 'the highest form of public library service'. In 1957 Ranganathan wrote that 'Reference service is the primary motive and the culmination of all library practices'. For the current generation too 'reference service is the peak of library activity' (Davinson, 1980). Even those librarians who are otherwise engaged usually agree that reference work is the one subject that should never be omitted from a librarian's professional preparation. A survey of library schools accredited by the American Library Association reported in 1990 that all 41 respondents offered at least one general reference course and at 90% of the schools such a course is compulsory.

Brian Neilson has argued that reference work has played a special role in the long struggle of librarianship for higher professional status. It is what sociologists call a 'core professional task', that is to say one that is shared by a large proportion of the members of a particular occupation and serves to make them distinctive as a group to the lay public. For lawyers the core task is arguing in court and for doctors it is consulting with individual patients. It matters little that in actual fact most lawyers do not appear regularly in court, or that doctor-patient interaction is frequently only perfunctory; 'the symbolic power of the "core task" in the public mind provides a ready identification for the profession as a whole that conveys status, the performance of special and esoteric skills and a sense of the critical role that the professional members play'.

What gives reference work this unique status, compared to, say, cataloguing, or collection-building, or library management, is firstly, its face-to-face character which makes it the most human of library services; and secondly, the assurance in advance that the effort exerted is not likely to be dissipated on the air but will be applied to the specific expressed need of an identifiable individual enquirer. In the circumstances it is not surprising that many librarians since Green and Poole have found intense satisfaction in reference work, a response still very evident even in a decade of belt-tightening and burnout. According to Ann T. Hinckley 'Reference librarians are among the most fortunate in our profession' (1980); for Ellen I. Watson 'Being a reference librarian is practically being in heaven' (1981); Robert C. Berring has told us 'I love reference work. ... I find reference work fun. I always have more energy at the end of a four hour shift than I had at the start' (1984); Isaacson too has found that 'It is fun to pursue answers to questions: my favorite reason for being a reference librarian' (1986). The first sentence in the fifth edition of the text by Katz reads: 'There is no more rewarding library work than being a reference librarian' (1987). Other have used words like 'exhilaration' (Hinckley, 1980), 'joy' (Charles A. Bunge, 1984), and 'satisfying' (Robert Hauptman, 1988).

Reference librarians feel too that they are in some way different. As Weech has explained, 'the diversity of the tasks of reference staff and the independent professionally isolated nature of many of these tasks tend to distinguish the reference function from many other library staff functions'. Others have noticed this too: Charles Ferguson called them 'a breed apart'. Over the years a number of reference librarians have used the word 'mystique' in writing about their profession (e.g., Caroline Spicer, 1973; Davinson, 1980; Mabel Shaw and Susan S. Whittle, 1986). This does not necessarily please other librarians, and those who have never sensed it may not understand, but there is no denying the fascination of what Naiman has called 'the dazzling unpredictability of reference questions', manifested day after day in a situation where 'The patron approaching the reference desk may have a question one has never heard before and will never hear again'. Katz makes a similar point from a slightly different angle: 'Most requests may fit into a general class, but, in a very real sense, every request is unique. Even if the librarian knew what type of questions he had been asked over the past thirty years, he still would have no assurance that the next one would not be an exception.' And the challenge inherent in the statistical fact that the resources at the librarian's disposal can probably be made to answer, in a large library, as many as 95% of all the questions asked, is one that never loses its savour.

*Further reading*
The following list of suggested readings (and each of the similar lists at the end of later chapters) is confined to periodical articles or conference papers or books that treat specifically the topics dealt with in the chapter, and have appeared since the previous edition of this book. It has been

compiled with students in mind and has been kept deliberately short in the hope that they may find the time to read most of the items listed. A list of general books on reference work follows the final chapter.

Radford, Neil A., 'Why bother with user education?', *New Zealand libraries*, **43**, 1980, 53 – 8.

Hopkins, Frances L., 'A century of bibliographic instruction: the historical claim to professional and academic legitimacy', *College and research libraries*, **43**, 1982, 192 – 8.

Land, Mary, 'Librarians' image and users' attitude to reference interviews', *Canadian library journal*, **45**, 1988, 15 – 20.

Eadie, Tom, 'Immodest proposals: user instruction for students does not work', *Library journal*, **115**, 15 October 1990, 42 – 5.

# — 2 —

## The reference question

The stimulus that sets in train the activity called reference work is a question from a library user. And therein lies the secret of the unshakeable belief of reference librarians that what they do is the very pith and marrow of librarianship. No need for them the anxious reminders about the 'centrality of the user': their whole craft is built round the user, whom they face daily.

Every year in England and Wales some 40 million reference enquiries are made in public libraries alone, according to estimates from the University of Loughborough Library and Information Statistics Unit. Similarly, Herbert Goldhor of the Library Research Center at the University of Illinois at Urbana-Champaign has estimated that the corresponding figure for the United States is over 100 million. Ann T. Hinckley believes that 'the intellectual challenge of responding to a wide variety of questions and research problems, combined with the excitement of working with people, is the most rewarding aspect of reference librarianship'. And in a gratifyingly high proportion of cases reference librarians are able to witness their users' satisfaction, acknowledge their appreciation, and quite often, enjoy their thanks.

Probably the first thing that the thoughtful young librarian will notice about the actual questions asked is that they fall into two broad groupings, according to the amount of help the user needs. The overwhelming majority of questions demand only limited assistance, not necessarily because they are easy, but on account of their essentially *self-limiting* nature. Questions as apparently diverse as 'What time do you close?', 'I am looking for a poem called "Ode to tobacco"', 'When is Halley's comet due again?' all fall into this class. In the first place, each of them has a specific, exact, and finite answer; secondly, once the information has been found the search is plainly at an end; and thirdly, during the course of the search the librarian is usually in no doubt as to whether the answer has been located or not. These three examples also serve to illustrate, respectively, the three different categories within this broad self-limiting grouping.

## Administrative and directional enquiries

The first category is what may be called administrative or directional enquiries, such as 'The photocopier appears to have broken down', 'Where can I see parish registers?', 'May I use your waste-paper basket?', 'Can you lend me a pair of scissors?', 'Do I have to book in advance to do a CD-ROM search?'.

Enquiries about such elementary and routine matters make no call on the bibliographical expertise of the staff, merely a basic general knowledge of where things are and how things are done in a particular institution. They are scarcely the type of questions that require professional librarians to answer them, but they are frequently and genuinely asked by users in need of help and any library has an obligation to make provision for them to be answered in a friendly and helpful manner. Most would agree, however, that in a well-ordered library many such queries could be anticipated by a clear system of signs and notices.

## Author/title enquiries

The second kind of question is the author/title enquiry, where the user is seeking a *particular work*. These have been called 'holdings transactions' by Mary Jo Lynch, because enquirers are in the first instance hoping to discover that the work they seek is held by the library. Of course in the majority of such instances users are able to find what they want for themselves, often through the catalogue, specifically provided for the purpose. But where the work cannot be located, or if it is of a kind that is not normally included in the catalogue, such as an article in a journal, or a government document, or where, as so often, the catalogue itself poses a barrier, users will frequently ask the librarian.

Typical of such enquiries are: 'I am looking for the Aquarian Gospel', 'Do you have the Universal Declaration of Human Rights?', 'I am trying to trace a play that Richard Burton was in called "The boy with a cart"', 'What is the earliest life of St Godric of Finchale?', 'Have you a book called *The Whig interpretation of history*? I think it is quite famous'. Questions of this type are described as 'known-item' or verification queries, because the work sought is definitely known to exist; what the librarian has to do is verify the details, where they are incomplete or inaccurate, and locate a copy of the work.

In some instances, however, the existence of the particular work asked for cannot be presumed, and such enquiries are therefore distinctly more speculative. They normally combine a specific author and/or title with a *bibliographic* specification, often form; for instance, 'Have you a translation of the Orkneyinga Saga?', 'Is it true that Hitler wrote a second book after *Mein Kampf*?', 'Did Sir David Brewster ever patent his invention of the kaleidoscope?', 'Is there a concordance to the poems of Gerard Manley Hopkins?', 'Didn't someone publish a reply to Desmond Morris's book *The naked ape*?' These are called 'not-known-item' or identification queries, and the librarian's first task is to see whether such works exist or not. If this is found to be so, they then become known-item queries.

Author/title queries are very common in all kinds of libraries, but particularly in large academic libraries, which for many students throughout their courses remain forbidding and mysterious. In most cases such questions arise from the enquirer's lack of familiarity with the mechanics of using a library to track down a separate bibliographical unit. To the librarian, therefore, they are usually easy, requiring tact and patience to resolve, but drawing upon detailed knowledge of a particular library's holdings and specific bibliographical training, rather than the broader professional education of the qualified librarian.

Once again, it might be argued that a higher proportion of these queries could be anticipated by the provision of catalogues that are more comprehensive and easier to understand, more positive indications within the library as to the supplementary role of bibliographies, indexes and abstracts, and so on.

### Fact-finding enquiries

The third category within this broad grouping of limited-help questions is made up of factual queries, sometimes known as quick-reference or ready-reference queries, but perhaps more usefully described as fact-finding enquiries. For their solution they demand the provision of *specific items of information* and statistically they form the bulk of the enquiries received in libraries of all kinds. There has been a tendency in recent years in the literature of reference work to disparage such factual questions as less worthy of the full attention of busy professional librarians. Yet the determination of specific facts is of immense importance in many major disciplines: historians, literary scholars, economists, lawyers, and many others will spend hours if not days in search of a single elusive fact. As for the scientist, T. H. Huxley paid graphic tribute to the power of facts when he spoke of 'the great tragedy of science – the slaying of a beautiful hypothesis by an ugly fact'.

In truth, the number and range of fact-finding enquiries asked in libraries demonstrates not only the value to business and industry and government and scholarship of the supply of accurate facts, but also the widespread fascination of people at large with precise factual knowledge, similarly reflected in the world-wide popularity of trivia games and radio and television quiz programmes.

Characteristic examples are 'What is Portuguese for "on" and "off"?', 'What is the frequency of the Copenhagen radio station?', 'Is there an international sign which indicates "this side up" on packing cases?', 'What is the name for an Arab man's head-dress?', 'Can you find the formula for calculating the surface area of a slice off the top of a sphere?'. Most enquiries of this kind require a single, factual answer, but in some cases the response, while still precise and limited, will consist of a series of facts: for example, 'Can you tell me where I can buy goldbeater's skin?', 'What is the derivation of "Alice" blue?', 'What is an isopach map?', 'I am trying to trace the budget of UNESCO?', 'How did the phrase "red letter day" originate?'.

Clausewitz said about strategy that 'It is simple, but it is not easy', and the young librarian should not be misled by the apparently simple character of fact-finding queries into assuming that they are easy to answer. To run to earth some facts can indeed be exceptionally difficult, measured by the time and effort required – for example: the original name for the Brownies (the youngest age group of the Girl Guides and Girl Scouts); the name of Pavlov's dog; whether Earl Mountbatten was related to Princess Pocohontas; the Bosanquet formula (magnetic induction); the registration number of the motor cycle on which Lawrence of Arabia was riding when he was killed.

It should scarcely need emphasizing here that the essentially limited commitment required by questions of this nature by no means implies that reference librarians are less sympathetic or concerned or attentive to the needs of their users. It is simply a consequence of this kind of question that there is no necessity or even opportunity to become closely involved in enquirers' problems. All that is required is the supply of an unambiguous factual answer. But of course, the transaction is still a personal affair and should be conducted in human manner. The librarian should be at pains to avoid the quick-fire response of the quiz contestant. Machine-like efficiency is not admired in personal relationships.

## Material-finding enquiries

A substantial minority of the queries posed by users do not exhibit this intrinsic self-limiting aspect: these are the questions that are *open-ended* in character, and thus demand more extended assistance from the reference librarian. They have sometimes been called subject or search queries, but are more graphically described as material-finding enquiries. What users require in such cases is the presentation to them of *a range of information* on the topic of their query. One enquirer may simply be looking for 'something on' (or even 'anything on') the subject and will be satisfied with any reasonable selection. Another may need to cover a topic exhaustively and will not rest content until all the material available has been produced. Examples of this kind of open-ended question are 'What have you got on the use of insects as food?', 'I am looking for designs for a maze', 'Can you find me something on famous gluttons?', 'Have you anything on making church vestments?', 'I am looking for something on absolute pitch'. All of these are plainly different in nature from the self-limiting questions quoted earlier. In the first place, none of them could be said to have a single definitive answer; secondly, a point is never reached when the search can be described as complete, because there always remains the possibility that further investigation will uncover additional information; thirdly, the librarian can only be sure that what has been provided is the 'right' answer, i.e. the range of information appropriate to the need, by observing the reaction of the enquirer.

In some instances questions are asked that are a little less open-ended, insofar as the subject asked about is also accompanied by a specification by form, e.g. 'Do you have an Eskimo dictionary?', 'Is there a discography of the British music hall?', 'Can you find me a life of R. D. Blackmore?', 'Have you got a sitar tutor?', 'Do you know if there are any patents on nutcrackers?'. Occasionally the specification is by form only: 'Can you find me some commonplace books?', 'I am looking for an example of a hocket [mediaeval technique of musical composition]', 'Have you any trade union rule-books?'.

Material-finding questions of this kind, in the words of James I. Wyer over 60 years ago, provide 'the staple and body of most reference work'. They are the most demanding kind of enquiries, calling into play the full repertoire of the reference librarian's skills, not merely bibliographical knowledge. Also needed is the confidence to initiate and sustain an intellectual partnership with the enquirer. The librarian must possess the sensitivity and perspicacity to observe the reactions of the enquirer to the progress of the search, and to elicit responses if necessary, so that its course can be adjusted and redirected more precisely towards the desired objective. Nice judgement will be called on throughout, but particularly for the decision to bring the search to a conclusion.

## Mutable enquiries

One minor phenomenon that the student should watch out for is the question that changes its character during the course of its investigation. As William A. Katz noted, 'Questions are mercurial' and an author/title enquiry may evolve into a fact-finding enquiry if inability to trace the work casts doubt on the accuracy of its description. A librarian who is asked for Michael Grant's *Latin readings* soon discovers that there is no such work, but further investigation reveals that the same author's *Latin literature* (1979) is in fact a revised reissue of his *Roman readings* (1958). Such is human fallibility, particularly in the matter of authors and titles, that problems of bibliographical verification are common in all libraries. The fault is not always the enquirer's: a 1979 study by Bert R. Boyce and Carolyn Sue Banning of the bibliographical citations in 10 major United States medical journals found 29% inaccurate; even in the *Journal of the American Society for Information Science* 13.6% of the citations were incorrect. Increasingly encountered too, as a direct result of the wider availability of bibliographical data online, is the simple 'Do you have?' question that later turns into 'Well, can you tell me who does?'.

Similarly what starts off as a fact-finding enquiry may emerge as a material-finding enquiry if the specific facts sought turn out to be disputed or obscure. If asked 'What is the origin of the scoring system in tennis?', the librarian soon discovers from the standard reference sources that the matter is disputed. If the enquirer wishes to pursue it further, the librarian then needs to find additional historical material explaining in more detail where the particular difficulty lies. Lynch has called such queries 'moving transactions'.

Not uncommonly enquirers too will change their stance during the course of the transaction: when presented with the answer to his query about the date of Gustav Holst's orchestral suite *The Planets*, one enquirer then asked 'How does it go?'. But this kind of shift should not come as a surprise; indeed, as Robert S. Taylor has pointed out, 'One of the results of the negotiations process is to alter the inquirer's *a priori* picture of what it is he expects'. This will be explored further in Chapter 4.

41

Should it be the policy of the library, or the librarian, to provide no more than a conservative or minimum or instructional service (see Chapter 1), the enquirer may find the transaction moving in the opposite direction, with a fact-finding or material-finding question being treated as if it were a directional question. A request such as 'Who was the architect of Broadcasting House?' might be dealt with by showing the enquirer where the guidebooks on London are kept; and a user seeking help on the part played by the Royal Navy in the suppression of the slave trade may find the librarian allowed to do no more than point out the slavery entries in the subject catalogue and the history bibliographies and indexes on the shelves.

## Research enquiries

From time to time librarians get asked questions, either of the fact-finding type or of the material-finding type, which turn out upon investigation to be really research enquiries. What is at issue here is 'real' or primary research, not research in the looser sense of that term to mean intensive searching. What usually happens is that the librarian discovers that the user's problem cannot be solved from the literature or from the various other sources, documentary or personal, that are available for consultation. In other words, both librarian and user find themselves standing at the very frontiers of knowledge. Should they wish to progress further, they will find that mere *searching* no longer suffices: what are needed are the more specialized tools of *research*, such as deduction, hypothesis, experiment, statistical analysis, critical judgement, observation, opinion surveys, historical method, and the like. Deploying such techniques, it is the research worker who carries the responsibility of adding to the sum of human knowledge. Reference librarians, as such, are not equipped with these tools, and in practice, except in very special cases, they are obliged to draw the line at original investigation. When on rare occasions they deliberately step over the line, for example in some special libraries, they are no longer practising reference work, but research. Explaining these complementary roles to an anxious enquirer is yet another task requiring from the reference librarian a more than common tact and patience.

Not all research enquiries are concerned with new knowledge. We have forgotten more than we have remembered and lost more than we have recorded. Much research involves trying to find it again. Archaeology provides the most dramatic example, but amateur genealogical enquiries furnish a typical illustration of the problem as it affects libraries. We know we all have ancestors: what has been lost is the link between them and us.

## Residual enquiries

Any representative sample, any cross-section, any week's harvest of queries in a busy library is sure to include a residuum that does not fit into any of the categories so far outlined. These are the questions that exhibit some internal inconsistency, some logical flaw, even some inherent impossibility, often quite invisible to the enquirer. Examples are 'Where is the centre of England?', 'How did Jesus wear his hair?', 'I am looking for a picture of Mollie Malone's wheelbarrow', 'I would like all the newsreel material you have of the Pilgrim Fathers first arriving in America', 'Can I have the magazine you showed my friend last week?'. Children have a particular propensity to ask such questions: 'How many grains of sand are there in a bucket-full?', 'Have you got a list of all the islands in the world?'.

It is scarcely possible to categorize these in any helpful way. Nevertheless, when questions like this are asked, the fact that they can have no true 'answer' does not leave the reference librarian free to ignore them. The enquirer still has to be dealt with, and in a civilized manner. In some instances, perhaps, librarians may feel like the character in James Thurber who knew a man 'who kept drawing on a piece of paper what the ringing of a telephone looks like', and from time to time may wonder why they did not become social workers. But it is often possible to furnish some kind of 'answer' that will satisfy a particular enquirer: there is, for instance, a village where 'A 500-year-old stone cross on the village green is said to mark the exact centre of England'; and there is information available on how Jewish men wore their hair 2,000 years ago. But in all such cases what the librarian has to do is to take time to explain, to persuade, to convince, and to send the enquirer home, if not better informed or wiser, at least more content.

## Unanswerable questions

Of course the world is full of questions that have no answer. Some of those just quoted are the kind that cannot have an answer, and librarians recognize them by virtue of their powers of reasoning: an answer is a logical impossibility.

There is a second category of unanswerable questions that do in theory have an answer, but which the librarian immediately recognizes from knowledge and experience as effectively unanswerable in practice. Many seemingly simple statistical enquiries are like this, such as 'How many hoboes are there in the United States?', 'I am looking for figures of life expectancy for every occupation', 'What is the Louisiana Purchase worth today?'. No one may have found it worthwhile to collect or maintain such figures. Other examples falling into this group are 'What is the current price of ivory? [trade has been banned since 1989]', 'What are the ingredients of Advocaat [a proprietary liqueur]?'. This last is a reminder that there is a large amount of information that is purposely kept dark: not only cloak-and-dagger state secrets, but vast quantities of confidential technical and commercial data, including details about business firms that may be household names but which are legally private companies. This veil of reticence even extends to seemingly innocuous information such as certain television viewing figures or the name of a person who has bought a valuable painting at auction or the unlisted telephone number of a best-selling author. It is often argued that access to such information by the citizen should be improved, by law if necessary. The problem that no society has yet solved is how to strike an acceptable balance between freedom of information on the one hand and the individual's right to privacy and the security of the state on the other.

The third category of unanswerable enquiries cannot be recognized at first sight: their nature is revealed only as a consequence of the librarian's search. Sometimes positive evidence is found that the answer is unknown. More usually such questions are deemed to be unanswerable when the search turns out to be negative, and it is decided either that further research or investigation will prove fruitless, or that it is not worth the effort. Examples are 'How many men fought at the Battle of Hastings?', 'Where does the word "loo" come from?', 'What is the origin of the custom of killing the bearer of bad tidings?', 'Who was the Betty Martin in the saying "All my eye and Betty Martin"?', 'How many children did Lady Macbeth have?'.

Some of these are found to be unanswerable because there is no answer, for example 'What is the English equivalent of *parvis* [a French word for the square in front of a church]?', 'I am looking for something on the Japanese alphabet', 'How can I copyright a song?', 'What are the names of the seven dwarfs?', 'How are loofahs manufactured?'. Once again, however, as always, there is a role for the reference librarian to play, even with unanswerable questions. There is often an explanation that can be offered to mitigate the disappointment: that there are many foreign terms without an English equivalent; that there are some languages that do not have an alphabet; that under English law copyright is automatic for an original work as soon as it is created; that in the original fairy story as collected by the Brothers Grimm in the early 19th century the seven dwarfs were all anonymous, and the names they are now known by were invented for the Walt Disney film in 1937; and that a loofah is a natural product, the pod of a plant.

## Question taxonomy and analysis
It is important that reference librarians should be able to look analytically in this way at the questions that are put to them, and in addition to the functional grouping that has been preferred here, the literature describes further methods of categorizing them along a variety of dimensions: by degree of difficulty, for example, or academic level; by length of time taken; by the type and number of sources used to answer them; or, of course, by subject. All of these methods have their value for particular purposes, whether for collection-building or staff evaluation or measurement of use. The advantage for study purposes of the grouping used in this chapter is that it is based on the nature of the practical response that the different categories require from the reference librarian – which is what this book is concerned with.

It is of course possible to take these broad groupings further. Fact-finding enquiries, for example, can be subdivided into those requiring statistical information ('How much is staked annually on football pools in Britain?'); quantitative information ('How many bones are there in the human body?'); a yes/no answer ('Were matches used in 1844?'); an illustration ('Can you find me a diagram of a pentacle?'); a meaning ('What is an oligopoly?'); a description ('What is Coade stone?'); a symbol ('What are the signs in stamp collecting for used and unused?'); a name ('Who was it said "All political lives end in failure"?'); a date ('When was the Northwest Passage found?'); a place ('Which is the cathedral where Chagall designed the stained glass?'); a word ('What is the fear of heights called?'); and so on and so forth.

Much interesting work has been done in the last decade or so on the analysis of *individual* reference questions. In Canada, drawing on a study of 5,721 questions asked in the University of Waterloo Engineering, Mathematics and Science Library, John P. Wilkinson and his colleagues have devised the 'step' approach, analysing questions 'in terms of the number of steps necessary to provide information – a "step" being regarded as a distinct and definable judgement leading to a decision, action, or recommendation'. Thus, 'Can you tell me where the patents collection is?' would be a one-step question; 'I am looking for a list of abrasive wheel manufacturers' would be a two-step question because the librarian has first to select an appropriate directory and then locate the information for the enquirer; 'Is there any literature on seat-belt injuries?' would be a multi-step question, with step one comprising the choice of appropriate bibliographical tools, step two the identification of relevant citations, and step three the location of the actual literature.

More recently Barbara M. Robinson has used the terms 'simple' and 'complex' to describe the characteristics of a reference question: 'If the question is simple, it is single-faceted. If it is complex, it is multi-faceted. In other words, if the question is short and has only one part, it is a simple question. If the question is long and contains many parts, such as clauses, it is complex.' 'Have you anything on baton-twirling?' would therefore be regarded as a simple question, and 'Can you find me something on duelling by students in Germany at the present time?' would be a complex question.

Particularly useful has been the work over more than a decade by Gerald Jahoda and his colleagues. An examination of more than 700 reference queries collected from academic and public libraries led them to 'the conclusion that each query statement consist of at least two categories of message words: those identifying the subject of the information need (called "givens") and those identifying the information desired about the subject (called "wanteds")'. In a query such as 'What is Paget's disease?' for instance, the 'given' is the disease while the 'wanted' is a definition or description. Others have followed with similar observations, though using different terminology. According to Richard L. Derr, for example, 'Questions possess a distinct structure. They consist of two parts: (1) *subject*: a term or terms that refers to an object in the world about which some type of determination is being sought, and (2) *query*: an expression that identifies the particular determination to be made regarding the subject of the question.' Of course such an analysis applies not only to reference questions, but to questions in general. The last 20 years or so have seen a particularly intense and thorough study of questions and their logic, and Nicholas J. Belkin and Alina Vickery have surveyed this research for its relevance to information retrieval. They too reported that 'An elementary question has two parts, a subject and a request. The subject presents a set of alternatives, and the request identifies how many of the true alternatives are desired in the answer and what sort of claims for completeness and distinctness are to be made.'

Of themselves none of these is a particularly penetrating insight, but the importance of Jahoda's research stems from his elaboration of the concept to provide not only an analytical instrument of considerable power but a practical tool to use in answering actual questions. His list of givens, for example, included: an abbreviation; a specifically named organization, person, or place; a term or subject (other than the specific types already listed); a specific publication. Among his list of wanteds were: date; illustration; numeric information (properties, scientifically measured, or statistics, involving counting); organization; person; address or general location; publication (bibliography, document location, or verification or completion of bibliographical data); textual information (definition or symbol, recommendation, general or background information).

With most queries the given is a subject and the wanted is textual information, as with 'How do you diagnose psittacosis in humans?' and 'I would like something on hysterical sneezing'. Examples of other permutations of givens and wanteds are 'Have you got a skeletal drawing of a horse?' (given: subject; wanted: illustration); 'I am looking for the text of Washington's first inaugural address' (given: specific publication; wanted: document location); 'What does *force majeure* mean on my holiday insurance policy?' (given: term; wanted: definition); 'What do you have on the Empress Tzu Hsi?' (given: specifically named person; wanted: general or background information); 'When was the first use of the term "welfare state"?' (given: term; wanted: date); 'What is Joyeuse-Garde [estate given by King Arthur to Sir Lancelot])?' (given: specifically named place; wanted: general or background information); 'Do you have a list of falconry clubs?' (given: subject; wanted: address or general location); 'How heavy is the blue whale?' (given: subject; wanted: numeric information [property, scientifically measured]). The use of Jahoda's technique as a searching tool will be illustrated in Chapter 5.

Most enquiries come from users who actually visit the library, but many are received by telephone. In certain kinds of libraries – such as business libraries – telephone queries may outnumber the others, and in some instances, e.g. in information and referral centres, may amount to 90% of all questions asked. And of course a proportion are received in writing by post, telex, or fax, and increasingly by electronic mail. Although there is no hard-and-fast rule, it is normal practice to respond using the same means where possible.

Inexperienced students often remark on the wide range of topics asked about, particularly in academic and special libraries. In the public library, the universal provider, it is perhaps less surprising to encounter the vast array of subjects that concern enquirers, but in special libraries one might expect the questions to be drawn from the special subject fields covered, and in academic libraries it might reasonably be assumed that the queries would be related to the subjects taught or the research areas under investigation. This is by no means true. While naturally most of the enquiries do fall into expected areas, there is a minority in all libraries which do not. The following three questions were asked in three different special libraries serving the chemical industry: 'What does a Lord-Lieutenant do?', 'What is the weight of the QE2?', 'Can you find illustrations of Italian army uniforms?'. Queries seeking quotations for speeches are common in at least one major university law library. And there is a government department library where one of the most frequently used quick-reference books is *The good food guide.*

There seems to be no limit to the subject range of the topics that may be asked about. Indeed, it can be stated as a rule: there is no area of knowledge that can be excluded as a possible subject for an enquiry in any library. Of course, that is not to say that all such queries will be answered; library policy in particular cases may prevent them even being accepted. But the reference librarian who is prepared for anything can at least refer such enquiries to the most likely source.

It also appears to be the case that a large proportion of the queries asked in libraries are devoid of any particular national or racial characteristics, other than the language in which they are expressed. The following queries come half-and-half from opposite sides of the globe: 'What does f.o.s. mean?' [free on steamer]?', 'How can I convert hectares to acres?', 'What is the national anthem of Sweden?', 'What is the address of the Development Bank of Singapore?', 'What is the chemical analysis of pineapple juice?', 'Have you any literature on cover crops?', 'What is it the poem says about Tuesday's child?', 'What are the seven wonders of the world?', 'What does q.h. mean in a prescription [*quaque hora*, Latin for every hour]?', 'What are the seating arrangements for an orchestra?', 'What is the central religious rite of Zoroastrianism?', 'Is there a list of famous people that were left-handed?'. Any British reference librarian, perched on or near the Greenwich Meridian, would recognize them all as just the kind that might be encountered any day, but would be quite unable to guess which half-dozen came from the western hemisphere and which from the eastern. It does appear to be true that the slogan 'Information – one world' is no exaggeration.

Not the least remarkable feature of reference work is the way that identical queries turn up again and again, in libraries of greatly varying types, often in different parts of the world and sometimes in the same library but at wide intervals of time. In his 1975 thesis on the history of reference in British public libraries, Kenneth Whittaker identified a 1913 article as the first of note wholly devoted to the subject of enquirers. He commented that 'the article certainly brings home that enquirers and their questions have hardly changed in the last sixty years'. And from the opposite end of the globe again, in 1978 the State Library of New South Wales had a number of enquiries for information on the use of hydrogen as fuel in internal-combustion engines; the records they had kept of requests showed that 'people were asking about this in the 1920s, the 1930s and the 1940s'.

There is an old joke that examiners in economics need never set the candidates new question papers because the answers change every year. The moral here for the young librarian is that the identical reference question may not always be adequately answered by the same reply, and not only because subjects change. As was described in Chapter 1, in reference work the librarian has to combine in a response a technically accurate reply to the question with a satisfactory fulfilment of the questioner's personal need. As Roger Horn has explained, 'How can you answer the same old questions over and over again? Well, it is just that the answers are different. For everyone who asks a question there is another answer: his or her answer to his or her question.'

*Further reading*
James, G. Rohan, 'Reference: analysis, management and training', *Library review*, **31**, 1982, 93 – 103.
Derr, Richard L., 'Questions: definitions, structure, and classification', *RQ*, **24**, 1984, 186 – 90.
Robinson, Barbara M., 'Reference services: a model of question handling', *RQ*, **29**, 1989, 48 – 61.

# — 3 —

# The reference process

While the term 'reference work' applies to the actual assistance given to the user in need of information, over the last 30 years or so the broader term 'reference process' has come to be used to describe the whole transaction with the enquirer in the course of which the reference work is carried out. This process centres on the initial point of contact where the enquirer puts the question to the librarian, but it stretches right back to the moment when the enquirer recognized the existence of the problem, and it extends through and beyond the librarian's search for the required information and the delivery of the response right up to the point where it can be mutually agreed that the original problem has been solved.

**Two phases**
It is important to recognize that the process has these two phases: reference work is not simply what librarians do to find the answers to the questions they are asked. It also includes the crucial prior stage where they examine with their enquirers the nature of their problems. The fact that in the majority of instances this preliminary stage need only be very brief has perhaps led to its neglect by earlier generations. Not the least of the valuable side-effects that the computer has had on reference work is an increased awareness of the critical significance of this pre-search stage in the reference process.

In 1964 Jesse Shera characterized the process as 'complex associative series of linkages, or events', and in 1966 Alan M. Rees explained how it involves 'not only the identification and manipulation of available bibliographical apparatus, but also the operation of psychological, sociological and environmental variables which are imperfectly understood at the present time'. In Gerald Jahoda's rather simpler terms it comprises 'the sum total of steps taken by the reference librarian in answering questions addressed to him'. But it is not a simple linear

50

process: these steps may involve a certain amount of preliminary backtracking over the question before looking for the answer, and occasional looping back during the course of the search. Unfortunately for the student of the process, the sequence and direction of these steps is often more impromptu than premeditated, and sometimes one step will merge into another. Indeed the whole process sometimes takes the form of a largely intuitive matching of requests, readers, resources, and responses by the reference librarian.

Nevertheless, it is essential not to lose sight of the transaction as a whole, 'essentially a process of interpersonal communication with the specific purpose of fulfilling others' information needs', in James Rettig's words. The fact of the matter is that the reference process is but one aspect of an individual's quest for knowledge and therefore always retains its distinctly human quality. To its practitioners this is the secret of its eternal appeal, but it is all too easily overlooked by the systems analysts and others who try to probe its mysteries.

## Eight steps

For purposes of study, nevertheless, it is helpful to set out the full logical sequence of interlinked decision-making steps that comprise the normal reference process.

1  *The problem*

The process normally has as its starting-point a problem which draws itself to the attention of a prospective library user. No one is immune to problems, and so in theory each member of the human race is a potential initiator of the reference process. The source of the problem may be external or internal. An external problem stems from the social or at least situational context of the individual; an internal problem is psychological or cognitive in origin, arising in the individual's mind. Many human problems, however, are not susceptible to solution by information; this is probably the case with most of those that arise in the course of our everyday life. Of the remainder which are possibly treatable, a large proportion are not recognized as such by those afflicted with them.

2  *The information need*

But those prospective users who form the opinion that to deal with their problem they need to know something, have then moved on to the second stage of their progress towards a solution. Their information need at this point may be vague and imprecise, though not necessarily so. But it will probably be unformed, and certainly unexpressed; it is what Robert S. Taylor called a 'visceral' need. This need may not in fact arise from a concrete 'problem' at all. The motivation may simply be the desire to know and understand, or even 'mere' curiosity, though we must not forget what Dr Johnson said: 'Curiosity is one of the permanent and certain characteristics of a vigorous intellect'. The exigency of the need too may range from 'It would be nice to know' to 'I can't go any further until I find out'.

The roots of information-seeking behaviour are indeed buried deep, but drawing on research in cognitive psychology a number of interesting theories have appeared in the literature of library and information science in recent years, following Taylor's seminal work in the 1960s. This will be investigated in more detail in Chapter 4.

There are of course a number of ways of finding out what one wants to know: observation, trial and error, experiment; asking someone; looking it up for oneself. The prospective user who tries any of the first three and is successful ceases to be a prospective user.

3  *The initial question*
One of the most important ways in which humans acquire knowledge is by asking questions, and if the potential user decides to ask someone then obviously it becomes necessary to give the need a sharper intellectual shape, to describe it in words, and to formulate it as a question. And those who wish to look it up for themselves may need to formalize the statement still further by deciding the precise words under which they will look it up.

So far the whole proceeding has been a matter entirely for the individual with the problem, and the communication has been what the psychologists call *intra*personal, involving a kind of mental rehearsal in anticipation of the expected *inter*personal encounter, the moment when the individual puts the question to someone else. Countless surveys have shown that comparatively few people think of the library when they need information, and even fewer turn to a librarian. But if a seeker after information does ask a librarian for help, the whole operation then becomes the reference process, with the steps already taken by the user compromising the first phase, and the second phase being a joint enterprise with the librarian.

4  *The negotiated question*
Though reference librarians cannot enter the reference process until

they receive the questions from the enquirers, they are vitally concerned about both its phases and all of its stages. Final success is dependent on each of the steps making up the first phase being correctly taken, and it is often necessary for librarians to retrace with their enquirers those first few steps they took on their own. The initial question as formulated by the enquirer may sometimes need further clarification or adjustment to ensure that it fits more closely the underlying information need. The question is then compared with the way information is organized generally in the library and more particularly in the specific information sources in its collections or elsewhere. This comparison often reveals that the question needs some redefinition or reordering to allow a more convenient matching with the terminology and structure of the sources to be searched.

5   *The search strategy*

Before the question as finally negotiated can be put to the information store, two technical decisions are necessary: how is the information store, whether local or distant, to be interrogated? and which parts are to be searched, in what order? The first is largely a matter of detailed analysis of the subject of the question, identifying its concepts and their relationships, and then translating them into an appropriate search statement in the access language of the information store. The enquirer can often be of great assistance to the librarian here.

The second decision involves choosing from among several possible routes. Success here depends on close knowledge of the various sources of information available for searching, experience in their use, and that intuitive sense which all reference librarians recognize and which has been much commented on but which no one can explain. It is normally a three-stage choice: first the category of source is selected, then the particular source within that category, and finally the specific access points within that source. And of course if this proves unfruitful another choice is made, of the next most promising category or source or access point, as appropriate. These are judgements almost entirely within the province of the librarian – and as suggested may sometimes be made at the subconscious level – but all can often be made more effective by a quick preliminary search to test the ground.

6   *The search procedure*

The conduct of the search of the information store is normally in the librarian's hands, though some like to have the enquirer at their elbow, ready to provide an instant reaction to what the search reveals. The most effective searches are those where the strategy is flexible enough to accommodate a change of course should the progress of the search indicate this. A well-prepared searcher will already have alternative strategies ready if need be: again, the presence of the enquirer facilitates such alterations of direction. Purists might argue that this is tactics rather than strategy, but so deficient in logical structure or internal consistency are many of the major sources of information that suppleness is a desirable attribute in a searcher.

7   *The answer*

In most cases a careful and experienced searcher will find an 'answer', but that is by no means the end of the process. What the librarian has at this stage is merely the product of the search. If the search has been carried out properly it should match, by and large, the search statement, as tactically modified, but it is necessary to make sure. The search may occasionally prove fruitless: this may also be an 'answer', but it is rarely satisfactory to present it to the enquirer baldly as such.

8   *The response*

An 'answer' is only a potential response: in some cases where there are no doubts in the librarian's mind as to its adequacy for the enquirer's purpose it may suffice in its unadorned form. But frequently for a complete response a degree of elucidation or explanation is necessary. It is also good practice for the librarian and the enquirer together to evaluate the 'product' of the search, and for both of them to give it their approval before it can be agreed that the reference process is complete.

This sequence represents the whole of the reference process from start to finish, but only in outline. It will be considered in more detail in Chapters 4, 5, and 6. It should not be forgotten, however, that there is usually one more, final stage: 'how [people] use the information or knowledge they accept as the answer', in the words of S. D. Neill. For the user this of course is the most important stage of all, the whole object of the exercise being to apply information to solve the initial problem, but as it occurs beyond the control of the librarian and after the user has left, it is difficult to see how it can be regarded as part of the *reference* process. Nevertheless, there are precautionary techniques which the alert librarian can deploy during the course of the interview, and these too will be discussed further in Chapter 4.

The process lends itself well to representation in diagrammatic form and there are many models in the literature, ranging from a simple sequential layout to elaborate and detailed flow charts, complete with decision boxes, branching, and feedback loops. These valuable aids to understanding are another benefit reference librarians owe to the advent of the computer: though the flow chart has been in use for many years in other fields, such as chemical engineering and work study, it is the computer systems analysts who have been most successful in adapting it to portray intellectual activities.

## A play for two characters

The industrial librarian who 20 years ago graphically described the reference process as a 'customer-librarian interactive drama' was not the only one to be struck by the analogy with the stage. In their 1987 book *The reference interview as a creative art* Elaine Zaremba Jennerich and Edward J. Jennerich justified the ' "theatrical" theme' of their title and chapter headings (The actor's tools, Supporting roles, One-person shows, Encore, Special performances, Finale, and half-a-dozen others) by asserting that 'the reference interview in particular is a performing art. Anyone who has worked at a reference desk has at some point had the feeling of being "on stage" and cast in a starring role', and they introduce their text by announcing 'And now . . . on with the show'.

All this should serve to remind the student that the reference process must not become a solo performance by the librarian: it should be a dialogue, with the enquirer and librarian playing complementary roles throughout. As has been described, the enquirer (most frequently male) makes his debut at the *reference interview*, the first act of the drama, where he has to ensure that his partner, the reference librarian (more often than not female), understands the nature of his problem. For the reference librarian her big scene is the *reference search*: the trap to be avoided here is playing the *prima donna*. An enquirer upstaged by a virtuoso parade of knowledge will not only feel uncomfortable but may be unwilling to venture into the limelight again. Third act, the *response*, comprises the denouement, when everything is made clear; the finale when the two players are reconciled; and the fall of the curtain, when they both live happily ever after.

**False impressions**

Just as when defining reference work it is necessary to explain what it is not, so in describing the reference process is it important to dispel certain lingering misconceptions as to what it comprises. It must be plain to everyone who has read this chapter so far that the objectives of the reference process are far broader than the routine supply of answers to questions asked by users of the library. The field of reference is strewn with failures, measured in the enquirer's terms, but where the reference librarian did provide a technically perfect answer to the question asked. Post-mortems on such cases always reveal a fault in the reference process.

If it is not sufficient then to describe the purpose of the process as answering questions, how best to characterize it briefly, short of a full academic definition? Of the many possibilities, the term 'problem-solving' is the one that fits most closely as a shorthand symbol. After all, as has been seen, it is the solution of the enquirer's problem that is the real object of the exercise. The asking and answering of a question is only the means. Neill indeed takes the view that 'The reference process from start to finish is a sequence of problems'. This matter will be explored further in Chapter 4.

The second mistaken view that still clings is that the process incorporates a 'reference method' that can be used as a guide to follow in all cases where the librarian seeks information in response to an enquiry. James I. Wyer knew this was not so as long ago as 1930: 'No such [step-by-step] statement of reference procedure can be made to fit every or perhaps any single question'. Two generations later, despite decades of attention from systems analysts and a whole portfolio of flow charts, Geraldine B. King felt obliged in her pamphlet on reference service in the small library to accompany her account of the reference process with the warning 'Of course any particular reference transaction will not neatly follow the parts in this description'. Precisely because the reference process – both the reference interview and the search – is a human activity, it is liable to infinite variation. This is its charm, and its challenge.

**The computer in the reference process**

Favourable mention has twice been made so far in this chapter of the effect of the computer on the reference process. The description of the eight steps of the reference process could apply equally well, without a word being altered, to either a manual or a computer search. In the remainder of this book the reader may notice that the computer has been similarly taken for granted as an everyday component of reference work. At first, in the late 1960s and early 1970s, it was seen by many as an alien interloper, and the common practice of setting up a distinct online search service, with the terminal located in a separate department, operated by specially selected and trained staff, reinforced this attitude. Integration is now the rule rather than the exception, and computer searching is now part of mainstream reference service in most (though by no means all) libraries. The increasing proportion of the reference librarian's traditional sources of information in the form of computerized databases, together with a number of brand-new tools, available for searching in a variety of new ways, has been an advance in reference work at least as great as the appearance in the mid-19th century of Poole's *Index* and the many other standard bibliographies and reference works mentioned in Chapter 1, an evolution which in many ways it resembles.

The use of computers has certainly enhanced the image of the reference librarian in the eyes of enquirers: by 1977 reference librarians were reporting that 'Users appear to be surprised to learn that librarians know more than how to point to the index table or the card catalog. Some have expressed the fact that they never realized how much specialized training being a librarian must require.' Part of the reason may be, as Jitka Hurych pointed out, that the service is 'usually based on appointments and ... The patron is, probably for the first time, given individual attention in the library.' It also produced some curious effects: a 1975 study of online users found that 'Engineers, scientists, and researchers more readily accept the results of online literature searching, even though the quality of the search is obviously still determined by the search prescription formulated by the librarian'.

But there were those who saw the coming of interactive computer searching as a golden opportunity for users to conduct their own searches, where previously they had to rely on intermediaries undertaking batch searches on their behalf. For reasons which one could have predicted, this never happened on anything like the scale some expected – in 1977 Carlos A. Cuadra reported that 'probably upwards of 95% of all online searches are carried out by information intermediaries' – although health warnings continued to appear about the fate of the reference librarian in the era of the computer. In 1983, for example, while acknowledging that information intermediaries 'almost monopolise expertise in handling online systems through local terminals', a British government document gave notice that 'they will have to rethink their role if they are not to lose all or most of it to end-users who have become familiar with computers'.

It is necessary to keep a sense of balance here: the spectre that has been raised of reference librarians as the charcoal burners and the handloom weavers of the library revolution when the 21st century dawns is as insubstantial as the prediction in the 1920s that the coming of radio meant the death sentence for the gramophone record. For whatever the computer might have done for library housekeeping routines (some of which it has abolished), or for acquisition and cataloguing methods (which it has revolutionized), it has so far only served to enhance traditional reference work. Professional intermediaries still carry out the overwhelming majority of computer searches.

Not the least interesting feature of the advance of the computer in the library is that it has affected different parts of the reference process in distinctly different ways. Its *direct* impact has so far only been felt on one stage of that process, namely the reference search. And even here in the overwhelming majority of cases a traditional manual search is still the preferred option. It is important to remember the success of a search is not measured according to the sources consulted or the medium employed, but by the answer obtained. Once that has been said, however, there is no doubt at all that in those instances where the librarian judges a computer search more appropriate, the effect is dramatic and obvious: a search at the terminal, with all that implies for search strategy and formulation, replaces a manual search at the shelves.

Its main impact on the reference interview has been to supply strong reinforcement to the cause argued for generations by traditional reference librarians that, as William Warner Bishop expressed it in 1908, 'The chief art of . . . a reference librarian is . . . the knack of divining by long experience what is actually wanted by enquirers'. Everyone who has examined the topic, librarians and non-librarians alike, has agreed that the reference interview is essential to the success of the computer search. William A. Katz insisted that it is 'an absolute requirement' and for Ching-Chih Chen it was 'the single most important phase of information retrieval'.

As for its effect on the information versus instruction debate, by 1982 Katz felt able to say 'the search is almost always performed by a librarian or search analyst. . . . The inevitable result is service on a maximum level, whether the librarian wishes it or not', and by 1985 Tze-Chung

Li had concluded that 'In online searching, the instructional function appears to be entirely eliminated from the reference service'. But the dispute is far from over. A vigorous rearguard continues to promote end-user searching: Dorice Des Chene, for example, argued strongly that 'In the future the role of teacher and consultant must become prominent for librarians, in the sense of enabling users to use online search capabilities ... effectively. The principal goal of librarians should be to teach users to find what they want for themselves.'

It is always likely to be the case that in many instances a human intermediary will be required between the enquirer and the machine: an enquirer's familiarity with the technology, its free availability, and its user-friendly nature are not the issues here. Just as experience has shown that a human link is often needed between the enquirer and the book, so will professional help continue to be called for with computerized databases, both online (including OPACs) and in CD-ROM format. In 1967 in the early days of computerized information retrieval Dorothy Sinclair predicted this in her article 'The next ten years in reference service': 'Today's users, even the most sophisticated, could spend their time making their own searches, but many of them call on us, preferring to devote their own time to their own productive work ... it seems probable that the skilled intermediary will still be necessary'. Evidence gathered 20 years on bears this out. In the famous 'Square Mile', the City (of London), there are probably more computer terminals than in any equivalent area of the globe, with the only possible contenders being Wall Street in New York and the financial district of Tokyo. Yet, much to their surprise, in a British Library-funded survey in 1987, David Nicholas and his colleagues found that 'In spite of ostensibly favourable conditions, end-user searching of online text retrieval systems among City firms is relatively uncommon. Online searching is flourishing but is very much the province of librarians'.

Surveys of library and information science schools show that virtually all now include instruction in database searching in the curriculum (though only a minority have integrated it into the general reference and subject bibliography courses), and in 1990 Linda Friend noted that in the United States 'Nearly every advertisement for a reference librarian now lists online searching as a qualification (either required or desirable)'.

Nevertheless, according to Barbara Quint, writing in 1989, 'To this day, many libraries still do not offer online searches to patrons as a standard professional information service. ... The view that online must always serve as a companion to print instead of a substitute pervades most library strategies.' A sample survey of 554 academic libraries in the United States reported in 1989 that 36% offered no online services at all. And Rosemarie Riechel, also writing in 1989, asserted that 'expertise in, or at least knowledge of, the application and operation of online systems seems to be sketchy. ... Automated information retrieval is still viewed by many librarians as a special function. ... Many "old" and "new" librarians are content with manual tools and resist change – viewing the machine as a cold intruder.'

It must not be overlooked that solving human problems is essentially a human activity, often demanding the infinite variety of response that can only be provided by another human. Over 60 years ago, long before computers, Wyer asserted in his famous textbook on reference work: 'Here is a service which defies and transcends machinery'. Even further back, in 1883 W. E. Foster was saying that 'Everyone of us knows perfectly well that, valuable as may be the aid and guidance rendered by the various species of inanimate contrivances ... nothing, after all, can take the place of the personal, individual, direct aid of the librarian'. As has been pointed out in Chapter 1, and as research has regularly confirmed, the questioner needs attention just as much as the question. But Lawrence S. Thompson was surely right when he argued that 'We must look forward to and promote aggressively the mechanization of librarianship, but with the primary objective of freeing superior minds with superior training for tasks which no machine can perform'.

## The librarian's personal attributes

One cannot study any aspect of the reference process without being made aware just how vitally dependent it is for its success on the librarian's personal attributes. By this is meant not professional accomplishments such as familiarity with reference sources or skill in searching databases or wide general knowledge or even experience in dealing with enquirers, but those individual human attributes, either innate or acquired, such as sympathy, resourcefulness, confidence, and the like. Of course such admirable qualities are to be desired in everyone, but for the service professions they are indispensable. Reference librarians deficient in such virtues labour under a constant burden which will often prove so crushing they will be unable to rise to meet their enquirers' needs fully.

The student can read almost as many opinions on the most desirable combinations of these human virtues as there are writers. In 1930 Wyer listed 27 'traits' 'in order of importance as determined by the vote of thirty-eight eminent librarians'. A couple of generations later Bob Duckett included 21 items on his 1989 'checklist of qualities needed', based on his experience of selecting staff over many years. Aside from differences in terminology, there is a very close correspondence between the two lists, with personal attributes such as dependability, courtesy, tact, interest in people, imagination, adaptability, initiative, industriousness, and patience far outweighing professional skills. The advance of technology has done little to alter the prescription. In her 1989 book on *Personnel needs and changing reference service* Riechel argues for the 'total integration of automated retrieval systems into the reference function' and lists 22 'attributes and characteristics ... of an ideal reference librarian and true information specialist'. Again the same basic requirements appear, though some are slightly modified for the electronic age, e.g. 'enthusiasm for new technologies' and 'ability to interact well with machines'.

One of the most influential contributions to this discussion was a much-quoted library school address delivered in 1948 by David C. Mearns of the Library of Congress, who identified seven attributes of the ideal reference librarian. Two of them might be called professional: literacy and a sense of media. The remaining five are distinctly qualities of character: imagination, enthusiasm, persistence, humility, and love of service. Today's students might not sit so willingly to be told of the necessity for such accomplishments, but they cannot fail to acknowledge the many research studies which show that these are just the kinds of qualities that users seek in their reference librarian, alongside (and sometimes ahead of) the professional competencies. They might find particularly persuasive the evidence reported in 1987 from a group of advanced reference course students sent to observe how their questions were treated in academic and public libraries: 'With amazing regularity, the students' satisfaction was found to depend on whether or not the librarian they encountered was friendly. So strong was this effect that high satisfaction was reported, even in the absence of acceptable answers to their questions, as long as the librarians seemed to be warm and interested.'

One quality appears on everyone's list: imagination. In what is still a greatly admired textbook on the subject, though published as long ago as 1944, Margaret Hutchins argued that 'Just as important as a good memory is a good imagination, that constructive power of the mind "which modifies and combines mental images so as to produce what is virtually new"'. Katz, the author of the most influential current text

61

on reference work, would agree: 'Substantive knowledge is a must, a liberal education a help, a scientific and technological background useful, but imagination is indispensable'. And while it is scarcely possible for departments of information and library studies to offer courses in imagination, or humility, or enthusiasm, or persistence, or dependability, still less to set examinations in them, and simple exhortations to such virtues might today fall on stony ground, the student will find the succeeding chapters of this book informed throughout by a conviction that these basic human virtues are every bit as vital a part of a reference librarian's equipment as professional expertise. Indeed, in the course of the reference process, as in all personal interactions, 'there is no human excellence which is not useful'. But as Mary Eileen Ahern recognized in the early years of the century, quoting from an even more ancient authority, the greatest of these is 'that charity which is not puffed up, does not behave itself unseemly, vaunteth not itself, but suffereth long and is kind'.

*Further reading*

Duckett, Bob, 'Reference work, staff selection and general knowledge', *Library review*, **38** (5), 1989, 14 – 21.
Jahoda, Gerald, 'Rules for performing steps in the reference process', *Reference librarian*, **25/26**, 1989, 557 – 67.

# — 4 —

## The reference interview

Most of the library users who put questions to the librarian know exactly what they need and ask for it clearly. It is important to make that point strongly at the beginning, because the rest of this chapter is concerned with those enquirers who do not fit this description. These, it will be found, make up a large minority in all libraries, and may be divided into two groups. The first comprises those who know what they need but have not put it into quite the right words; the second group is made up of those who are not certain what it is they need.

Described in terms of the steps involved in the reference process, this first group of enquirers have identified their problem, recognized their information need, but have not clearly and fully expressed it in the form of a question that will allow the search to begin immediately. The second group have not even got this far: they are aware that they have a problem and that information may assist in its solution, but they have not identified any more precisely than that the nature of the information they need. Of course, when they approach the librarian they may voice their plea for help in the shape of a question of some kind, but it is unlikely to have more than an indirect bearing on the problem they have to solve. The alert reader of this book will have noticed that some of the questions given as examples in Chapter 2 are of this kind. In the form that they have been quoted they cannot be answered satisfactorily.

Before any assistance can be given to such enquirers, and certainly before any search can begin, the question as first stated needs to be *negotiated*. In other words the true subject of the enquiry has to be identified, elucidated, and if necessary refined. This is done at the reference interview, the heart of the reference process. Studies have shown that such an interview, defined as a transaction where the reference librarian has to ask the enquirer one or more questions, is necessary in quite a large minority of cases. Mary Jo Lynch's Rutgers

PhD investigation of four New Jersey public libraries in 1976 found that interviews took place for 49% of the enquiries.

Probing further into an enquirer's question is not always to everyone's taste. Some librarians find it more comfortable to stifle their professional consciences and take every question at its face value, disregarding any suspicion they may feel that it is not what the enquirer really needs. Obviously, the supply of even an accurate answer in such cases is not going to solve the enquirer's problem. An unobtrusive survey of such 'faulty information' questions in two Midwest United States university libraries in 1977 revealed this clearly: in 33% of the cases 'This reluctance to attempt the difficult interview ... was a major source of professional failure'. For non-professional staff the failure rate was 72%.

### Reasons for an interview

It is important for the student to understand why so much of the librarian's attention has to be devoted to what is only a minority of questions. Quite apart from the basic policy point that no enquiry should be regarded as unimportant, the arithmetical truth of the matter is that it is the mishandling of interviews with enquirers who are not sure what they need that is responsible for a high proportion of incorrect or inadequate answers and unsatisfied users. In what is now regarded as a classic unobtrusive test carried out in 60 public library outlets in Maryland it was found that an enquirer was likely to obtain an accurate answer to a question only 55% of the time. Particularly relevant in the context of this chapter, deliberate use was made of '*negotiation* or *escalator* questions where the librarian needed to identify and understand the patron's request through a series of probing questions'. Based on a detailed analysis of the findings, Ralph Gers and Lillie J. Seward reported in 1985: 'Of the 720 "escalator" questions asked ... there was no instance of a user receiving a correct answer when the librarian failed to elicit the specific question. The librarian who does not probe to the most specific level is likely to almost never provide a correct answer.' Einstein used to say that if you ask a question carefully and accurately you are half-way to finding the correct answer.

Interestingly, this was found to be a particular problem in the early days of computer searching. In 1971, after a four-year laboratory enquiry, Tefko Saracevic reported that 'The human factor ... seems to be the major factor affecting the performance of every and all components of an information retrieval system'. In 1973 S. D. Neill was even more pointed: the reason for 'the failure of the information scientists to provide solutions to the information problems of ordinary people ... has been present in information science from the very beginning, when the decision was made to ignore the human element. ... What is lacking is communication ... one-to-one face-to-face communication with a specific individual about his specific requirements.' In 1978 William A. Katz shrewdly predicted: 'Paradoxically, the introduction of the machine into the reference process will force even the most reluctant reference librarian to participate as one human being interacting with another'.

But the lesson was learned, and by 1985 Nicholas J. Belkin and Alina Vickery were able to report 'a shift in emphasis in the profession from the study of document or text representations and associated search techniques, to study of the users of IR systems, characteristics of the questions or problems which they bring to them, and interactions of users with intermediaries'. They saw this as 'an explicit recognition of the integrated nature of the information system as a whole, and especially of the importance of understanding and dealing with the entire information search process'.

There may be a dozen possible reasons for an interview, many of which are concerned with minor adjustments to the question – as will be seen in a moment – but Lynch discovered that in as many as 13% of the interviews that she recorded, the question originally asked was different from the 'real' question revealed by the librarian's probing. Earlier surveys of academic libraries had shown that as much as a fifth or a quarter of the questions asked do not represent the enquirer's actual needs.

There are a number of indications in the question or in the enquirer's approach that the librarian needs to watch for as a sign that an interview may be required. Some are obvious: ambiguity, for example; others are less immediately identifiable, such as the incomplete query. Gerald Jahoda and Judith Schiek Braunagel have advised that 'certain types of givens or wanteds provide clues that indicate the real query may not have been asked', and they instance a request for a specific reference title or a specific type of tool. The enquiry phrased in very broad terms almost always needs narrowing down. The librarian may suspect that the enquirer's motive is not yet clear. Quite often, of course, the difficulty may lie on the other side of the desk: if the librarian does not understand the question or is not familiar with the subject, it may be necessary to ask the enquirer to explain further. An interview may also be required for technical purposes even where the subject has been quite precisely delineated: the librarian may need to know how much information the enquirer wants, and at what level. There may be constraints of language or period or geography or format or time that need to be determined. It is sometimes helpful to know the sources that the enquirer has already consulted. And so on.

Here is an appropriate point to re-emphasize the assertion made in the first sentence of this chapter: most queries do not need negotiating, and therefore most enquirers do not need interviewing. The question asked is the question meant. It is necessary to say this because the case for interviewing has been overstated in the literature, for example by Raymund F. Wood: 'It is a rare questioner who blurts out what he (or she) really wants to know in the very first moment'; and by Ellis Mount: 'more often than not, the question that is asked at the reference desk bears little resemblance to the question that should have been posed'. There are genuine dangers in this kind of attitude, but fortunately others have issued warnings: 'people who attempt to negotiate every question develop mechanical, stereotyped behaviors that are unattractive' (Sandra M. Naiman); 'Sometimes the reference interview impedes the flow of information' (Fred Batt); 'librarians may pose counter-questions simply because they are inept, inefficient, incapable of answering, or unable to locate material' (Robert Hauptman). Jahoda and Braunagel's words are worth keeping in mind: 'The first step in successful negotiation is identifying queries that require negotiation and eliminating those that do not'.

But the student should be cautioned that the question that must be negotiated bears no unequivocal mark for all to see. Recognizing such questions requires judgement and experience: this is one of the reasons why reference work, as the student will remember from Chapter 1, is a profession, and not a clerical skill.

## Interview procedure

A number of writers on the reference process have compared it to a chain. The analogy reminds one of the old proverb that a chain is only as strong as its weakest link: it is clear that the whole reference process could collapse if there is a break at any point along its length, stretching from the enquirer's basic problem right through to its agreed solution. But, as has been said, the reference librarian only enters the process at the end of its first phase, when the enquirer has already forged a number of these links, for example between the information need and its expression in the shape of a question. If, as someone once said, an interview is 'a conversation with a purpose', then the purpose of the interview is to allow the librarian to start testing the links of the reference chain. It follows from this that reference librarians need to be as adept at asking questions as they are at answering them. This has tended to be overlooked until comparatively recently, particularly during their professional education.

Indeed this is the stage in the reference process where a librarian's basic education and general range of interests show to their best advantage. It is commonly but mistakenly thought that it is for the reference *search* that subject expertise and a wide range of general knowledge are so desirable. Ellsworth and Joan Mason were of the opinion that it 'takes about ten years of avid reading in a broad range of fields, after a good liberal education' just to provide the perspective for even the first step in answering a reference query. This depth of background knowledge is particularly valuable in resolving 'faulty information' questions, where the enquiry contains some error. Bob Duckett was even more positive: 'The knowledge learned at university is not generally the sort of knowledge required in everyday enquiry work. ... What I seek most from prospective staff is a good old-fashioned liberal education ... it is general knowledge that we need, not necessarily knowledge of any particular subject, although a good knowledge of current affairs is important.' To help choose staff for Bradford Reference Library he devised a 30-question test of general knowledge, orally administered at the interview. Charles A. D'Aniello believed that this 'cultural literacy is different from, and serves a different purpose than, detailed subject knowledge', and that 'sometimes it is the interpretive ability of the librarian, a major determinant of which is the level of general or particular knowledge he or she possesses, that is the major factor in either success or failure of a transaction'.

In fact, Katz has argued that 'the librarian is in the unique position of being the "master of the interdisciplinary"' and that 'this ability to look outside a narrow scope is what makes reference work a speciality ... the specialization of the broad view, which makes reference librarians a unique link in the information chain'. He also believed that 'one convincing argument that the reference librarian can be both a specialist and a generalist is to be found in the development of reference services outside the formal structure of a library'. Support for this view can be found among the information brokers themselves: Susan R. LaForte has said that 'Success depends not so much on subject specialization, but on being expert at locating information in any field, and being "willing to spend the time and effort" to do so'; and in the opinion of Barbara Whyte Felicetti 'it is far more important for the broker to understand the bibliographic nature of information and to be able to conduct a first-rate reference interview than to be specifically subject-oriented'.

Furthermore, at the search stage of the process, as will be seen later, the librarian has a whole series of aids ready to hand, ranging from a host of bibliographical tools (including the library catalogues) to the collective experience of colleagues. The reference interview, on the other hand, follows a much less clearly charted route, where the librarian, single-handed, has the task, in conversation with the enquirer, of distinguishing from the whole universe of knowledge that particular segment that matches the often imperfectly expressed need.

As an *aide-mémoire* to the questions they should consider putting to the enquirer during the course of the interview, three generations at least of reference librarians have quoted to themselves Rudyard Kipling's quatrain from the *Just so stories* (1902):

I keep six honest serving men
  (They taught me all I knew);
Their names are What and Why and When
  And How and Where and Who.

Kipling of course was originally a journalist, and these have been called the 'standard interrogatories'. It is interesting to note that they were quickly added to the online searcher's armoury, being cited by Sara D. Knapp (1978), Stuart J. Kolner (1981), and Donna R. Dolan (1982). In 1989 they were used by the *Encyclopaedia Britannica* in an advertising campaign.

Robert S. Taylor's research in the 1960s on the negotiation of questions marked a major advance in librarians' understanding of the reference interview. He likened the procedure by which a librarian's questions to the user successively refine the subject of the enquiry to a series of 'five filters through which a question passes, and from which the librarian selects significant data to aid him in his search'. Though he quite rightly claimed that 'they have not been put together in rational form before', they do match quite closely Kipling's 'six honest serving men'.

**The subject of the enquiry**
In order to begin the interview all the librarian needs to do is to pass

the enquiry through the first of Taylor's filters, which he has labelled 'Determination of subject'; or (and this amounts to the same thing) the librarian can summon the first of the six serving men to ask the question 'What?'.

There are two distinct aspects to establishing exactly what the enquiry is about. The first is basically a matter of *terminology*: the librarian has to understand what the words mean. If asked 'Have you anything on cimbaloms?' or 'Where does oolong come from?' or 'Can you find me some illustrations of Vijayanagar?' or 'I would like something on the Decroly method' or 'What have you got on scumbling?', and the librarian has not met any of these terms before, the first step must be to discover what they are. The most natural way out is to ask the enquirer, who will usually know, or at least will be able to put the librarian on the right track. Where this does not suffice, consulting a dictionary or encyclopaedia is the remedy (all are in the *Encyclopaedia Britannica* [*Micropaedia*]). This may also be necessary if the words in the question are recognized but the librarian is still uncertain of their meaning in the context, e.g. phantom limbs, knot gardens, Manchester goods, dog days, rice Christians.

Another wise precaution at this preliminary stage is to make sure that one has heard aright. Libraries are not the silent and sepulchral halls of popular myth, but busy and often noisy workplaces, and mishearing is not uncommon. All librarians can tell tales of being caught out in this way, to learn of their error only when the answer has been produced: something on oranges and peaches when *The origin of species* (by Charles Darwin) was asked for; information on blood pressure when what was wanted was something on Glubb Pasha (commander of the Arab Legion). One of the easiest ways to obviate such mishaps is for the librarian immediately to restate the enquirer's question; such paraphrasing is a standard interviewing technique. As a bonus a response of this kind will often prompt further helpful details from the enquirer.

Ambiguity is another terminological hazard to negotiate. If asked for illustrations of Mount Vernon it is important to discover whether it is George Washington's home that is wanted or the many other places (cities, mountains, etc.) with the same name. Similar vigilance has enabled librarians asked about the Clan Ross to determine that the enquirer wanted the ship of that name and not the Scottish clan; asked about the Isle of the Dead to find that it is a painting and not a place; and in the course of helping the searcher after St Pancras to ascertain that he was not interested in the district of London or in the railway station, but in the saint himself, stoned to death in Sicily in the first century. One should take the utmost care never to jump to conclusions. Aural ambiguity is a particular snare and librarians fall victim every day: providing information on Patmos (Greek island) rather than Pat Moss (racing driver); or producing the definition of a carrot rather than a carat. But at least such homophones can be detected by a librarian on the alert.

This clearing of the terminological undergrowth is only half the battle. Though now understanding the meaning of the question, the librarian may still be unfamiliar with the subject. This is no cause for alarm, however: often in reference work, as Poe said about chess, 'What is only complex is mistaken for what is profound'. Samuel Swett Green encountered this well over a hundred years ago: 'A librarian is frequently asked to give information in regard to things and processes which he knows nothing about'. Indeed this is one of the most delightful prospects offered by reference work, providing every day a new intellectual challenge. Charles A. Bunge has expressed this well: 'There is a particular joy, I think, in helping someone to learn and know. And as a bonus, our own knowledge grows in the process.' Commenting on Green's paper, Otis Hall Robinson confessed 'I sometimes think students get more from me when they inquire about subjects that I know least about'.

No librarian should ever hesitate to display ignorance to the enquirer. As Will Rogers truly said, 'Everybody is ignorant, only on different subjects', and most library users know this well enough. They no longer believe that the librarian has read all the books in the library, and are usually only too pleased to combine their subject background with the librarian's knowledge of information sources and skill in their use. This is indeed an excellent way of starting off the friendly collaboration that all such transactions should be.

Librarians, and particularly the young, underrate their professional ability to master a brief, and rapidly to come to terms with an unfamiliar subject. And young and old alike still have to grasp the full potential of systematic bibliography – their own basic discipline – as an immensely powerful tool of intellectual enquiry. It was left to a non-librarian, the great journalist H. L. Mencken, to make the claim that 'In three weeks one could become the second best authority on any subject, given access to a decent library with a good librarian'.

## The incomplete enquiry

As was said earlier, terminology is only one facet of determining exactly what the enquiry is about: there remains the important matter of ensuring that the question is *complete* as an expression of the enquirer's information need. Unlike ambiguity, which the wide-awake librarian can always recognize, the incomplete question may not always signal its presence at the outset. What librarians do know from long experience, however, is that such questions are very common indeed. For whatever reason, many enquirers do neglect to set out their full information need in precise verbal form.

In the proceedings of the pioneer 1876 Conference of Librarians we can read that 'Mr Edmands gave some amusing illustrations to show that readers had only the most vague idea of what they really wanted'. In the 1890s Silas H. Berry was telling his colleagues at the New York Library Club 'It is so hard to get a fellow to tell you what he is really after'. There has been no change in all the hundred years since, except that librarians have become less patronizing and more understanding. It remains true, as Frederic J. Mosher remarked, that 'most librarians will verify the astonishing fact that it is more difficult apparently to ask than to answer'.

Probably the most frequent form that this tendency takes is for the user to ask for material on a general or large subject when what is really wanted is something quite specific or detailed. Katz claimed that this is 'the average complaint of every working librarian'. In her 1981 Sheffield PhD thesis Marian Barnes reported on her study of 280 enquirers in two large public libraries in the north of England: 'A much higher percentage of users said [to the investigator] they were seeking specific information than were observed to frame their enquiry in a way that indicated that a specific item of information was being sought'.

Enquirers who ask 'What have you got on wars?' or 'Have you anything on electrical engineering?' are easy to help: there is little doubt in such cases that they have generalized their more specific need and a tactful librarian can soon arrive at the heart of the matter. Eleanor B. Woodruff was one of the first to point out in 1897 that 'the ability by skilful questioning, without appearance of curiosity or impertinence, to extract from the vaguest, most general requests, a clear idea of what the enquirer really needs' is 'one of the greatest gifts of a successful librarian'. She gave as an example a request for 'a book that will tell everything about all kinds of birds' when what was wanted was a book on the diseases of chickens.

71

More difficult to detect are the enquirers who ask where the law books are or the section on religion, for instance. This may well be what they want, of course, and they might rightly resent an officious librarian assuming they really need something else. But if what they actually require are the weekly income tax tables or books on the architecture of abbeys they may look in vain, because in many libraries the former might well be in the finance or business section and the latter with the other architectural books. What has gone wrong here is that the generalization has been made incorrectly: in terms of the reference process a break in the chain has occurred between the information need and the initial question.

The serious interruptions to the reference process that follow such inadequate generalizations should obviously be prevented if at all possible. Unfortunately, no one has yet totally explained why it is such enquirers do not ask for what they know they need. It is not always correct to conclude, as K. Sankaraiah has warned, that if they fail to frame their questions more specifically it is because they are incapable of doing so. It has been suggested that they may feel that a broader question is 'easier' for the librarian than a specific request: surveys in academic libraries have shown that some students at least do not believe the librarian would understand or be able to answer anything other than a general question. Theories from the field of interpersonal communication have also been drawn on for clues. In a face-to-face dialogue the messages exchanged between the participants carry three kinds of information: cognitive – concerned with facts, ideas, the 'meaning'; affective – conveying attitudes and feelings, consciously or subconsciously; and cooperative – organizing and regulating the interaction. So far as concerns spoken messages, everyone knows that in virtually all such situations speech is sometimes used to convey general sociability rather than specific meaning, particularly near the beginning of an encounter – for example, exchanges of politeness, remarks about the weather, enquiries about health. Though the exact meaning of the words used is largely irrelevant, this is more than talk for the sake of talk: it contributes to the process of interaction regulation.

The opening speech act in the reference encounter is no different, in principle. Health and the weather perhaps do not figure to any great extent, but Thomas Lee Eichman pointed out in 1978 that an enquirer is simply following standard operational procedure by opening with 'a deliberate move to a less specific concept that what he or she has fully in mind ... with the effort directed ... at establishing a mind-to-mind channel'. The interpersonal component in the reference interview will be explored in more detail later in this chapter.

Similarly, in 1983 Joan C. Durrance drew on the suggestions of the social psychologist Erving Goffman for 'the reasons behind the frequent preference of users for starting with the general question rather than by asking for what is really needed. "When individuals are unfamiliar with each other's opinions and statuses, a feeling-out process occurs whereby one individual admits his views or statuses to another a little at a time. After dropping a guard just a little he waits for the other to do this".'

Anita Schiller has another explanation to offer: 'Perhaps the necessity for such psychological detective work comes, in part, not so much from the patron's inability to express himself, as from his feeling that he is not really entitled to request specific information'. This astonishing state of affairs, after over a century of reference work, has already been discussed in Chapter 1. Norma J. Shosid explained further: 'Some of the librarians' communication troubles arise from the fact that so many of the people with whom they are dealing do not know what to expect from them. People are not sure how to behave in differing library situations.' According to this argument, the users are indeed in real need of specific assistance but fear that the librarian would expect them to be able to help themselves. Their generalized request is therefore by way of an offered compromise: 'At least put us on the right track; we will then find the rest of the way on our own'.

A minor variation of this theme is the request for a particular book which the enquirer believes may contain the answer to the question. Sometimes it does not, or at least not in convenient form; this approach has been characterized as 'misplaced independence' and manifests itself in the case of the enquirer who asks for a list of all the inventions in the world when what he is after is the man (or woman) who discovered the quadratic equation. The librarian's difficulty here of course is to distinguish between, on the one hand, the enquirer who asks to see *Who's who* because that is what he wants; and on the other, the enquirer who asks to see *Who's who* because he wants to know when Errol Flynn died, and has assumed, incorrectly, that he will find him included there. But Patrick Wilson has reminded us that 'Librarians are in a special position to help a person avoid waste of time and energy looking in wholly inappropriate sources'.

Similar problems can arise with an enquirer who starts off by saying 'I would like to order a computer search'. It is also not uncommon for a request for a specific title to mask a material-finding enquiry that would be satisfied by any book, etc., on the topic.

There will also be those who have decided what they need but are afflicted by the paralysis of 'unverbalized thought'. Highly literate people like librarians do not always appreciate the difficulty many people have in putting their thoughts into words. It is a mistake to think that this inarticulateness is confined to the ill-educated or dull-witted: Frederick W. Lanchester, a university graduate, one of England's greatest engineers, and the builder of the first British car, used to claim that he found it easier to think up a new invention than to describe it in words later.

An incomplete question will usually be defective in either its 'wanted' or its 'given' element (as explained in Chapter 2), and occasionally in both. What is normally required is for the faulty component to be either elaborated, with more data, or refined, by narrowing it down. To take some specific cases: a request for books on Mu has as its wanted the location of specific documents, but its given, 'Mu', is obscure and needs elaborating (it is a supposed lost continent in the Pacific). In a query seeking information on Gustav Mayrink (Austrian novelist) the given is quite clear – a person – but the wanted could be any or all of several: illustration, bibliography, document location, general or background information (biographical or literary); it needs refining. Similarly, an enquirer seeking 'the diary of an old lady – very much spoken of some months ago' needs to be asked to elaborate further on the given; and someone looking for information on the Gospel of Nicodemus (a fifth-century Apocryphal work) should be encouraged to be more specific about the wanted.

Some enquiries turn out to be incomplete for purely incidental reasons. They may be unambiguous and precise and apparently complete in both their givens and their wanteds, but for practical purposes they still need some redefinition, either on account of their own complexity or because of the way they are treated in the literature. Unfortunately for the inexperienced librarian, such enquiries can appear deceptively simple, e.g. 'I am looking for statistics on infant mortality in Britain'. The obvious first source is the *Annual abstract of statistics*, where there is a double-page spread devoted to the topic. But this does not give figures for 'Britain'. What do appear are separate statistics for the United Kingdom, England and Wales, Scotland, and Northern Ireland. The second problem is that the numbers given are not actual deaths but rates of deaths per thousand live births, thus making it impossible to derive totals for Britain by adding the figures for England and Wales to those for Scotland, or by subtracting those for Northern Ireland from those for the United Kingdom. The final difficulty is that the statistics are divided into still births, perinatal deaths, neonatal deaths, and post-neonatal deaths, with no totals and no immediately obvious indication as to what these terms mean. The next step an experienced reference librarian might take would be to consult the Central Statistical Office *Guide to official statistics*, an excellent reference work and winner of the Library Association Besterman medal. This lists no fewer than 18 'regular sources' and 5 'occasional sources' on infant mortality.

In practice, the librarian may judge that the most satisfactory response is simply to produce the relevant documents open at the appropriate page, with an invitation to ask again if not satisfied. This is to treat the question in its incomplete state, trusting that the enquirer will be able to complete it by examining the materials provided. But this would only be after a rapid and almost instinctive assessment of the kind of enquirer; in other cases the librarian may deem it more prudent to offer to explain, or to try and ascertain by questioning if there are any more precise requirements.

### The unsure enquirer

Discussion so far in this chapter has concentrated on those enquirers who know what they need but have not asked their question in quite the right way. It is now time to study the second group referred to at the beginning of the chapter: those who are not certain what it is they need. They have indeed asked a question, even though it may have been prefaced by 'I am not quite sure what I want, but ...'. They also know that they have a problem, and they have decided that it is one that information may help to resolve, but they are hesitant over what kind of information they need. When they present themselves to the librarian most enquirers of this kind will ask 'questions' about 'subjects', even though such a 'question' may in fact be no more than a hypothesis on the part of the enquirer as to where a solution may be found. By no means all of them will make clear that they are unsure, and unless the librarian is attentive enough to detect this, either immediately or during the subsequent conversation, the process will run into trouble.

As mentioned briefly in Chapter 1, cognitive psychologists now have a lot to tell us about how problems arise in people's minds, and linguistic psychologists have similarly investigated the process of asking questions.

Drawing on this research, much recent attention has been given in our profession to the way reference questions originate. One of the first librarians to attempt an explanation was D. J. Foskett in 1958: 'When a research worker begins to make a search, he has become aware of a gap in his knowledge that he wants to fill, but he cannot know the extent of his ignorance. When he formulates the question he asks, it is more likely to be in terms of what he knows than what he does not know.' In 1960 D. M. MacKay, a professor of communication, elaborated further, suggesting that an individual's information need represents 'a certain incompleteness in his picture of the world, an inadequacy in what we might call his "state of readiness" to interact purposefully with the world around him'. In his 1962 Western Reserve PhD dissertation Paul Sprosty made a particularly useful contribution: 'A question follows the detection of a gap in what can be termed ... one's cognitive map of an area. But it seems likely that as soon as this gap is identified the thinker bridges it with some concept or idea based on the knowledge he has at hand. Furthermore, the extent to which he can communicate the nature of this "bridge" varies. ... Questions, then, are not simply requests for information. The information that [an enquirer] seemingly requests and receives, actually confirms or refutes ... the cognitive bridge he has already erected to close a cognitive gap.'

The most fully worked out model to appear in the library literature was constructed by Taylor in 1962. It made a major impact on our understanding of the reference interview and laid the groundwork for virtually every subsequent study. He identified four levels of information need, corresponding to the sequence of four stages of question formulation which 'shade into one another along the question spectrum'. The first is the *visceral* need, the actual but unexpressed need, of which the enquirer may not yet be fully conscious; 'It may only be a vague sort of dissatisfaction. It is probably inexpressible in linguistic terms.' It is not yet really a question. The second level is the *conscious* need, the realized mental description an enquirer forms as to what information is needed; 'It will probably be an ambiguous and rambling statement'. The third level is the *formalized* need, the concrete terms the enquirer uses to describe the area of doubt; it is 'a qualified and rational statement of his question'. The fourth level is the *compromised* need, represented by the form of words presented to the information system (of which the librarian is usually seen as a part); 'the question is recast in anticipation of what the files can deliver'.

In 1981 in the course of developing Taylor's model further in the context of the online pre-search interview, Karen Markey likened his description of the 'visceral' need to Leon Festinger's theory of cognitive dissonance which states that we seek an internal consistency between our beliefs and our actions or between one belief and another. The absence of such consistency, this conceptual conflict, this mental discord, is known as cognitive dissonance, and we consciously strive to reduce it by various means, including the seeking of information.

Perhaps the most eclectic elaboration of the theories of Taylor and others is to be seen in the work of Nicholas J. Belkin in his 1977 London PhD dissertation and several more recent publications. As he explained in 1985, 'people, when they do engage in information-seeking behaviour, do so because their states of knowledge concerning some particular situation or topic are recognized by them as somehow being "insufficient" or "inadequate" for that situation; that is, there are *anomalies* (gaps, uncertainties, lack of relations or concepts, etc.) in their conceptual state of knowledge concerning the topic, which they perceive as needing to be resolved in order to achieve their goals'. Although he conceded 'This concept is not wholly original but rather a synthesis of a number of previous suggestions' and its basis 'can be seen in Taylor's schema of levels of question', he has devised a felicitous acronym, ASK (anomalous state of knowledge), and his contribution has shed fresh light on the way reference questions originate.

It is scarcely surprising, therefore, that some enquirers present themselves at the reference desk with questions that will not resolve their problems, although by no means all of them show symptoms of uncertainty. As Jahoda and Braunagel explain, 'If the information need is stated in the form of a query at the first or second stages of development when the requestor has not clearly defined it, the result will most likely be a query that is stated vaguely or ambiguously'. In Taylor's words, 'The skill of the reference librarian is to work with the inquirer back to the formalized need, possibly even to the conscious need, and *then* to translate these needs into a research strategy'.

But if an incomplete question is difficult to detect at the initial stage, to recognize those instances where the question is inappropriate to the underlying need requires almost a sixth sense, or at least an uncommon shrewdness. Useful too is what many years ago William Warner Bishop described as 'the curious ability to sense the real point at issue'. Whatever form it takes it should be the kind of insight that would lead a librarian to suspect that behind an enquiry such as 'Where would I find the section on transport?' might lie a need for illustrations of sedan chairs; or that a request for 'Any books about St Paul' conceals a requirement for the emblems associated with him (a sword and a book). This is the time for what James I. Wyer called 'Library mind-reading ... how to give people what they do not know they want'. Taylor is certainly right to claim that 'Without doubt, the negotiation of reference questions is one of the most complex acts of human communication. In this act, one person tries to describe for another person not something he knows, but rather something he does not know.'

## The mistaken enquirer

Even more arcane are enquiries from users who have not even completed the first step of the process successfully, that is to say they have failed to identify their problem. The librarian's difficulty in helping such enquirers stems from the fact that they confidently believe that they have. They are not aware that their hypothesis as to what information will solve their problem is not soundly based; they may even be unaware that it is only a hypothesis. In other words, not only do they not know what they need, but they do not know that they do not know. The questions they ask, moreover, are quite likely to be positive, precise, and clear. But they are the *wrong* questions: answers that are supplied will not solve the original problems because they were incorrectly diagnosed in the first place.

It requires an extraordinarily astute librarian to uncover this at the interview stage. The technique used to fathom the mystery is, of course, asking questions, but the stumbling-block with this kind of enquiry is knowing when to ask. There are risks in assuming that the enquirer has got it all wrong; and volunteering to answer a query that has not been asked is like helping blind pedestrians to the other side of the street without first making sure that they want to cross. One suspects that here the librarian is approaching the boundaries of that region where technique is of little use. Of this facet of the reference interview George W. Horner has warned: 'certain of its recurring difficulties may belong to a fairly labyrinthine area of permanent human responses'. In some cases the real question that needs to be answered may indeed turn out to be, as Winston Churchill once said about Russia, 'a riddle wrapped in a mystery inside an enigma'. A good general education and fund of sympathy, resourcefulness, and confidence are a great help, but it would be foolish to ignore the important role intuition plays here as in other parts of the reference process. The elder Oliver Wendell Holmes once said that 'A moment's insight is sometimes worth a life's experience'.

## Motive and context

Calling up another of Kipling's serving men by asking 'Why?' may coax valuable information from unsure or mistaken enquirers. In Taylor's terms, this is his second filter, 'Motivation and objective of the inquirer', which he regarded as 'probably the most critical'. What the librarian does is attempt to discover the purpose for which the information is required.

Traditionally, of course, in the words of Robert L. Collison in his 1950 textbook *Library assistance to readers*, 'The job of the librarian is to provide information without questioning the purpose to which it may be put or the circumstances which gave rise to the query'. Jahoda and Braunagel in 1980 were of the same mind in their textbook, maintaining that the librarian 'should *never* ask *why* the client-patron wants the information requested'. The experience of Mount was that 'An enquirer does not willingly reveal his reason for needing the information', and in any case it is often difficult to ask outright without appearing impertinently curious. Barbara M. Robinson reported in 1989 that 'Some practitioners believe that probing is an infringement on client privacy', but she also reminded us that 'Asking why has long been a source of controversy within the profession'. Norman J. Crum argued in 1969 that 'Finding out *why* the customer wants the information cuts the search time in half and usually determines the priority, depth, and form of response'. His side of the argument has been given strong reinforcement from the research front over the last decade or so. As Belkin and Vickery explained in 1985, 'A major implication of this cognitively oriented work is that there is no such thing as an information need in the abstract, but rather circumstances which lead to information behaviour ... the human needs which might give rise to information behaviour form a highly complex, interactive group of cognitive, affective, social and political factors'. This gives us, as Brenda Dervin and Patricia Dewdney put it, a 'fundamentally different' picture of information: not a commodity, not 'an autonomous object that can be stored, accessed and transferred', but something that 'does not have an independent existence but is rather a construct of the user. It follows that "information" that helps one person at a particular time and place may not help another. It may not help even that same person somewhat later.' Catherine Sheldrick Ross drew a useful distinction between 'the *"correct"* answer for the disembedded, contextless question and the *helpful* answer for a particular person in a particular situation'. Wilson has spelled out the implications: 'The only *clear* sense in which we can speak of people needing information is in relation to further purposes, goals, or standards ... without information about purpose, there is no basis for judgment about need, nor any good way of discovering "real" wants'. In other words, context is all.

What certainly does seem to be the case in practice is that the librarian who is able to establish in the enquirer's mind at this early stage the collaborative nature of the reference process usually finds that explanations follow. Wilson has encouraged us to 'remember how often people do spontaneously give information about purposes, and how many opportunities can be given them to do so'. But the warning given by Jahoda and Braunagel should also be heeded: we must 'be sensitive to signals communicated by the user that indicate he does not want to divulge any additional information'. The lesson to be learned here, in Taylor's words, is that 'Enquirers frequently cannot define what they want, but they can discuss why they need it'. Such discussions enable the librarian and enquirer together to work out what is required and to formulate the question that the enquirer wanted to ask.

### Open and closed questions
The 'skilful questioning' referred to by Woodruff in 1897 is still the reference librarian's main negotiating instrument. But it must not be used as a bludgeon, or even as a scalpel. The reason an interview is necessary in the first place is because the librarian has not been told enough about what is wanted, and so any line of questioning must be designed to get the enquirer to talk. What experience teaches us is that 'open' questions are more likely to achieve this than 'closed' questions, which limit the kind of answer that can be given, either to a simple yes/no, or to one of a set of specified possibilities. Open questions, as their name suggests, are much less restrictive in nature, leaving the decision as to the amount and kind of information in the reply much more in the hands of the person being asked.

To take a particular case, to a not untypical request such as 'What have you got on corkscrews?' the reference librarian might not unreasonably respond: 'Is it something on their history or collecting them that you want?' – an obvious closed question. A timid enquirer, or one offended by such a response, might simply reply 'No', in which case the librarian has to start all over again. The second attempt (unless the librarian is particularly obtuse) would almost certainly be an open question: 'What sort of thing would you like to know about corkscrews?'. The enquirer would then be obliged to say, and in all probability would provide sufficient information for the librarian to work on – for example, 'I've just invented a new kind of corkscrew and I want to know if anyone else has had the idea before'.

Likewise, if the librarian's response to queries such as 'I am looking for something on Bertrand Russell' or 'Have you anything on Dylan Thomas?' was 'Do you want information on his life or his writings?' that would clearly be a closed question, and could well confuse and even annoy an enquirer simply wanting to know whether Bertrand Russell had a title (he succeeded his brother as 3rd Earl in 1931) or where Dylan Thomas first appeared in print (in a school magazine).

Closed questions usually begin with words like 'is', 'do', 'can', 'will', 'has', and normally have a rising intonation pattern. They imply that the librarian has already made a judgement or at least an assumption as to what the enquirer wants. They are the tools of cross-examination. Open questions start with 'what', 'when', 'where', 'who', 'which', 'why', 'how', etc., and have a falling intonation pattern. They sometimes produce a bonus in the form of useful additional information about the query for which the librarian would not have thought of asking.

But even with open questions the way is not always smooth: if it is a mistake to treat the reference interview as a forensic interrogation, it is equally undesirable that it should be a casual conversation, and handing the initiative to the enquirer runs that risk. Every reference interview has a purpose and time is never unlimited; as Taylor argues, 'This requires both direction and structure on the part of the information specialist'. Now and then one encounters enquirers unwilling to talk, as Jahoda and Braunagel were suggesting above, perhaps because they prefer to keep their business to themselves; someone who has just invented a new kind of corkscrew may well feel like this. Experienced reference librarians have found that a precisely formulated closed question at the appropriate juncture – often based on an educated guess – can be very effective. Marilyn Domas White has distinguished three sequences of questions: 'the funnel sequence, moving from broad, open questions to closed, restrictive ones; ... the reverse-funnel sequence, moving from closed to open questions; ... the tunnel sequence, using a series of the same type of question, either open or closed'.

Dervin and Dewdney have argued for the use of 'neutral' questions, based on the cognitive theory of 'sense-making'. The reference query is an attempt to fill a *gap* which appears when individuals feel themselves in the *situation* of being unable to make progress without forming some kind of new 'sense' about something. The *use* to be made of the answer to the query is the third element. A neutral question is a particular kind of open question that seeks to uncover the underlying situation, the gap faced, and the expected use of the information requested, e.g. 'How would you like this information to help you?'. Neutral questions obviously probe the motive and address the context of the query.

## Specification of the response

If the primary objective of the reference interview is to determine the subject of the question, obviously an important secondary aim in appropriate cases is to glance forward in the direction of the likely answer in order to anticipate its probable shape insofar as this is possible at this preliminary stage. This is a matter of getting a rough idea from the enquirers of the *amount*, and the *level*, and the *form* of the material they want. It often involves discovering what they already know, including where they may have looked already, and something of their personal characteristics. In Taylor's scheme this corresponds to his filters three and five: 'Personal background of the enquirer' and 'What kind of answer will the inquirer accept'. The librarian asks Kipling's questions 'Who?' and 'How?'. It is important to note here that these filters, or questions from the librarian, are not brought to bear in a fixed, pre-ordained sequence: as Taylor points out, 'they may occur simultaneously', and so some knowledge of the enquirer may already have been gathered if questions regarding motive and context have been asked.

Indeed, a question such as 'I want to know all about baking powder' is impossible to answer in any useful sense without applying Taylor's filters. Similarly, if asked 'How do heat pumps on refrigerators work?', most librarians would feel obliged to adjust the amount and level of material in the response to the individual enquirer, who might be doing a school project, solving a domestic problem, satisfying curiosity, or a whole range of other possibilities. As to the form the response might take, an enquirer seeking information about chalk figures on hillsides in England would surely be disappointed by material without illustrations.

This is the point where the librarian may be surprised to learn that one of the personal characteristics of the enquirer is that he, or more usually she, is actually asking on behalf of someone else. Donald Davinson has warned that 'Enquiries made through agents can be very difficult indeed to deal with. Unfortunately, they are most commonly found in areas where the information sought is quite complex and specialized – in business and commercial enquiries where the executive is too busy to come to the library in person.' G. W. Horner hit the mark in 1965: 'Out of the secretarial world it comes, the prime example of the untethered query, bobbing uselessly about until one can tell what caused it to be launched'. He called it a 'third-hand' enquiry. A survey some years ago in Manchester Commercial Library found that one-third of the telephone enquiries were of this kind. According to Jack B. King, 'The bashful male mechanic, hanging back, while his female companion makes an enquiry on his behalf about the location of a repair manual for a Ford truck, is commonplace in a public library'. Even in academic libraries it is far from unusual: students regularly ask for each other, but here too women seem to ask more for their men friends than the other way round.

If the enquiry looks as if it might take more than a few minutes to satisfy there is one further important matter for the librarian to ask about: the urgency. The standard interrogatory 'When?' is used. As long ago as 1911 Marilla Waite Freeman began her paper on this topic by quoting a popular song of the day: 'I want what I want when I want it'. The song may have been forgotten but among library users the sentiment lingers on. In the library of London Weekend Television 70% of the enquiries must be answered immediately, and a further 15% by the following day. Without doubt, enquiries take time, and one has come to expect users to be puzzled when the librarian starts asking questions rather than finding answers, but, in truth, librarians forget too easily that many enquirers are in a hurry, and hardly any are under no time constraint at all. It may often be judged preferable for the enquirer to leave the question in the hands of the librarian to investigate and report on in due course.

This secondary objective of the reference interview is no mere matter of form or routine. It can quite markedly alter the nature of the subsequent search. As was emphasized at the end of Chapter 2, and in discussing motive and context earlier in this chapter, identical questions from different people may demand quite different answers: though the subject may be the same, the amount and level and form of material may not.

## Limits
By this stage the librarian will probably also have ascertained if there are any of the other standard constraints on the query such as language, time, or place. Restrictions as to language are fairly obvious. If asked

to help trace reports on the Allied bombing of German cities in World War II, the librarian will need to know if the enquirer would be able to read material in German. Time or period restraints can be crucial: an enquirer seeking the route of the Tour de France cycle race must be asked to specify the date because it varies from year to year. To discover if there are limitations as to place, the librarian will need to summon the last of Kipling's serving men and ask 'Where?'. To a question about famous women travellers it might seem appropriate for the librarian to ask if the enquirer is interested in a particular region of the world; it would certainly make the search simpler and therefore more immediately productive.

In practice as often as not such limits are assumed rather than stated, at least in a manual search. A human searcher looking for the effects of recent political changes on banking systems in the countries of Eastern Europe would not be likely to produce papers in Polish or Hungarian unless there was good reason to believe the enquirer could read them. A request for a book on the Great Fire of London would normally be met by the offer of a recent title, even though books on the topic have been appearing since 1666. Computers, as is well known, lack such common sense, and will only eliminate unintelligible papers or out-of-date books if specifically instructed to do so.

Indeed the deliberate incorporation of such restraints into a search formulation in advance is a particularly useful device used by computer searchers to guard against unwanted citations. A search for information on the design of hospital operating theatres might be limited in advance to papers in English, of US and UK origin, during the last five years.

### The interview for a computer search
Otherwise, as many reference librarians have discovered somewhat to their surprise, the reference process for a computer search is *in principle* no different, up to this stage. Ethel Auster has carefully compared the online negotiation process with the 'long and well documented scholarly tradition centering around the reference interview', and has found the same underlying structure. As Prudence W. Dalrymple concluded in 1984, 'The introduction of online searching into reference services has not had a dramatic effect on the nature of the librarian-user interaction'. But one thing it has done, as mentioned in Chapter 3, is to confirm the significance of the interview in the reference process. In *Online search strategies*, the text that he edited in 1980, Ryan E. Hoover claimed that 'The importance of the reference interview cannot be overstressed'.

Simone Klugman explained why she believes that interviewing skills have acquired 'a new importance with online searching': 'overlooking any of these steps might have immediately visible disastrous consequences'.

It has of course affected some of the finer detail, and this is worth spelling out. The interview before a computer search is normally longer (though the search itself is usually shorter): in 1977 Arleen N. Somerville found a range of between 5 and 60 minutes, with most interviews taking between 20 and 40 minutes, and other investigations have confirmed this. But these are figures for the interviews preceding formalized, by-appointment, online literature searches, designed to produce perhaps 50 bibliographical references, or similar extended searches of source databases. Over the last decade there has been a marked growth in impromptu quick-reference searches, taking no more than a few minutes at the terminal and with a correspondingly brief interview. These will be described further in Chapter 5.

As suggested, interviews for searches other than the simplest are more formal. Most commonly they take place away from the reference desk, in a separate area of the library, sometimes in a private office. It is usually the case that greater pains are taken to clarify the topic, partly on grounds of cost: it can be expensive to refine a search topic while online. Normally, a search form has to be filled in, usually by the librarian with the assistance of the enquirer, but sometimes in advance by the enquirer alone. There is some evidence that search results can be improved if the topic is first described in the enquirer's own words. Tina Roose explained the reason for a form: 'Somehow the computer is more exacting than printed sources, and we librarians are less willing to try a search that costs money . . . without more concrete information about what exactly the patron wants'.

Because computer searching is highly language-dependent, much more attention has to be paid to terminology, and the librarian needs to grasp the opportunity offered by the interview to obtain as much help as possible from the enquirer by way of technical vocabulary, synonyms, abbreviations, jargon, etc., particularly in a specialist field.

It used to be the case that enquirers were normally more professional and business-like in their approach, and more certain about what they wanted, but this was in the early days when online search services were on offer only to specialists. A much wider range of clientele is found nowadays, and so, particularly with naïve users, librarians may find themselves explaining just what it is that a computer can, and often more importantly cannot, do. It may well be that at an early stage in the interview agreement is reached that a search of printed sources would be more appropriate. Based on her experience as Coordinator of Online Searching in the library of the University of California, Davis, Sandra J. Lamprecht itemized some of the more common misconceptions of the user: '(1) The computer can "think" like a human and therefore it will automatically understand his topic. It will know just what he needs. (2) The computer has access to all of the written material in the world going back for many years and all of this information is stored in one large database. (3) The computer contains the library call numbers for the journals cited in the search results for whatever library the patron wishes to use, or, the computer will provide a full text access automatically to all articles at no additional cost. (4) All databases selected provide excellent book as well as journal coverage. (5) There is a database for every area of research. . . . (6) Little effort is required to retrieve what one needs with no in-depth thinking required. (7) There is no need to investigate a topic further once the computer search has been completed.'

The nature of the desired response needs specifying in much more detail for a computer search. In the case of a bibliographical search it is usual to ask if the enquirer has views as to the optimum number of citations required, and whether high recall or high precision (explained to the user if necessary) is preferred. Or would just a few recent articles do? Output format too needs discussing: citations alone or with abstracts; sorted in a particular order; screen display only or printout; online or offline; downloaded for further manipulation; and so on and so forth. Mention was made above of the explicit inclusion in the search formulation of certain restraints such as language, time, or place, but computerized systems offer a much wider range of non-subject limitations that can similarly be specified in advance. These vary considerably from one database to another, even among those from the same vendor, but typically might include limiting the search to in-print materials, or certain document types, or particular publishers, or materials of a particular length, or illustrated material, and many others.

Of course, the building of all these requirements into the actual search itself is a task for the librarian at the search stage of the reference process which follows, but they will all obviously need to be discussed with the enquirer at the interview. It follows from this that the librarian needs to be much more fully informed about search system features and the databases themselves than is strictly necessary with a search confined to printed sources. Bunge believes that this is a difference that has not been sufficiently stressed in the literature. Of course one would hope that all reference librarians are at all times fully aware of the nature and content of all the information sources at their disposal; but with manual sources, including the card catalogue, as was noted in Chapter 1, it is often possible to 'fumble and stumble' one's way to an answer in a way that is not possible with a computer search.

As with a manual search, the interview continues intermittently throughout the search stage and beyond, as will be described in Chapters 5 and 6, and so there have been suggestions that the term 'pre-search interview', commonly used in the context of computer searching, is a misnomer. Peter Ingwersen wrote: 'It is worth noting that the common pattern in search and negotiation in IR involves continuous search interviewing and parallel searching processes. One ought therefore to advise information researchers to abandon the concept of the "pre-search" interview and concentrate on the "search" interview, in which the former plays only a small part.'

### 'The little things'

Perhaps only rarely will it be necessary to pursue a reference interview to its fullest extent: this is a matter for the librarian's judgement in the light of individual circumstances. The Lynch study that was quoted at the beginning of this chapter found that in only about a quarter of the interviews was there need for more than a couple of questions from the reference librarian. But few among that large minority of enquirers with which this chapter is concerned will supply all the missing details without some gentle prompting, or even quite close questioning. This is not because they are secretive, as a rule, or even reluctant. As Ross has explained, they 'often don't understand what the librarian needs to know before she can answer their information needs more efficiently'. For this they are not to blame: they cannot be expected to be fully aware of the resources available to meet their needs. It is a similar unawareness that sometimes leads them to present their questions in compromised form, as we have seen, with their demands adjusted in advance in accordance with their expectations of the library, and, sometimes, of the librarian. In other words, they ask for what they think the library can provide rather than what they want.

The advantage at this stage of the game lies with the librarian, as the one who knows the rules best – i.e., the organization, structure, vocabulary, and location of the sources of information, and especially of the keys to those sources, the catalogues, bibliographies, and reference tools. And by virtue of their training librarians are able to pick up clues that others would overlook. As Sherlock Holmes once said, 'It has long been an axiom of mine that the little things are infinitely the most important'.

In this, as in many fields of human activity, there is a world of difference between professional and amateur performance; indeed the very standards of judgement are different. It is this undeniable fact, rather than a claim to intellectual superiority, that the student should regard as the explanation for advice given in the literature about never taking for granted the accuracy of the enquirer's facts or the sources claimed to have been consulted. The simple truth of the matter is that the librarian is obliged to maintain a higher standard of accuracy with regard to, for instance, the precise spelling of names, or exact dates, because of their crucial significance in searching catalogues and bibliographies and reference books, or in interrogating a computerized database. Again, on the matter of sources already consulted by enquirers, the implication is not that they are unreliable or deceitful, but that in looking in the *Encyclopaedia Britannica* they may not be aware of the index, for example; or in looking up a word in *Webster's third new international dictionary* they may not have noticed the supplements. The reference librarian, however, like another Great Detective, R. Austin Freeman's Dr Thorndyke, must constantly be on the alert for 'the unexpected significance of trivial circumstances'. A third member of the brotherhood, Earl Derr Biggers' Charlie Chan, once explained that 'Detective business consist of one insignificant detail placed beside other of same'. This is also true of much of reference work: for example, devising a computer search formulation.

**Interpersonal communication**
More than a generation ago Lee W. Anderson made a brief plea for reference librarians to receive 'more academic preparation in the fields of psychology and human relations', and posed the question 'In working with people as intimately as reference librarians do, isn't an understanding of the individual library patron as important as a successful response to the intellectual content of his question?'. So far this chapter has concentrated almost exclusively on the intellectual component of the reference interview, which has as its central objective the negotiation of the question by the reference librarian. But there is more to the role than this. If the librarian is not to be regarded as a

mere functionary, and is truly practising a humane profession, it is axiomatic that this librarian-enquirer exchange must not be just a transfer of information. Inevitably it is a social act, but it has to be recognized on both sides as even more than that – as a human relationship, however brief. And even those many reference questions that do not require an interview are similarly acts of interpersonal communication. What might otherwise be merely a transaction must be given a human face. It would be to overstate the case to compare this partnership, as some have done, with the doctor-patient or even the lawyer-client relationship, but even at an everyday level there are consequences that flow from the acknowledgement by the librarian that such a human bond, however tenuous, must inevitably be there. There are dangers here in taking too literally the mechanistic chain analogy referred to earlier: the overall shape of the interview is not in fact linear – making use of a single channel – but circular, cyclic, and multi-channel, with considerable interaction between the participants – often quite subtle – and constant feedback, as in any face-to-face dialogue.

Some librarians have realized the importance of this interpersonal element for many years: in her 1897 paper Woodruff declared that she was 'almost prepared to put tact in meeting strangers and making them feel at home in the library . . . in the same category as [knowledge of information sources]'. The analogy with a doctor is closer here, inasmuch as it is well known that a good 'bedside manner' is often quite as important as skill at diagnosis. In 1973 Ric Calabrese commented that 'Studies in other disciplines have . . . verified that from the client's, patient's, customer's, student's, patron's, etc., point of view, the professional's manner in his interpersonal relationships, his way of interacting with others, is far more influential than either his knowledge, intellectual training, or orientation in his field'.

It is only quite recently that Anderson's plea has been given the attention it deserves, and much of the impetus has come from the findings of research into the way users measure the success of their encounter with a librarian. In 1977, in the context of online searching, Judith A. Tessier and her colleagues set out four aspects of user satisfaction: the output of the search; the user's view of the library as a whole; the particular 'service' that the library provides; user interaction with the library staff. This last aspect, she reported, 'is not now measured, but surely it is on the mind of the user and affects user satisfaction. Moreover, it is especially worth measuring because it is under the immediate control of the librarian.' Although user satisfaction is not a totally reliable indicator of the quality of some aspects of the service they receive, for reasons which will be explored further in Chapter 6, users are well placed to evaluate the interpersonal aspects of their interaction with the librarian, such as attitude and personality. By 1983 Alma Christine Vathis was able to claim that 'patrons have been shown to evaluate satisfaction first on an interpersonal level and second on an intellectual level'. In 1986 Desmond B. Hatchard and Phyllis Toy reported on a survey of Australian college libraries: 'There was agreement by both staff and student users concerning the qualities which library staff ought to possess. Above all else, they must be out-going, friendly, approachable, able to make users feel comfortable and have communication skills. Library personnel must also be helpful, patient and have a sound knowledge of all the library resources.' Naiman has translated this into concrete terms: 'it is more important to be regarded by our clients as friendly, self-confident, trustworthy, and dependable than to be regarded as "walking encyclopedias"'.

**Users' unease**
Research has repeatedly shown that many people feel uncomfortable in libraries. Maurice Line's survey of Southampton University students showed that 19% found the library intimidating and 48% found it mildly intimidating – a total of two out of every three users. It is difficult for librarians to recall this feeling, especially if they rarely visit a strange library themselves. Nor do they appreciate the vulnerable psychological position in which enquirers find themselves: they are not simply asking, as in a department store which might be every bit as imposing as any library, for goods or services which they need and which it is the business of the store to supply – they are openly admitting their ignorance. The seminal investigations of T. J. Allen in the 1960s showed that engineers and scientists often do regard the asking of a question in this light, and fear of losing prestige among their fellows does indeed strongly inhibit their use of information sources. And on grounds of status, some are particularly unwilling to admit their information need to the librarian, especially if they are uncertain about its nature.

Possibly this reluctance is only a special case of the general discomfort many of us feel in asking for assistance, especially from a stranger, and 'library anxiety', as it has been termed, may simply be one facet of the 'communication apprehension' syndrome. Hatchard and Toy found that only a third of their sample of Australian college library users had no problem in approaching other people for help in everyday life. As long ago as 1911 in an article entitled 'The shy enquirer' James Duff Brown suggested that 'The subject is well worth discussion, as indeed is the whole question of the psychology of readers in general'.

There is some research evidence that lack of privacy also bothers some users. It is, of course, an absolute rule that a user's enquiry is as confidential as a discussion with a doctor or a lawyer, but this fine theory normally has to operate in the context of a reference interview in full public view. Private consulting rooms such as those routinely used for online search interviews are scarcely a practical solution for everyday queries, and they might deter more than they would attract. As so often with this very human activity, what is needed is a nice balance of common sense and discretion.

Mooers' Law too may come into play here. A specific application to our field of the well-known Principle of Least Effort, it states: 'An information retrieval system will tend not to be used when it is more painful and troublesome for a customer to have information than for him not to have it'.

The barriers users face are often physical in nature, and many libraries still fail to provide what Katz specified as 'easy-to-see, easy-to-use access points where a librarian is on duty'. In a 1989 study of reference interviews in 142 United States libraries, 'Many observers [library school students] had trouble identifying the reference desk'. One study of reference desk placing in a United States university library reported that at one of the desks the enquirers often began by asking 'Do you work here?'. Unlike many other interview situations it is common for the user to have to stand while the professional remains seated. In the course of the study to be described later in this chapter Edward Kazlauskas found that users were more likely to put a question to a librarian who was standing rather than sitting. Linda Morgan reported that library users at the University of Houston were more willing to approach a [high] counter than a reference desk because of 'less formality, better eye contact, and less tendency to appear busy'.

Margaret Forster, a distinguished biographer and novelist, writing on the 'life begins at 40' theme, had this to say: 'I like going into an impressive library and not being intimidated; I like not being afraid to display my ignorance and ask for help. I like the confidence that middle age brings.' But years of experience do not always dispel the sense of unease: the speaker who confessed to a conference of over 100 reference librarians 'I still hate to ask questions and would rather flounder round on my own!' was a librarian, a professor, and a former

President of the Reference Services Division of the American Library Association.

## Unasked questions

Discussed earlier in this chapter was the reluctance of some enquirers to ask in specific terms for what they want. A matter of much more serious concern is the clear research evidence now confirming what some reference librarians have long suspected: users frequently fail to ask any questions at all even when they obviously wish to know the answers. Surveys have shown that even in large academic libraries, with perhaps as much as 90% of the material that users are seeking, something like 40% of readers trying to find a book will leave empty-handed rather than ask a librarian for help.

Their reasons are always the same: they thought their query too trivial to bother a busy librarian with; they did not wish to reveal their ignorance; they were not sure it was the librarian's job to help with problems like theirs; they did not think the librarian was capable of helping them; and so on. When the students in Line's University of Southampton survey were asked whether they thought the library staff might be able to help with a 'subject query' which they were not sure how to tackle, 51% replied that the possibility had not occurred to them. Informal surveys at the State University of New York at Albany discovered that students 'thought they were supposed to do "all [their] own work", and calling on a librarian was unfair'. Students are not alone in their ignorance: a survey of six academic libraries in California found that 'the average faculty member ... was aware of only 50 per cent of the reference services available', indeed 'there were individuals who desired the service without knowing it was already being offered'.

Paradoxically, as the Southampton survey showed, although asking the library staff was one of the two least-favoured methods of finding material on a new topic, for those students who did overcome their reluctance it was by far the most successful, with a 97% satisfaction rate.

At a deeper level F. W. Lancaster is surely correct in his speculation that 'The answers to many questions may never be sought because the individuals, in whose minds the questions are raised, believe (perhaps quite erroneously) that no recorded answers exist'. In their 1981 textbook Diana M. Thomas and her co-authors state that 'most [users] remain unaware of the extent to which librarians are able to help and advise them' and 'Ironically, at a time when librarians are prepared to do more than ever before, it does not occur to most people to consult them'.

Molly Sandock has remarked that 'It is distressing that misunderstanding, ignorance or ill-feeling may prevent persons who could profit from the help of the reference staff from consulting them'. This is no new phenomenon. In 1891 W. E. Foster was complaining that 'so modest is the average reader, and afraid of giving trouble, that the librarian is very sure that readers have sometimes wandered in and wandered out without obtaining what was wanted for lack of assistance that would have been gladly rendered'. A century on, however, the expansion of knowledge and the information explosion has multiplied the problem a hundredfold. Add to that the problems caused by the enormous complexity of urban life in the later 20th century, and there is explanation enough for the vast pools of unanswered questions that research continues to uncover in every section of the community. 'At no time in history', according to Geoffrey Langley, 'did people of all types and classes stand more in need of information, or rather of answers to questions, on all manner of matters great and small.'

But as King emphasized, 'Users have a tendency to try to solve their information problems outside the library'. This is putting it mildly: they will do anything rather than ask a librarian. They will ask neighbours, friends, people at work. They will ask in the local newsagents, the post office, the corner shop. They will even stop the police on their beat, and postal workers on their delivery round. In 1986 the National Consumer Council reported: 'We have found that a large number of people take up the invitation by parts of the media, either radio, television, newspapers or journals to write or call for information and advice. An even larger number write or try to ring well known media people to get help.' They will also write the mayor, their local councillor, or their Member of Parliament.

Anyone who doubts this should examine the queries that are asked on radio programmes or in the 'Answers to correspondents' columns of many local newspapers and popular magazines. Actual recent examples include 'How are magistrates chosen?', 'What was the date of the first crossword puzzle?', 'Who was "Jack Robinson" in the famous proverb?', 'Why does a judge wear a wig?', 'Who invented snooker?', 'What does "time immemorial" mean?', 'Who originated the phrase "the man on the Clapham omnibus"?'. As will perhaps be obvious, all of these are typical 'library-type' enquiries, so typical indeed that some years earlier each and every one had appeared in published collections of reference work case-studies, serving to demonstrate the point made in Chapter 2 about identical queries turning up again and again. It is worth noting that the queries that are actually broadcast or printed are merely the tip of the iceberg. Indeed a number of newspapers have recently realized how vast is this demand for information and have begun to market their reference skills, typically charging a flat fee for a phone call of up to five minutes. One UK national daily employs nine staff to deal with telephone enquiries alone. Though the scale is now infinitely greater, this is no new phenomenon: as long ago as 1910 J. D. Stewart was complaining that 'Most of the questions that people ask the editors of their favourite papers could be answered at once by their local reference libraries'.

King suggested one explanation for this behaviour: 'The profession has long encouraged users in self-help practices, and it seems quite possible that some users at least are reluctant to admit that their self-help measures have failed'. Claire Turnbull reminded us that such an enquirer 'is sensitive about his lack of knowledge of the library. He feels that he has failed because he has to turn to the librarian. This situation presents itself as a threat to his ego.' But even with those well-informed users who are fully aware that librarians are actually there to answer questions, there remains the problem, as Katz reminds us, that 'our user can never be quite sure that this ideal reference librarian is going to be behind the reference desk'. And as we have noted, even finding the reference desk is not always easy: after visiting 13 major university libraries in the United States Florence Blakely reported, 'As a stranger enters the portals of the libraries being surveyed, he is not overwhelmed by the high visibility of a reference or information desk'.

Yet another unexpected benefit from the introduction of computer searching facilities was noticed by James M. Kusack in 1979 and has since been reported by many libraries: 'Computers give library patrons an excuse to approach librarians . . . the patron is not expected to know anything about on-line searching and is therefore free to ask as many questions as necessary with no threat to a delicate ego'. A similar phenomenon had been remarked earlier with microform catalogues, with users 'free to admit difficulties . . . and ask for help with the "machine"'.

**Librarians unwelcoming**
There seems little doubt that librarians themselves must share some of the blame for users' unease and unasked questions. Time and again, research studies, such as those at Southampton and at Syracuse cited in Chapter 1, show that users, and even more significantly the much

94

more numerous non-users, find librarians unreceptive. Maxine Budd has drawn our attention to the fact that 'Readers in libraries often communicate with staff whose job is not specifically to communicate with them. For example, they will ignore the enquiry desk and ask a question of some person pushing a trolleyload of books.' An experiment at the University of New Hampshire with specially trained non-professional 'aides', selected from current undergraduate students, found that students with problems, but reluctant to consult a librarian, would willingly accept help from another undergraduate.

One quite serious barrier to improvement in the past has been the reluctance of users to tell librarians of their feelings about the matter. Even when captured by an opinion survey and asked a straight question they are often too nice to say what they really think. From time to time librarians do catch a fleeting glimpse of how others see them when some professional with the public ear – often a journalist or academic – does articulate this widely held view of them as unsympathetic, so mystifying to librarians. In a competition for a 'Bastards of the Year' award, according to Rosemary McLeod, a New Zealand journalist, 'Librarians would score on their attitude, especially being patronizing and unapproachable. They'd do well on failing to be helpful, an area where they specialize in denying that any author or book exists that they haven't heard of.' In a front-page article in the *Sunday Times Weekly Review* John Carey, professor of English literature at Oxford, referred in passing to librarians and their 'high-minded dislike of anyone who actually wants to use the commodities they're in charge of'.

But it is not just users who find librarians inhospitable. Studies by more professionally aware observers tell the same story. In 1989 Durrance recorded the reaction of a University of Michigan library school student helping in an unobtrusive test: 'This reference interview couldn't have been more unsatisfactory. The librarian made me feel intrusive. She sighed noisily when I asked my question, was uninterested in my needs, and didn't help me with any alternative suggestions for seeking the information. She never knew whether or not I had been successful.' In her 1980 Sheffield MA dissertation, Nicola Brown, another library school student, described an online pre-search interview in a university library, when the librarian was fully aware that she was being observed: 'when the user entered the room and sat down, the intermediary moved her chair back but did not look up. She kept her hand to her face which made it difficult to hear what she was saying, often frowned but never smiled and never met the user's eyes. She did not encourage discussion of the user's question and several times interrupted the user or ignored what he was saying. The interview lasted only twelve minutes and the observer felt that the user still had more that he wanted to say. The intermediary appeared uninterested and unfriendly.' There seems no doubt that some librarians have become specialists in what D. J. Campbell called 'inter-personal un-cooperation'. They put one in mind of the celebrated Gattling, in Stephen Potter's *Lifemanship*, who had the power 'by his *opening remarks* . . . of creating a sense of dis-ease'.

Even mature and experienced professional observers have found the same. To Sally E. Gibbs, a library school lecturer, 'The library staff can often seem unapproachable, and even I as a practising librarian often find myself intimidated by the staff of my local reference library'. Indeed, Davinson believed that 'The biggest single problem facing the user in making an enquiry in a reference library is the librarian'.

It is still far from well understood by librarians that the success of the reference process is dependent to a high degree on the user's view of the librarian. One useful measure of satisfaction used in other spheres is whether the enquirer feels inclined to return to the library on another occasion. A survey of students at the University of Nebraska found that they 'assumed that all reference assistance given is either good or bad depending on the past assistance they have received'. It does sometimes happen, as Pamela Tibbetts has reminded us, that 'The librarian may find exactly what the person has asked for, but made him feel so miserable in the process that he will never come in again'. Any hint of mutual antipathy is usually fatal to the reference interview and adds further to the future toll of unasked questions.

## Avoidance behaviour

It is perhaps not without significance that some writers on the reference interview use the term 'encounter'. The *Concise Oxford dictionary* defines this as 'meet as adversary', 'meeting in combat'. In recent years some of the more outspoken librarians have been taking a very cool look at their colleagues. Drawing largely on investigative work done on other professions, they have suggested that reference librarians too exhibit symptoms of what has been called 'avoidance behaviour'. Squeezed between the upper and nether millstones of increasing demand and dwindling resources, enmeshed in the bureaucratic structure that many libraries have become, under pressure from colleagues, superiors, and families to perform well, and sometimes set goals that conflict with their ideal of professional service, as Jane Robbins has pointed out, 'Individual librarians develop ways in which to make their jobs easier. Many of the mechanisms which they employ are largely psychological.'

Manoeuvres that have been used, as the percipient observer well knows, include simplifications and routines to save time, such as excluding certain categories of questions, or stereotyping users ('students', 'housewives', 'old people', 'ethnic minorities'). In her study of 1,000 reference interviews Barnes commented that 'the tendency of library staff to react to enquiries normatively rather than uniquely is an example of prevalent response to people and situations by which individuals look for the familiar elements to which they know how to respond and tend to ignore the unfamiliar or inconsistent aspects'.

Other ploys include redefining the librarian's role by choosing only one of several conflicting expectations, and the activation of what psychologists call 'threat-reduction mechanisms'. A quite common example is giving a spurious impression of busyness at the reference desk, what Davinson well described as 'bibliothecal pyrotechnics which are designed to impress and overawe the user with the mystical prowess of the librarian'. A similar stratagem is deliberately to contrive an authoritarian atmosphere, either institutional by means of rules and regulation, or personal by means of academic status, for example. Sometimes both institutional and personal one-upmanship can be combined in the way the reference desk is designed and located. As Robbins quite plainly warned, 'It is essential that librarians . . . realise that as these mechanisms come into accepted use they become an institutionalized expression of antagonism towards users'.

Librarians may also be shouldering other psychological burdens: the fear that the next question will be too technical, or not understood, or impossible to answer. They may take an instant dislike to an enquirer, or may have developed a general distaste for certain categories of users, or may feel unable to cope with the user's psychological problems. And *pace* the stereotype discounted in Chapter 1, in her observation of reference interviews in public libraries Barnes did find 'a lack of professional self-assertiveness and confidence in interaction with users'.

The donning of what Sidney M. Jourard has called 'character armour' is another behavioural syndrome with a similar objective. It commonly takes the form of a 'professional' manner deliberately adopted to keep the client at a distance, to hide one's real self, and often to protect one's personality from too much bruising. The classic example quoted by Jourard (and perhaps now a dying breed) is the brisk, super-efficient nurse, whose manner appears to be something she 'puts on when she dons her uniform'. Librarians too, as Edward J. Jennerich has pointed out, 'tend to be more formal (professional is a frequently used synonym) than is necessary or even desirable'. It does appear to be the case, as Janet E. Corson noted in the context of online searching, that 'Even a coolly professional key, as when the librarian asks simply what the patron's question is, may not be appropriate to facilitate the exchange of information needed for many, if not most searches'. The particular professional 'armour' that librarians assume includes moving rapidly about from place to place during the course of the enquiry, becoming preoccupied with answering the question or solving the problem rather than helping the enquirer, and making a parade of special knowledge. What has been called 'rocking-chair reference' or the 'sit and point' technique is also to be observed widely.

It is important to understand that it is not mere courteous recognition or polite interest that users look for; the 'empty sincerity' of the greeting one might exchange on passing a neighbour on the street is not sufficient for reference enquirers. The positive attribute they seek here is genuineness, where in the words of Manuel Lopez and Richard Rubacher, the individual librarian is 'without bureaucratic facade or professional mask, able and willing to be himself'.

For a decade and more Durrance has argued that librarians should drop the cloak of anonymity that is uniform in the profession: 'Certainly the attorney-client, the physician-client, the pastor-client, and the educator-client relationships are enhanced because the client knows the name of the professional he/she is dealing with. Likewise the nurse-client and the bureaucrat-client relationships are weak because the client has difficulty in maintaining the relationship due to the anonymity factor.' Her research has demonstrated some of the effects of this policy of professional anonymity: a 1984 interview survey of 429 users of three United States academic libraries found that users find it hard to distinguish librarians from other staff members, indeed have only a vague idea of staff differentiation, and are unaware of the credentials of librarians. Student observers in a 1989 unobtrusive survey of 142 libraries of all kinds were uncertain as to whether they had been attended to by a librarian: 68% thought they had, but only 35% of them felt quite sure. Samuel Rothstein has spelled out one significant implication: 'patrons, being confused about the kind of person they are dealing with, hesitate to ask for more than the minimum assistance or to follow up an inquiry'. A homely example of *vox pop* support for

Durrance's case came from the Hillingdon Libraries project in London in 1976: 'It would be nice if they had a badge that said what they were, because these librarians they spend a lot of time learning, actually what they've studied, then the people could possibly go up and ask them about the books'.

There are hopeful signs that the lessons are being learned. With increasing frequency advertisements for reference librarians and similar information posts include specifications such as 'good interpersonal skills', 'excellent communication and interpersonal skills', 'interpersonal skills are mandatory', 'strong interpersonal skills are prerequisites', 'exceptional interpersonal skills are essential', 'excellent interpersonal skills are clearly vital', 'interpersonal skills are a must'. It is interesting to note that the advent of computer searching has not changed matters: according to Somerville, 'Person-to-person communication skills ... are among the most critical for conducting an effective interview', and 'These are the same as for all reference interviews'. Harry M. Kibirige believes that 'profound interpersonal communication is still needed in spite of automation'.

## Approachability

The concept of approachability has been referred to a number of times in this chapter. Margaret Hutchins, the author of what is still the best book on the subject and probably the first to use the term 'reference interview' almost 50 years ago, always maintained that approachability is the first requirement of the reference librarian. It is interesting to note the main conclusion drawn by Kazlauskas from his observation of reference interviews in academic libraries a whole generation later: 'It seems that in the reference area "approachability" is of utmost importance'.

In his 1876 paper Green advised his audience 'Receive investigators with something of the cordiality displayed by an old-time innkeeper'. Sadly, old-time innkeepers are even more scarce now and in any case their hearty style of welcome is probably too bluff and simple for our sophisticated times. What methods then are open to today's reference librarians to encourage users to bring their questions to them? As William Donovan pointed out, 'Friendliness and approachability can neither be trained in classes nor assumed at will by individuals'.

Going up to puzzled users in the library is sometimes advocated, by Trisha Gillis, for example, with her view of the 'librarian as floorwalker' and her philosophy of 'attack the patron'; though her opinion that

99

'people *like* being approached' is not one with which all reference librarians would agree. But the experience of J. Richard Madaus, also an advocate of 'aggressive reference service' was that more questions were answered from the floor than the desk. Simply moving about more among users has a similar effect. Larry D. Benson and H. Jolene Butler were able to put a figure on this: 'leaving the desk to walk round the reference area has increased the number of reference assists by 25%'.

But librarianship is a multi-disciplinary field, and reference work, though squarely based on systematic bibliography, owes more than most areas of the subject to other disciplines. It is worth stressing again the relevance to the point at issue of the investigations of the social psychologists in the field of interpersonal communication, including nonverbal communication. As others have pointed out, for the most part reference librarians are medium-oriented rather than client-oriented: not the least value of the study of interpersonal communication is its emphasis on the personal rather than the material.

Perhaps a small warning would not be out of place here: statistically, as has been said, the great majority of reference transactions can by their nature be no more than fleeting exchanges, whereas most of the relevant work in social psychology relates to deeper and more extended relationships. A 1973 study of a week's sample of nearly 6,000 enquiries in six public libraries in England found an average time per question of 6.23 minutes. A generation earlier a survey of a month's queries in Detroit Public Library found that the average was 8.4 minutes. An analysis of over 11,000 queries in 14 large city libraries in England in 1982 showed that 70% took less than 10 minutes. And these figures include the search and response time as well as the time spent on the interview. Barnes found that in one of the two libraries she investigated 'policy was actively to discourage staff from taking more than five minutes in dealing with any one enquiry'.

It would be a mistake to forget statistics such as these, and try to equate the reference interview with social work interviews or consultations with lawyers and doctors. Indeed, while drawing on a number of fields for comparison, Elaine Z. Jennerich has told us that 'Personally, I believe the reference interview is unique among the professions'. Moreover, as White emphasized, 'Other professions where interviewing is used extensively ... have been able to categorize interviews to a greater extent. As a result, they can predict content. types of behavior, and likely problem areas and develop approaches that accommodate the usual patterns.' But reference interviews are 'so diverse and unpredictable'. Dana E. Smith has said that 'Like snowflakes, no two reference transactions are identical'.

There is one conclusion of the psychologists about interviews that is of particular relevance for librarians: the crucial importance of the initial impact, 'the first four minutes'. As explained by Leonard and Natalie Zunin, 'In essence, getting through the four minute barrier can be compared to a supersonic aircraft breaking the sound barrier: after the initial turbulence ... the chance of smoother progress is predictably improved'.

## Nonverbal communication

Without any doubt, the aspect of interpersonal communication that has had the greatest impact on reference librarians over the last two decades or so has been nonverbal communication, that is to say the exchange of face-to-face messages between individuals by means other than words, examples of which have already been described: noisy sighing, the moving back of one's chair, covering one's face with a hand, frowning, and avoiding looking at people. Language is only one channel, but, in Dean Barlund's words, 'Communication involves the total personality. Despite all efforts to divide body and mind, reason and emotion, thought and action, meanings continue to be generated by the whole organism.'

This is a topic far more complex and varied than might at first be imagined, and the social psychologists have identified and described no fewer than seven channels of nonverbal communication, making up what has popularly been called our 'body-language', which can be analysed, learned, interpreted, and used like speech in quite systematic fashion. One oft-quoted estimate is that 65% of the social meaning in a two-person conversation is conveyed by nonverbal means.

The general field of bodily movements is known as kinesics (facial expression, gaze, gesture, posture), but nonverbal communication also includes paralinguistics (grunts, sighs, tone of voice, silent pauses, etc.), proxemics (spatial behaviour, e.g. placing in relation to others), bodily contact (touching, etc.), clothes and other aspects of appearance, and so on. Of course we are all aware of this to some extent. Everyone knows how difficult it is to talk to someone who won't look at you. As children we learn in daily communication with our parents the significance of a firmly closed mouth, or fidgeting hands, or raised eyebrows, or a sigh, or a caress. Many years ago there was a popular music-hall song that began 'Every little movement has a meaning of its own/Every thought

101

and feeling by some posture can be shown'. Those who have travelled widely may know that these familiar signals do not mean the same everywhere: some are culture-specific. Shaking the head from side to side means 'yes' in some countries, 'no' in others; Ross and Dewdney have reminded us that 'Eye contact, for example, is understood in Western cultures as a sign of attentive listening, but in Eastern cultures may be taken as a sign of disrespect'. It is even more significant among Arabs, who find it difficult to talk when side by side or wearing dark glasses.

These nonverbal channels play a central part in human social behaviour. Indeed, according to Michael Argyle, a social psychologist at Oxford, 'the expression of emotion and the negotiation of interpersonal relationships ... is done almost entirely non-verbally'. This is an aspect of human behaviour that holds a considerable fascination for everyone; indeed some of the popularizations in book form have reached the best-seller lists. Its immediate relevance to the reference interview is obvious and it has been the focus of much attention. One of the first to grasp its implications was Shosid, significantly a business librarian, who reported in 1966 on observations made of reference encounters at the University of Southern California. She discovered that there was indeed considerable nonverbal communication going on, but that both librarians and enquirers were not always aware of the fact. She concluded that 'Librarians must become sensitive to this continuous nonverbal communication and harness it into their total communications strategy'.

Every later study has served to confirm this, sometimes inadvertently. The 1972 Lynch investigation of public libraries in New Jersey involved the use of a radio microphone to tape-record the interviews, and it was found that sometimes the actual words used made little sense in the absence of any record of the nonverbal communication that must have accompanied them, such as 'a glance, a facial expression, or a shrug of the shoulders'.

In spite of this quite powerful impact, one feature that distinguishes nonverbal communication from speech is that it often operates at low levels of awareness, even unconsciously. This cuts both ways, of course: recipients may be unaware that they are receiving and reacting to nonverbal signals from the sender; they are also likely to be oblivious of the signals that they themselves are sending inadvertently. In the context of the reference interview therefore, librarians need to be constantly reminded, as Marie L. Radford did in 1989, that 'in addition to *giving* content information in response to the user's request, they are also *giving off* interpersonal and relational information'. Indeed, in such a situation 'You cannot NOT communicate', as Anne J. Mathews emphasized. Even total silence and complete immobility convey their own message. Moreover, such an attitude is not interpreted by its recipient as a sign of neutrality or detachment, but as distinctly unfriendly, even hostile.

There is one further characteristic of nonverbal communication that is significant in the context of reference. It is perfectly possible for the nonverbal message to conflict or even contradict the verbal message; in spite of what they might be saying, people often cannot prevent their real feelings showing through, as our everyday experience tells us. This has been well described as nonverbal 'leakage', and its importance lies in the fact that, as Robert E. Brundin reported in 1989, 'studies indicate that when verbal and non-verbal messages differ, people will most often believe the non-verbal'.

An experimental study at Edinburgh University library in 1978 revealed that 'the rate of approach [by enquirers to the information desk] during [artificially contrived] "not busy" conditions was significantly higher than for "busy" conditions'. Similar findings had been reported earlier in the classic study by Kazlauskas based on observations at 10 service points in four academic libraries in Southern California: 'Those reference personnel who appeared receptive tended to be inundated with requests from patrons, while those who exhibited nonreceptivity were oftentimes left alone by patrons'. He too commented that 'The body language, if opposite to the verbal language, may tell us what the person is really saying. And naturally, there are some situations in which only nonverbal language is available, such as the observation by patrons of an individual at a reference or information desk. A reading of the reference librarian's body language may tell the patron whether or not to approach.'

More specifically, he took the opportunity to draw up lists of typical nonverbal behaviours exhibited. Of these the most significant are the negative behaviours, because they directly contradict what on the face of it is the stated or understood position, namely that reference librarians waiting at service points would welcome enquiries. As recorded at the time, their nonverbal signals included the following:

1  Lack of an immediate nonverbal acknowledgement of a patron waiting to ask a question;

2   No perceptible change in any body movement upon the movement of a patron into the traditional space for transaction of impersonal business;

3   A staff member in a sitting position with hand held on the brow covering the eye vision and engrossed in reading, filing, or some other activity;

4   Tapping the finger(s) on the counter when a request is made and twitching the mouth upon movement to fulfil the request;

5   Pacing behind the counter when the patron is using an item at the counter.

He made one further percipient comment about the effect on other potential enquirers who notice these negative behaviours: this can make them 'apprehensive of similar interactions or can even dramatically turn them away from any interaction at all'.

It has to be said that the response of the profession to this emphasis on nonverbal behaviour was not entirely favourable. Katz, for example, in the 1978 edition of his text, complained that 'Useful as kinesic analysis may be at the reference desk, it often comes close to the ridiculous . . . [with] ponderous, sometimes fatuous conclusions'. Perhaps the warning was necessary, but those who believe that there is no problem here should sit for half an hour in many of the libraries where enquiries are dealt with, and then make a judgement as to whether students of the reference process should be alerted to the effect on users of negative nonverbal behaviour. To see ourselves as others see us, as Robert Burns well knew, is a rare gift, but as he went on to say, 'It wad frae mony a blunder free us'. Making a positive effort now and then to stand in the enquirer's shoes is good for the reference librarian's soul. So often the way one sees things depends on one's personal standpoint.

Argyle believes that 'Any socially skilled behaviour requires correct use of NVC at a number of points'. Although the head nod is the most common, two of the most basic nonverbal signals are the smile and the frown: we now know that babies can recognize such expressions at a few weeks old; in fact, research at the University of Wales at Cardiff has shown that only 10 or 15 minutes after birth babies are attracted by an animated face. To require reference librarians to wear a permanent smile would perhaps not be welcome, and it might alarm more enquirers than it would attract. Even to suggest that they smile occasionally might not be acceptable: like many whose vocation it is to serve, from New York cab drivers to Parisian café waiters, they do not always feel like smiling. But at least they could be asked to frown less. An instructive field exercise for any student is to visit a library and count the number of librarians with a frown. Most often, of course, such an expression merely reflects the intense mental effort inseparable from the daily work of the librarian; unfortunately it also conveys a clear nonverbal message to any potential enquirer.

Research has now demonstrated that Bernard Vavrek was right in 1974 when he claimed that 'While it may not seem as important as [knowledge of reference sources], one's facial posture can vastly affect the willingness of the patron to pose a question and certainly it can influence the manner in which the question is asked'. It can also have a quite marked effect on the user's judgement of a librarian's ability. In a controlled experiment using 320 public library users as volunteer observers, Roma M. Harris and B. Gillian Michell found in 1986 that 'Despite the fact that each observer watched a competent reference interview [scripted, using professional actors, on videotape] in which the librarian successfully responded to the patron's question, the perception of competence, including the likelihood of obtaining a useful answer to a question, was affected by whether the librarian smiled, spoke warmly, and looked at the patron during the interview'.

Of course, this kind of wordless communication is a two-way process, and the librarian must be doubly on the alert to read the nonverbal signals transmitted by the user. Indeed Katz by his 1982 edition had come to believe that 'The true value of nonverbal communication lies not so much in helping the reference librarian to shape up for the encounter as in assisting that librarian to understand the person who wants help'. For example, according to Virginia Boucher, in a scholarly though not entirely humourless paper, 'The Irate Patron stance is characterized by very erect posture, an angry facial expression, sustained eye contact, dilated pupils, emphatic head nods, and in rare cases, clenched fists'. She also gives valuable advice on distinguishing between the Lost Sheep and Confidence Personified.

More seriously, Lynch believes that 'The reference librarian probably also gains information from such clues as how the patron is dressed, what objects he or she is carrying, how confident he or she seems to be about using the library'. But the warning given by Joanna López Muñoz is worth remembering: 'People tend to manipulate their appearance in order to send messages about their social status or occupation'; and more generally, just as with verbal messages, nonverbal signals can be sent with deliberate intent to mislead.

Finally, reference librarians must not forget that much of their reading of these nonverbal clues will be happening at the subconscious level, and helping to form their attitudes towards the users.

## Listening

Earlier in this chapter it was claimed that the reference librarian's main negotiating instrument is skilful questioning, and its purpose is to get the enquirer to talk. It therefore follows that the librarian must be a good listener, and this too is a distinct technique that requires skill to perform well. In our literate modern societies it is not as highly developed as it used to be.

The first step towards being a good listener is to stop talking: Mathews has reminded us that 'we have two ears and one mouth, which we should use in the same proportion'. Reference librarians need to become as fully aware as other professional interviewers of the tactical value of the pause in encouraging the enquirer to volunteer more information.

Mention has already been made of paraphrasing, defined in this context by Nathan M. Smith and Stephen D. Fitt as 'sending back to the patron a straight-forward, albeit tentative, interpretation of his message'. Theodore P. Peck has explained how this is mutually beneficial: 'it sharpens the librarian's ability to listen and informs the interviewee that his problem has been understood'. It has been called active listening.

Premature diagnosis is a common fault: as Davinson warned, 'So often after the user begins a statement of need, the librarian stops listening with complete attention and begins to bend the needs of the user to fit his own conception of the bibliographic structures – the librarian begins to think of a solution before really knowing the question'. Edward J. Jennerich has noticed that 'reference students selectively listen to a query until some word or concept makes contact with an information source they know; then they stop listening and wait for a suitable conversational opening so that they can run and get a book'.

Patrick Penland is right to warn that 'Genuine listening is hard work and requires that the librarian be alert to all the verbal and non-verbal cues which occur. Interviewing involves the hearing of the way things are said, the tones used, the expressions and gestures employed.'

## Reaction

The transplanting of so many insights from the psychological and social sciences into the library literature during the 1970s and early 1980s 'provided a challenge to widely held assumptions about the reference interview', according to Bunge in 1984, and provoked, perhaps not unexpectedly, 'a sort of common sense backlash', and not only in the area of nonverbal communication. Among the mildest rebukes was that from Archie G. Rugh in 1976: 'Any training in the library schools for reference work is – or ought to be – principally training in bibliography, not personal relations or interpersonal communication'. Ten years later, though he had modified his view somewhat, he was still gently warning: 'To be sure, our work may be enhanced and improved by applying the interviewing techniques perfected by the behavioral sciences, but without solid training in bibliography there is no point in a reference librarian interviewing anyone in the first place. ... The reference interview is a technique for formulating a bibliographical problem and a bibliographical strategy.'

Others were less inhibited. Fred Oser wrote of 'the "tormented" or "tragic sense" of the reference interview', and Joseph Rosenblum declared that 'something is rotten in the state of reference librarianship'. Particular scorn was directed at the language used by the protagonists of the interpersonal dimension: 'so cloaked in difficult and obscure language as to totally defeat comprehension' (Davinson); 'frequently written in an unnecessarily inflated jargon whose major effect is to make the self-evident seem to be a revelation or the simplistic seem to be profound' (David Isaacson); 'The jargon of communication often is enough to leave one speechless. ... The amount of sheer nonsense written about two or more people talking together is almost as objectionable as it is humorous' (Katz).

Of course psychologists have long become inured to the lay view that their work consists largely of 'the monotonous discovery of common sense', and that, as one of them himself put it in his standard text, 'psychologists only appear to say in ridiculously long words what most people know already to be a fact of life'. Indeed the word 'psychobabble' was specifically coined to describe their jargon. Among the social psychologists too, Argyle at least was aware of the common lay reaction to academic analyses of nonverbal communication, which is not only the oldest form of communication but also a commonplace, everyday experience: he acknowledged that 'The reader may feel that he is in the position of Molière's Monsieur Jourdain, who discovered that he had been speaking prose all those years'.

But for our profession, Rothstein, as he has done so often, recently provided a balanced view, based on the experience of a lifetime: 'I myself doubt both the validity and value of such [a standardized and teachable set of] procedures, but I welcome the fact that reference librarians are now becoming more sensitive to and knowledgeable about the psychological factors in reference work'.

## The professional attitude

The humane attitude towards enquirers that is outlined in the second part of this chapter should never be assumed as a mere veneer of politeness, or exploited as a manipulative technique to make them feel good, or undertaken as any form of public relations. It should be adopted, firstly, for hard practical reasons: such an approach has a positive effect on the willingness of the user to cooperate in providing the further information that is needed; moreover, as Benson and Butler have noted, 'it is this concern and warmth that bridges the gap between the idealistic service one would hope to offer and the realistic service one is often forced to give'. But secondly, and far more importantly, it is the only stance that can be taken by a true professional. It is one of the chief characteristics of a profession that the role of its practitioners is not merely the delivery of a service but the acceptance of a degree of responsibility for the welfare of their clients.

*Further reading*

Belkin, Nicholas J., 'Anomalous states of knowledge as a basis for information retrieval', *Canadian journal of information science*, **5**, 1980, 133 – 43.

Smith, Nathan M. and Fitt, Stephen D., 'Active listening at the reference desk', *RQ*, **21**, 1982, 247 – 9.

Somerville, Arleen N., 'The pre-search reference interview – a step by step guide', *Database*, **5**, February 1982, 32 – 8.

White, Marilyn D., 'The reference encounter model', *Drexel library quarterly*, **19**, Spring 1983, 38 – 55.

Bunge, Charles A., 'Interpersonal dimensions of the reference interview: a historical review of the literature', *Drexel library quarterly*, **20**, 1984, 4 – 23.

Oser, Fred, 'Referens simplex or the mysteries of reference interviewing revealed', *Reference librarian*, **16**, 1986, 53 – 78.

Ross, Catherine Sheldrick, 'How to find out what people really want to know', *Reference librarian*, **16**, 1986, 19 – 30.

Wilson, Patrick, 'The face value rule in reference work', *RQ*, **25**, 1986, 468 – 75.

Jennerich, Elaine Zaremba and Jennerich, Edward J., *The reference interview as a creative art*, Littleton, CO, Libraries Unlimited, 1987.

Radford, Marie L., 'Interpersonal communication theory in the library context: a review of current perspectives', *Library and information science annual*, **5**, 1989, 3 – 10.

# — 5 —

# The search

With many of the author/title or fact-finding enquiries, a 'search' as such is scarcely necessary. Certainly, the answer has to be found, but a professional knowledge of bibliographical and reference sources – not only specific titles but general categories – supplemented by experience, and aided by a good memory, quite often ensure that the reference librarian knows just where to look. A request for details of international paper sizes, or a list of the Catholic bishops in Scotland, or the magnetic declination in 1960, or last year's winner of the Irish Sweeps Derby, or how the Muslim calendar works, or the salary of the Lord Chief Justice of England, will be answered almost spontaneously from *Whitaker's almanack*. In such cases the only element of decision may be in choosing from a number of equally suitable sources.

What seems to happen in this kind of 'automatic mental retrieval', as Marcia J. Bates has called it, is that the librarian either knows from memory that the answer is there, or has learned a simple set procedure for finding the answer to certain types of question. These procedures are not algorithms, that is to say well-defined rules to be followed in order to accomplish a particular task, and which are known to produce the required effect in all instances, such as the mathematical rules for long division. The reference librarian's repertoire of tactics in this particular context are rather 'rules of thumb', or heuristics – procedures that tend to produce useful results, but which are not guaranteed in all cases. They are learned by experience and practice. Such a rule of thumb might state that for specific details about prominent British people, still living, the first source to try is *Who's who*, although of course not all heuristics are so simple. It has been said that the reference search is much more like doing crossword puzzles than solving algebraic equations or even playing chess.

Even some of the material-finding enquiries need no search in anything like the usual sense. All that is required in many cases is simply

110

a small selection of what is available on the topic – perhaps no more than a single book. The librarian can normally trace sufficient material in the classified sequence on the shelves with little or no fresh intellectual effort. Once again the decisions required are minimal: the selection of one source rather than another where there is a choice, and an assessment of when sufficient material has been supplied. Typical examples of enquiries of this kind that should be satisfied within minutes in any reasonably stocked library are 'I am looking for something about the effects of television on children', 'Have you anything on acupuncture?', 'I want a good readable book on the Black Death', 'I would like something on the Bloomsbury Group', 'Do you know of anything on bell ringing?'.

Routine though such enquiries may seem to the librarian, the speed and assurance of the response does seem like sorcery to many users. Gratifyingly often, their reaction is delight and gratitude. The student should remember, however, that the effortless ease of such replies does conceal from the enquirer the extensive anticipatory effort of the librarian in studying the sources of information and prior experience in their use – not to mention a familiarity with the classification system and the arrangement of the collections. In addition to the heuristics already mentioned there is a whole battery of minor skills and special techniques, intellectual and manual, for using particular sources of information: they have to be mastered one at a time and committed to memory. It is also likely that as librarians go about seeking answers their minds are working on the problem at the subconscious level too.

In many libraries enquiries of this fairly elementary nature – so far as method is concerned – will comprise a good majority of the total. The bulk of the remainder, however, will be made up of two important categories requiring more minute attention. Firstly, there will be those material-finding enquiries where merely 'something on' the topic will not suffice; as was mentioned in Chapter 2, not uncommonly the user will need to see everything that is available, on, for example, prison suicides, or seat-belt injuries, or snake meat as a delicacy, or coal carving. To satisfy such needs a careful and systematic search is necessary. Secondly, in every library there will always remain a substantial number of enquiries, both fact-finding and material-finding, where no particular source immediately suggests itself; and to these must be added those where an obvious source has proved fruitless. In such instances, instead of providing virtually an automatic response, the librarian has to take the alternative approach of looking in any source

111

that seems likely. In other words, here also a real search is necessary.

**Pause for thought**
There is a distinct danger at this point that the enthusiastic but inexperienced librarian will fall into the common error of mistaking motion for action: it is usually a mistake to head straight for the catalogue or the shelves or to sit down at the computer terminal without at least pausing for a couple of minutes or so to think. But as A. E. Housman once said, 'Thought is irksome and three minutes is a long time', and it has to be admitted that librarians who should know better do sometimes plunge into what are not simple searches with only the sketchiest idea of a strategy. Perhaps regrettably, their flair will often carry them through, but the likelihood of failure and the consequent disappointment of the enquirer can almost always be reduced by taking thought.

Leonard Woolf observed that 'The grinding of the intellect is for most people as painful as the dentist's drill'. Reference librarians are no exception, unfortunately, and so they often need consciously to force themselves to bring their minds rather than their muscles to bear on the problem before them. Margaret Hutchins' advice cannot be improved upon: 'Answering questions is a reasoning process ... it should be thought through before a step is taken or a hand lifted towards a book'.

By this stage in the reference process the librarian is faced with *two* problems. One is the enquirer's problem, expressed in the form of a question, the solution of which is the whole object of the exercise; the second is the librarian's own problem, which is how to go about finding this solution. It is important for the student not to confuse the two: the librarian's problem is not a 'subject' or substantive knowledge problem like the enquirer's, it is a problem of technique or methodological knowledge. But of course both these problems interact, with the subject of the query influencing the mode of searching and the search findings feeding back and possibly modifying the user's view of the subject.

The successful prosecution of any search, other than the simplest, depends on the twin series of interlocking decisions which together constitute the search strategy. The first group of decisions controls the form in which the enquirer's question is put to the information store; at its most basic this is a matter of choosing the keywords to use when looking the subject up. The second group of decisions concerns the planning of the search route through the information store; this is a question of which sources of information are to be included in the search and what sequence is to be followed. Each of these two sets of strategic decisions normally encompasses a host of subsidiary decisions, often closely linked with one another and with the corresponding or subsidiary decisions in the other series.

The decisions in this twin battery are not necessarily taken in logical or even in consecutive order. And once taken they are not at any point or in any way regarded as final: each is perhaps best regarded as no more than a hypothesis to be tested. Indeed, in some instances, reference librarians may not even be aware that they have taken a decision: Charles A. Bunge's study of the process led him to conclude that 'In manual or more traditional systems the formation of search strategies by reference librarians seems to take place primarily at the subconscious level'. A good part of the explanation for any apparent lack of logic or system must lie in the arbitrary and uncoordinated nature of many of the sources of information themselves, despite the efforts of librarians, bibliographers, indexers, database managers, and sundry compilers of reference works.

The same explanation accounts to some extent for the lack referred to in Chapter 3 of a generally applicable search method. In the words of William A. Katz, 'Because of the variables of both human judgement and resources, it is impossible to give a definitive outline of a search process'. All experienced searchers know this. It is true there are topics, usually of very narrow compass, where the literature, for special reasons, has so distinctive a cast that it is indeed possible to outline a common search path that will lead to the solution of most enquiries. Two examples, from quite dissimilar fields, and certainly markedly different in subject content, are heraldry and patents. As F.S. Stych has shown, it is possible to systematize the identification of coats of arms, setting it out in the form of a flow chart that leads the searcher by way of a whole series of interconnected or alternative paths to the various reference works that should provide the answer. Similarly, one can devise a step-by-step approach to a search for British patent specifications on a specific subject.

It is not easy to think of subject fields where such a pre-programmed search is possible: certain specific areas of law is one, chemical compounds another; there may be a few more. What is clear from an examination of such search methods is that they are all quite different one from another. The idea that there could ever be devised a search strategy applicable over more than the most closely defined area has to be abandoned in the face of such evidence.

What has been developed at the general level, notably by Bates but also by Gerald Jahoda and his colleagues, are a number of search *tactics*, which not only give a clearer insight into the search process as it has been practised by reference librarians for generations, but also provide specific tools to apply at appropriate stages in the search. Some are probably heuristics already in regular use, but which have not been so clearly set out before.

## The librarian's instinct

If there is then no search method, does the librarian proceed solely by instinct? The answer of course is no, but before proceeding further with an explanation, it would be as well to pause and consider the value of an experienced librarian's instinct. The *Concise Oxford dictionary* defines instinct as an 'innate propensity to certain seemingly rational acts performed without conscious intention'. There seems no doubt that when faced, for instance, with a range of equally likely (or equally unlikely) search paths to follow, the frequency with which the experienced (or perhaps gifted) reference librarian will choose the right one owes more to some capacity of an instinctual nature than could be attributed to the operation of chance. D. J. Foskett called this 'flair', but he claimed that it is acquired by experience. Stych wrote of 'those intuitive leaps and . . . those irrational hunches which, in the experienced worker, are probably the result of a rapid, subconscious review of stored knowledge'. Mary W. George indeed believed that 'Search strategy . . . is no more than the step-by-step arrangement of the reference librarian's instantaneous flashes'.

What certainly happens without a doubt is that the experienced librarian, consciously or not, does telescope into what may appear to be a single instantaneous decision a whole series of logically connected search steps that the less experienced (or less gifted) librarian has to take one at a time at a more deliberate pace.

At this point the student could well be excused for wondering what profit there lies in attempting to understand a search method consisting of a strategy arrived at largely subconsciously and a procedure mainly intuitive. It is indeed true that this remains a corner of reference work that research has done little to illuminate, despite attempts by observation, questionnaire, and running self-commentary. According to Bates, probably the most penetrating thinker on the topic, 'For all the developments in automated and semiautomated information retrieval, nothing yet matches the ability of experienced human searchers – whether known as "information specialists" or "reference librarians" – who move skilfully among the enormous range of resources, both manual and online, to develop bibliographies or to answer questions. We know discouragingly little about just what those skills are and how they develop; we cannot define yet what it is that an experienced searcher knows that a beginner does not.' What follows in the next few pages, therefore, is simply a brief outline description, covering the formulation of the search statement, the choice of sources, the selection of the search route, and the procedure of the actual search itself.

## Search strategy: formulation of statement

Access to the subject content of the various sources making up the information store is by means of words: whether the item of information is in an encyclopaedia article, a textbook, a patent specification, an autograph letter, a citation in a bibliographical database, a trade catalogue, a newspaper clipping, a video-cassette, or any possible alternative, it can only be traced by utilizing the access language of the store, or, if different, the access language of that particular section of the store where the item is located. These access or control languages consist of those subject terms used in the cataloguing and indexing of the individual units in the store – subject headings, keywords, descriptors, index entries, etc.

It is obvious that the enquirer's question (or negotiated question if an interview has been necessary) will be in natural language, this is to say in ordinary words. It is unlikely that this will correspond exactly to the language used in the information store, and so what the librarian has to do is to 'translate' the question into terminology acceptable to the system. It has to be made to match the keywords used in the subject catalogue and the classification system and in the indexes to bibliographies, reference works and other materials in the library, or in the equivalent computerized databases that might be searched. Even in a free-text or natural language computer search the input is rarely in exactly the form used by the enquirer: what is used is a subset of the enquirer's words, selected to represent the essential subject information in the query statement; very common words and the so-called 'function' words are omitted, and some of the remainder may well be truncated. This is the stage at which the question passes through the last (actually the fourth) of Robert S. Taylor's five filters as described in Chapter 4: 'Relationship of inquiry description to file organization'.

For those questions which have already been modified at the interview stage this is, of course, a further redefinition.

The operation normally starts with a detailed analysis of the subject of the question into its various concepts. Foskett advised: 'Before consulting any source, the searcher must be sure that he has placed the subject of the enquiry in its correct part of the field of knowledge, and he does this by classifying it. In other words, he must analyse the subject into its various facets, which not only clarifies it in his own mind, but also provides him with the key words under which he will have to look when he comes to indexes and catalogues.' For such a task librarians are particularly well fitted by their professional education: bringing to bear the analytical power of classification should be second nature to them. Facet analysis in particular can be helpful at this stage, using, for example, Ranganathan's five fundamental categories of Personality, Matter, Energy, Space, and Time; or more probably one or more of the later refinements by Brian C. Vickery and others.

Each of the half-dozen or more facets of an enquiry such as 'the socio-economic prospects of immigrants in Britain' would then in their turn be analysed in order to provide appropriate keywords for the search, not forgetting more generic and more specific terms. In building up lists of search terms librarians are not obliged to rely entirely on their own mental resources. They might consult an encyclopaedia article on the topic, check for likely terms in appropriate dictionaries, including dictionaries of synonyms, examine classification schedules, consult bibliographies and indexes in the field, and perhaps most useful of all, study any lists of subject headings, thesauri, or other authority lists that seem likely to be of assistance. Jahoda has called these 'vocabulary-bridging tools', and 42,000 terms from a number of them have been consolidated in a particularly handy volume, *Cross-reference index: a guide to search-terms*. This is the point at which a dip into the literature in the form of a quick trial search of the field can also reap dividends.

Taking as an example the enquiry quoted, and concentrating for the moment on one of its most distinct facets – 'immigrants' – at the end of an exercise of this kind the librarian would have a list of terms such as the following, under any one of which relevant information may be found when the time comes to consult the materials in the information store: aliens, assimilation, asylum, brain drain, citizenship, colonies, deportation, displaced persons, emigrants, emigration, emigrés, empire, ethnic groups, ethnic minorities, evacuees, exiles, expatriates, foreign populations, foreigners, fugitives, guest workers, immigrant families, immigrant labour, immigrant personnel, immigrants, immigration, incomers, migrants, migration, minorities, nationality, naturalization, patriotism, population transfers, race, refugees, repatriation, residents, settlers, stateless persons, transients. This is not an exhaustive list: it does not include the names of countries or regions from which immigrants come, such as Bangladesh or the Caribbean; nor does it include the names of nationalities or other groupings, such as Vietnamese or Sikhs.

Of course in an ideal world it would not be necessary to look under all these terms for what is after all just one subject, and a clearly defined one at that. At the very least one would expect to be directed to the right term should one be so misguided as to try the wrong one first. There is an extensive literature on alphabetical subject indexing which it is not possible even to summarize here, but it is still far from an exact science. Morale in what has been called this 'currently dismal scene' is low, with words like 'jungle', 'muddle', and 'trauma' appearing in the titles of articles on the topic. As a consequence, attempting to translate an enquiry into a search statement that matches the indexing patterns of the various sources in the information store is still a chancy business. Katz has concluded that 'There is probably no entirely satisfactory method for the reference librarian to master the subject heading approach to the information file'. However, although the computer still has to make its full impact on the underlying intellectual problem of subject indexing, in the search the chance to use the Boolean OR for combining synonymous search terms into concept clusters, and to use truncation for simplifying the listing of terms with common stems is a distinct contribution.

It will be obvious to any student that no such search statement can be prepared in a vacuum: constantly in mind must be the various and varying sources that will be searched. Nor can a single global search statement be prepared: the general analysis of the subject will of course hold good in searching any source, but the finer points of synonymy and cross-referencing and component order in composite headings and searching for combinations of concepts will need constant readjustment as the search moves from one source in the information store to another. The decisions as to the choice of sources and the selection of the search route are not merely complementary to the formulation of the search statement, they are inextricably linked to it as components of the total search strategy.

## Search strategy: choice of sources

A routine, step-by-step, exhaustive search through the whole of the information store would of course locate the answer, if it is there. Serendipitous browsing too, of pastures that seem promising, might suffice, and indeed has sometimes to be resorted to in the absence of any other strategy. But what seems to happen in practice is that the librarian forms a series of hypotheses as to the most likely sources where the required information may be found. These in turn are tested during the actual search procedure and their validity proved or disproved. The choice that is open to the librarian lies among the four basic sources, common to all libraries, that make up the information store: the library catalogues, bibliographical sources, reference materials, and the literature in the field. In most libraries the great bulk of such sources will be in printed form, mainly books. Increasingly, they are available in computerized format, sometimes as an alternative to the printed version, but also uniquely. Audiovisual formats too are widely found, but outside the worlds of education and the media normally comprise only a small proportion of the total information resources. There are of course special sources that vary from library to library: confidential research reports in industrial and governmental libraries, for instance, or unpublished dissertations in university libraries. In a category of its own is a fifth information resource, also common to all libraries: the library staff.

By far the largest of these sources is the literature in the field. It is also the most important source, central to the function of the library in society. It comprises primary literature like original monographs, learned journals, conference proceedings, research reports, official publications, theses, manuscripts and archives; as well as secondary literature in the shape of the more familiar books and periodicals. They are all basically designed to be read, or studied, rather than consulted. Within each subject field they form the record of what is known and what has been done; indeed, in library terms, they *are* the subject. The collection, organization, preservation, and exploitation of all these subject literatures is the *raison d'être* of the library.

It is to the literature on the subject that the average lay enquirer with an information problem would probably turn first – to 'see if there is a book on it'. For such searchers the great advantage of the library is not merely that it acquires books for their use, but that it arranges the individual items in classified order, so that all the titles on the same topic are shelved together. So much taken for granted is this major contribution by librarians to the organization of knowledge that most library users would be completely at a loss if faced with any alternative. Library classification, indeed, is an intellectual instrument of great power for the prosecution of any search in a library: its twin features of collocation and order alone must have been instrumental in satisfying the information needs of millions of enquirers. Richard A. Gray has reminded us that 'Library classification schemes are cognitive maps by which librarians and library patrons plot their present positions and plan their horizontal and vertical movements within a database – the database in this instance being a library's total collections'.

But, as is well known to librarians, classification has its limitations, quite apart from the deficiencies of the actual schemes. Despite what lay users think, it does not gather together all the material on a topic. As Grace O. Kelley showed over 50 years ago – though her conclusions have been much misunderstood – a logical classification conceals as much as it reveals: information on specific animals, say beavers, to take her example, is also to be found in some of the general books on animals, and in periodical articles and encyclopaedias and so on, which are not placed with the books specifically devoted to beavers. Her findings were that only 15.8% of the material on beavers that could be traced through the catalogue was under the specific class number on the shelves.

No one has explained this dilemma more strikingly than Foskett: 'Classification does, after all, attempt to arrange the dynamic, multi-dimensional continuum of knowledge into a linear sequence: it is a compromise between the ideal and the possible – the ideal being to have a copy of every document alongside copies of every other document to which it is relevant, which would easily cover the entire surface of the earth with libraries; and the possible being to reduce knowledge to a linear sequence and to call on other techniques to fill up the resulting gaps'.

The two most valuable of these techniques are those embodied in the library catalogues and in the various kinds of bibliographies. As has been mentioned, these, together with the reference works, comprise the remaining three basic sources making up the information store. All three – but particularly the bibliographies and reference books – fall very much into the reference librarian's domain, the major part of whose professional education is occupied in their study. They comprise the subject matter of the basic discipline – systematic bibliography; they are the sources turned to first; and it is their use and exploitation, particularly as keys to the literature in the field, that provides the foundation of the librarian's professional practice.

Two of them, the library catalogues and the various types of bibliographies, are often compared and contrasted. Both are obviously secondary sources, as is the third part of the trinity, the reference tools, inasmuch as the information they contain is compiled from the primary sources; but unlike reference works, catalogues and bibliographies do not contain substantive information – 'subject' knowledge – at all. They comprise only citations, which indicate content but do not supply it. Even if a catalogue contains annotations or a bibliography carries abstracts, they are but summaries of and surrogates for the true content of the item cited. For the reference librarian contemplating a search, therefore, they are unlikely to furnish a substantive answer, except in the case of an enquiry of the author/title or otherwise strictly bibliographical kind, e.g. the date or publisher of a book.

Received wisdom enshrined over a century ago in the words of Justin Winsor, President of the American Library Association and the most influential librarian of his day, is that 'There is no factor in the efficiency of the library equal to the catalog'. In 1934 Isadore G. Mudge believed it was 'The most important single reference tool in the library'. These sentiments found their echo in 1990 from Elaine K. Rast, a university library head of cataloguing: 'The public catalog, whether a card or an online catalog, is the directory to the library much like an index is to a book. Its importance cannot be underestimated.' Yet this traditional stance conceals an ancient feud between cataloguers and reference librarians over the true function of what F. W. Lancaster too has called 'the single most important key to a library's collection': is its objective to provide an informative bibliographical tool, supplying a subject analysis of the contents of the library, or should it aim to be only a finding list? What has been called this 'relentless warfare' has, if anything, intensified over the last couple of decades, with the two camps moving further apart rather than closer together.

There are two separate problems here. The first is that even as finding lists, most catalogues are incomplete inasmuch as they list only works that are published separately, without attempting to distinguish, for example, individual contributions in collected conference proceedings, or chapters by individual authors in books. And of course it is exceedingly rare to find a library catalogue that analyses the contents of periodicals in its collection. The second problem is the plain inadequacy of the subject indexing, both in quantity and in specificity, whether it takes the form of subject headings in a dictionary catalogue or a subject index to the classification scheme in a classified catalogue. This is a far more difficult problem to resolve. Kelley's classic study of information on beavers demonstrated the overall effect of these deficiencies, showing that the subject catalogue indicated no more than 37.3% of the material on the topic that was available in the library.

According to Richard D. Altick, an eminent literary scholar, 'a library card catalogue is not a tool of scholarly bibliography . . . it should never be resorted to for the guidance that thorough research requires'. D. W. Krummel, a music bibliographer as well as professor of library and information science, believed that 'Subject access to the world's literature is one of the major failings of modern library cataloguing'. Samuel Rothstein pointed out in 1964 that 'reference librarians . . . probably more often than not do not even have to consult [the catalogue] in their searches'. Diane M. Brown's 1985 survey of 648 telephone reference questions in the Chattanooga-Hamilton (Tennessee) Public Library showed that in only 15% of cases was the card catalogue searched.

Online public access catalogues deploying the power of the computer may well have the potential to modify this pattern. Keyword searching for subjects, for all its crudity, is certainly an enhancement, and the ability to undertake known-item searches using only fragments of a record or author/title acronym keys can reduce failure in cases where the searcher starts with inaccurate or defective bibliographic information. Experimental studies have shown that enhancing standard catalogue records by adding subject terms taken from tables of contents can produce a dramatic increase in document retrieval. And for those libraries without a classified catalogue, notably in the United States, the opportunity to search by class number adds a new weapon to their arsenal.

Unfortunately, for a number of years after the introduction of OPACs, they were seen as not much more than a mechanized version of the card catalogue, 'a card catalogue on wheels' as someone put it. In 1987 James R. Dwyer was still able to claim that 'many products represented as online catalogs are merely jerry-built circulation systems that don't even begin to function as the card catalogs they are meant to replace', and the conclusion of Charles R. Hildreth in 1989 was that although 'The best of today's online catalogs have transcended the limitations of the earlier forms of the library catalog (i.e., book, card, and microform). . . . The potential of the online catalog to provide improved access to library materials and the information they contain is still largely untapped.'

Many of these OPACs are available for wider consultation, over telecommunication links such as the Joint Academic Network (JANET) linking universities and other academic sites (including the British Library) in the United Kingdom. As it forthrightly proclaimed, 'JANET opens the doors of the databases and online services of the UK academic community at no cost, in the same way that the community's libraries open *their* doors, at no cost to the community at large'. Here too one should note the great bibliographical utilities such as the Online Computer Library Center (OCLC), originally designed primarily as cataloguing support tools but now increasingly used in reference work.

It is useful to recall what Jesse H. Shera told his audience at a conference in 1966: 'the reference librarian, I think, historically came into being because there was this gap between the key to library resources [i.e., the catalogue] and the resources themselves. In other words the key was only an imperfect key. It only unlocked certain doors. And there were a lot of other doors around that the key wouldn't fit. So in a sense the reference librarian is the keeper of the keys and has all these other resources to investigate.'

Pre-eminent among these other resources are the bibliographies, especially the lists, indexes, and abstracts of periodicals. It is hardly necessary to emphasize here the absolute indispensability of bibliographies and indexes for reference work. It will suffice just to remind the student of the way they complement the library catalogues and extend the service provided. Firstly, they index several major categories of material normally excluded from library catalogues, such as periodical articles, official publications, individual poems in anthologies, patent specifications, and many others. As an immediate indication of the importance of the first two categories, for example, it might be mentioned that many academic and special libraries spend more than half their acquisitions budget on periodicals; and Her Majesty's Stationery Office and the United States Government Printing Office are the largest publishers in their respective countries.

The second way that bibliographies and indexes extend the service provided is that they do not confine themselves to the collections of a particular library, and thus provide at least bibliographical access to the whole world of information.

The fourth basic source making up the information store are the reference tools, compilations specifically designed to provide items of information in the most convenient form. The main conventional categories are encyclopaedias, dictionaries, directories, yearbooks,

122

biographical sources, and geographical sources. They are widely regarded as very much the librarian's province, although as was made clear in Chapter 1 the mastery of reference sources is only part of the reference librarian's repertoire.

As already noted, many important bibliographies and reference tools are now available in the form of computerized databases: some correspond to already existing printed versions, but many do not, thus providing a unique source of information. Currently there are over 5,000 publicly available for searching online, and perhaps 1,500 in 'portable' format (but with many titles overlapping), mainly CD-ROM but also diskette and magnetic tape. These make up a substantial resource and are now routinely considered in many searches, as appropriate. It is nevertheless important to preserve a sense of balance here: 5,000 is a large number, but it does not begin to compare to the numbers of printed reference tools – there are, for instance, over 7,000 dictionaries of the English language alone. Computer searching will be discussed later in this chapter.

A word needs to be said here about teletext and videotext, available in many libraries, providing access to distant computerized databases by means of a domestic television set and a simple keypad (though dedicated terminals are available and microcomputers can also be used, with appropriate software). Developed originally in the United Kingdom, they have now spread to many countries under various names, often proprietary, but have tended to remain national rather than international systems. Teletext is a broadcast system, providing perhaps up to 3,000 pages of regularly updated information accessible by keying in page numbers found by way of a menu and/or an index. Best regarded as an electronic newspaper, it comprises news headlines and brief summaries, weather forecasts, travel news, details of radio and television programmes, sports news, financial information such as exchange and commodity prices, cookery recipes, etc. There is no charge for use. Videotext is an interactive system, using telephone lines and available to subscribers only. The amount of information available is much more extensive, with over 400,000 pages currently available in the UK. Access is basically by means of menus guiding the searcher through a series of hierarchically structured pages, but simple keyword searching is also possible, though this requires an alphabetic keyboard. It could be seen as an electronic quick-reference collection, but as a mass medium it has failed to appeal. With almost four million of the television sets in the UK able to receive the service, less than 100,000 are current subscribers. Consequently, specific markets have been targeted, such as agriculture, business, education, etc., though its full potential has still to be realized. Interesting comparisons have been made with other technological innovations such as the telephone and the typewriter, which were quickly taken up by business and industry but penetrated the domestic market much more slowly.

An important information source found in all libraries, but given surprisingly scant attention in the literature until recently, is the library staff themselves. As Ann T. Hinckley reminded us, 'a reference librarian's best source may be another librarian'. Whether long-serving or recently arrived, the members together must obviously have experience greater and interests wider than any single individual, and this unique source of knowledge is a major asset in any library. There is some reason to believe that it is not drawn on as much as it might be – often for personal reasons – but each member should learn to regard it as one of the alternative sources of information to be consulted as a matter of course in any appropriate search. Each reference librarian should accept the role, in the words of William Warner Bishop as long ago as 1915, of 'a guide not only to the books, but to the library's resources in personnel'.

Some libraries take this more seriously than others, and have quite firm conventions about consulting colleagues; many have an unwritten rule that a negative answer should only be given after all available staff members have been asked. Jan Kemp and Dennis Dillon made an important point when they noted that 'when librarians do not ask for assistance they abrogate the responsibility to maintain an ethos of collaboration among staff members'.

In many libraries an attempt has been made to embody the collective memory of the staff in permanent form in the shape of a staff information index. Called by an extraordinary variety of names – query file, information file, curio file, catch file, rough-reference file, hard question file, useful reference file, answered queries file – it is normally quite an informal affair, on cards, arranged alphabetically by subject. The items are contributed by the staff themselves, as and when appropriate. Eleanor B. Woodruff gave advice on what to include as long ago as 1897: 'All material . . . which has been found with difficulty and after long search should be recorded in some permanent form. Experience has shown that certain questions come around with the regularity of the seasons, and the references to them once found and noted are available for all time. . . . In this index references are in place to all sorts of odds and ends of information that you pick up in your reading, or attract your attention in going through the magazines, clippings from newspapers, and items that no index, however complete, will bring out, which you will surely need and would otherwise be at a loss to know where to find.' Sometimes included, and surprisingly useful, are queries that were *not* answered, despite a thorough search. Typically, such files include much local information: obituaries from the local paper, an index of the library's own correspondence, a list of local experts, and so on.

There may of course be more than one file: actual examples include indexes to ships built locally, freelance translators, prominent demolished buildings, reproductions of famous paintings, television theme tunes, plays with trial or court-room scenes. They could be regarded as reference works in embryo; indeed many are deliberately designed to supplement existing reference tools, and there are quite a number of useful published reference books that started life as an informal card file in a library. Two examples, from opposite sides of the Atlantic, are *'Isms: a dictionary of words ending in -ism, -ology, and -phobia* from Sheffield City Libraries, and *Respectfully quoted: a dictionary of quotations requested from the Congressional Reference Service*, published by the Library of Congress. Some files are very large, filling 200 drawers in Chicago Public Library, for example. A number of them have been computerized: in 1989 it was reported that four such ready-reference files had been merged at the University of California at Los Angeles. Any librarian who has had the opportunity of working with such files and indexes (and they are normally for staff use only) will vouch for their importance as an alternative information source in their own right. Mabel Conat's 1947 survey in Detroit Public Library found that almost 16% of the 18,701 sources checked to answer 12,292 questions were 'departmental information files'. In 1982 Bronwyn W. Parhad reported that Chicago Public Library was answering 30% of the 1,000 quick-reference phone queries each day from 'Special files'.

It is now a platitude to assert that no library can ever be self-sufficient. The corollary to this is that outside sources must be regularly drawn upon in the course of meeting enquirers' needs. Referral, or the passing of the enquirer (or the enquiry in written form) on to another library or other source of information, will be discussed in Chapter 6. In the context of the search itself, the use of outside resources means their direct consultation by the librarian as one of the alternative information sources.

## Search strategy: selection of route

The decision as to the order in which the series of search hypotheses is tested is itself a component of the total search strategy. In its complete form this decision comprises three stages: firstly, a general category of source is selected; secondly, a specific title within that category is picked out; finally, a choice is made about the precise mode of access that will be used to locate the required information within the specific title chosen. Experienced reference librarians often appear to combine the first two stages in one mental operation. For the librarian with less experience or limited prior knowledge there are what Jahoda and Braunagel called 'lead-in tools' that have been specifically developed to serve as a bridge between the general category and the specific title. The best known of these, of course, are the reference librarians' twin 'bibles', Walford and Sheehy, which even the most omniscient reference librarian will regularly consult.

Once again it must be stressed that there is no formula, no routine, no operation that can be prescribed. As Jahoda and Braunagel conceded, 'There is undoubtedly an optimum search sequence, but the present level of knowledge in reference has not yet provided for any generalizations about the best sequence for searching potentially useful reference tools'. Basic search principles are occasionally encountered in the literature: 'move from the general to the specific', 'go from the known to the unknown'. These are so general as to be meaningless; in any case they are disregarded daily by every busy reference librarian.

More useful are attempts by a number of writers to isolate certain features of the question that may suggest a particular approach to the search. James I. Wyer called these 'handles that may be laid hold of' in proceeding towards the solution of a problem. These are in fact aspects of the question secondary to the actual subject, which is of course the first 'handle'. The other five he identified are biographic, bibliographic, time, language or nationality, and form. He suggested that an indirect approach from one of these five aspects may well locate the answer more quickly. Stych has identified a series of 'general factors which impose decisions on the searcher concerning the path to be followed and concerning the order in which steps are to be taken'. They comprise perhaps a dozen or so features of the question such as subject field, time, space, language, level, amount, and certain other special factors such as the skill and experience of the librarian – all of which clearly contribute to the decisions on the search strategy to be followed. Several of these are matters that crop up in the interview: his suggestion was that they be systematically checked off as a kind of 'mental kerb-drill' before stepping out on the search route proper.

The most carefully elaborated approach to question analysis as an aid to the search is the work of Jahoda and his colleagues, described in Chapter 2. He has explained that 'Like queries, which can be characterized by givens and wanteds, each group of reference tools can be categorized by combinations of givens and wanteds'. Having dissected the query into its given and its wanted according to Jahoda's scheme, the librarian then attempts to find a reference tool with matching givens and wanteds. To illustrate, if asked 'How many people live on the island of Herm [one of the Channel Islands]?', the librarian would note that the given is a specifically named place, and the wanted is numeric information (statistics). One category of reference tool characterized by such givens and wanteds is a gazetteer; and the answer can indeed be found in a gazetteer. Similarly, a request for the 'correct name for the whippoorwill' has a term or subject as its given and textual information (definition) as its wanted. The reference tool with corresponding givens and wanteds is a dictionary, where the answer can easily be located.

The student should remember what Katz has said: 'the search process can be as subjective and intuitive as the reference interview'. Wyer himself believed that the choice in any particular case as to which is the most promising of his 'handles' is a matter of 'reference instinct'. And although Stych maintained with regard to the factors he isolated that 'reference librarians are basing decisions on them constantly', he admits that they do so 'largely unconsciously'. This remains true for computer searching also, which Barbara Newlin has found to be 'highly creative. Your best solutions come with hunches and flashes of insight.'

As was described at the beginning of this chapter, the natural starting-point for many subject enquiries is those materials on the topic in the classified sequence on the shelves. In some instances, however, the enquirer may require an exhaustive search – that is to say all the material available, not just 'something on' the topic; in others, the librarian may be less sure which is the most appropriate part of the classified sequence, or experience may warn that little would be found there anyway. Indispensable though classification is, its limitations as outlined earlier may mean that in such cases the librarian is less likely to go to the classified sequence direct. It is to one of the other three basic sources – the library catalogues, bibliographies, or reference works – that eyes would be turned first.

As has been said, library catalogues and the various forms of bibliographies do not by their nature provide substantive answers, but what they do serve as, *par excellence*, is a point of departure when no other source seems more promising. As E. J. Coates put it, 'The subject catalogue enters into the work of the reference librarian at the point at which his personal knowledge or recollection of the material in the library fails. ... A busy reference department would be crippled if every subject enquiry had to be routed through the catalogue, if there was no one available with the necessary knowledge of bibliographical short cuts and the accumulated acquaintance with sources derived from constant handling of enquiries.' Foskett's advice was that 'Only where the answer is provided by an analytical entry is the "catalogue first" method quicker, and the proportion of this type to the whole is definitely not high enough to justify a longer routine for *all* requests'.

## Computer searching

An increasingly common choice facing many reference librarians is whether the question is appropriate for a computer search, usually online but also CD-ROM. The choice of a computer search is of course a strategic decision, but it is only one of many such interlocking decisions, as was explained earlier in this chapter. It is sometimes necessary for the librarian to make a deliberate effort to see it in this light, because there are many instances where a manual search would be more effective and more efficient. This is often true even in cases where the enquirer has actually asked for a computer search: as was mentioned in Chapter 4 one of the duties of the librarian in a particular case may be to explain what the computer can *not* do. As Jane I. Thesing tellingly explained: 'Just as a surgeon should not hesitate to recommend alternative treatments which might be more beneficial to a prospective patient, so must an online searcher evaluate other options available to the user before carrying out an online search. An online search is not the best answer for everyone.'

This is the point at which the librarian should remember Abraham Kaplan's Law of the Instrument, as stated in its most homely form: 'Give a small boy a hammer and it will turn out that everything that he encounters needs pounding'. A computer should never be used in a search simply because it is there. The advice of Stuart J. Kolner, an experienced MEDLARS searcher, is worth quoting: 'If the requester wants nothing more comprehensive or exhaustive than what is provided in a printed tool, there is no reason to draw it from an on-line source.

Using the computer as a copying machine wastes searcher time and system time, and prevents other searchers' access to the terminal.'

A computer search is the preferred option if what is required is an exhaustive examination of the literature, especially over a period of years. Similarly, it is to be preferred where a number of indexes are to be searched, and the search system permits them to be searched together. A computer search might also be chosen where the indexes, etc., in their printed form are difficult to search on account of their size or complexity. It is particularly suited to a question requiring the coordination of two or more topics, especially if qualified by requirements such as document type, date, language, etc. The computer is also helpful in coordinating search terms for topics that can be expressed in a variety of ways, such as variant spellings, abbreviations, synonyms, etc. Similarly, if the question involves new terminology, or jargon (particularly journalese), or slang, unlikely to be indexed in the printed version, and a free-text search is desired, then obviously a computer search would be fitting. And if the matter is urgent, and a computer search would save time, this consideration might override all others.

In some instances, of course, there is no alternative to a computer search: for material too recent for the printed indexes; where the particular point of access that is required is provided only in the computerized version; where customized output is a requirement; for a full-text search, in databases where this is possible; in databases with no printed equivalent. The reasons might be entirely local or domestic: if the printed version is not available for consultation, either because the library does not hold it, or key volumes are on loan, missing, or binding.

Those instances where a computer search is contra-indicated are not so easy to recognize because the signs are less distinct, though none the less valid. Broad, vague topics are usually unsuitable, especially if the vocabulary of the field is imprecise, as often in the humanities and the social sciences. Any question that is not clearly formulated should be avoided, though a search of the printed indexes can often help to clarify such a topic, thus making a computer search more feasible. A search where browsing or serendipity might be important is better undertaken manually. In certain cases even very precise questions may also be inappropriate: as Donna R. Dolan explained, 'Any question in which the qualitative, the temporal or the quantitative is a significant aspect presents a problem. At least part of the difficulty is that many of the words expressing these concepts – above, below, more, less, etc. – are stopwords. In other words, the data base vendors regard them as too insignificant to be loaded as searchable terms, although they can make cataclysmic differences in a search.' In a similar way, the limited nature of the Boolean logic used in a computer search formulation can make it impracticable to deal with questions involving comparisons or indeed any relationships other than the simple AND, OR, NOT.

### Quick-reference computer searching

Conventional wisdom used to be that a computer search was inappropriate for simple author/title or fact-finding enquiries, or simple material-finding enquiries of the 'something on' type, where no more than two or three citations are required. This view has altered sharply over the last dozen or so years with the spread of quick-reference searching of computer databases, as mentioned in Chapter 4. This was defined by Virgil P. Diodato in 1989 as 'the use of online search services to answer questions at a reference or information desk while the patron waits'.

In 1984 Eileen Hitchingham and her colleagues complained that 'manual searching of some reference questions, when online searching is possible, is like using a quill pen to communicate when a word processor is in the next room'. A number of libraries had already seen the light, and others were swift to follow, so much so that in many libraries such quick-reference searches now outnumber the others, and the new service has played a major part in bringing computer searching into the mainstream of reference. General agreement was soon reached on a number of basic ground rules. Searches should be brief, lasting no more than five or 10 minutes. The response should be limited to five or at the most 10 citations in a search of a bibliographical database or an equivalent amount of data from a source database. The decision to undertake a computer search must always be at the discretion of the librarian. The search should be free of charge to the enquirer.

Not surprisingly, at first there was considerable uncertainty among reference librarians over precisely which quick-reference questions were suited for online searching, especially as the cost would be borne entirely by the library. But eventually, with experience, there has emerged a series of tactical indicators suggesting to the searcher when, or when not, an online search would be preferable to a manual search. As with the other kinds of questions, where a manual search can be done at least as quickly and effectively as a computer search it obviously makes sense to choose it, if only to maximize a library's fixed investment in its collections. The clearest pointer to a computer search is to be seen in those instances where retrieval from the printed source would obviously be more difficult, perhaps because of insufficient access points, or because indexes appear late, or do not cumulate. A similar sign would be a requirement for highly current or time-sensitive information. Another positive indication is an enquiry giving the opportunity to exploit special facilities offered by the search system or particular features of individual databases allowing aspects to be searched that are not normally indexed in the printed versions. And a computer search should always at least be considered after the failure of a manual search.

Bibliographical verification and identification enquiries have been found particularly apt for computer quick-reference searches, and as with OPACs, as noted above, the facility to search using fragments of a record or author/title acronym keys is a powerful tool. In the case of fact-finding enquiries, there are two categories where a computer search may be called for. The first comprises those seeking facts which the arrangement or indexing of the corresponding printed source is unable to reveal: a number of source databases are full-text files, and often contain facts that cannot be extracted through the conventional index. The second category consists of those enquiries for directory-type or other information where it is essential to be absolutely up to date. News databases in particular are well suited to providing answers to fact-finding reference queries seeking current information, and most of the use made of full-text news databases consists of quick-reference searches.

Material-finding enquiries comprising a single narrow concept that can be described using a specific term or phrase, particularly if spanning a number of years, have also been found quite suitable for quick-reference searches, as have the more familiar searches requiring the coordination of two or more concepts, provided the enquirer wants no more than a handful of pertinent citations.

Surveys have shown that the time spent at the terminal averages between four and six minutes. Typical results have been characterized by Maurita Peterson Holland thus: 'Usually searches provide two or three references on two or three search terms in one or two files'. One important early conclusion reported by Greg Byerly in 1984 was that 'online searching can answer certain reference questions that would literally be impossible to answer using conventional print reference tools'.

But it does still appear necessary to offer encouragement to those

131

librarians hesitating over the computer. In 1988 in a paper on the challenges of automation, Elizabeth Bramm Dunn felt obliged to say that 'it is important that we be not timid about incorporating automated sources into routine reference work. ... We should not look on the use of automated sources as "cheating".'

## CD-ROM searching

As soon as they appeared on the market it was stated by Tony Feldman – not a librarian – that 'Quite clearly CD-ROMs have a natural application in libraries and few industry figures doubt that this is the first major area of use that will become commonplace'. By 1990, after surveys of libraries in the United States and 18 western European countries, Ching-Chih Chen and David I. Raitt were able to confirm this prediction: 'Since the introduction of the first library-related CD-ROM products in late 1984, CD-ROM has exploded onto the general library marketplace'.

It is perhaps worth explaining at this point that from where the user sits – whether an end-user or an intermediary – a CD-ROM search and an online search seem broadly similar. The databases are often the same, at least superficially, the search system is command-driven or menu-driven or a mixture of both, subject searching is by controlled vocabulary or keywords or both, employing Boolean logic if needed, and screen output can be printed out or saved to disk as desired. Indeed, with some systems, such as Wilsondisc/Wilsonline it is possible in the course of a search to move almost imperceptibly from the CD-ROM database to the online database with a single keystroke. There are of course differences, one of the most noticeable being a much greater variety of search software with CD-ROMs, often specifically devised for a particular database, and sometimes offering different levels of sophistication for novice or skilled searchers. It is this that makes CD-ROM so much more user-friendly, with the better databases providing context-specific help screens, imaginative displays (often in colour), windows, pull-down menus, etc. Updates of continuing databases are usually only quarterly, so they are invariably less current than the online equivalent. Response time is usually slower, but then of course there are no connect charges.

## Computer search formulation

It is at the stage of the formulation of the actual search statement itself that the computer search becomes markedly different from a manual search. As described above, the subject of the question will already have been analysed into its various concepts and all the possible terms for expressing these concepts will have been identified. For a computer search this has to be done with elaborate and exhaustive care – noting alternative spellings and singular and plural forms, for instance – because the actual matching of the terms will be done by an inflexible machine rather than a human searcher able to interact and adjust almost instinctively to what the search reveals at any point. Search aids available in the system, such as indexes, and thesauri and classification codes where they exist for individual databases, can be displayed on the screen to assist the process. The essential difference between a search of printed sources and a database search stems from the need to follow strict rules of presentation and logic as to form and sequence when putting the search statement to the system; and unless menu searching is available, the instructions for the processing of the statement have to be given in the command language of the system. As a rule, for searches other than the simplest, the search statement is written down in advance.

Search system features such as truncation, word proximity operators, the facility for restricting the search to particular fields, are also exploited as necessary at this point. A decision also needs to be taken whether to use a controlled vocabulary or natural language search (or a combination of the two).

It is also necessary at this juncture to incorporate into the search formulation any of the particular restraints or limitations ascertained at the interview, such as date or language or country of publication or document type and so on. Also taken account of must be the enquirer's wishes with regard to the number of citations required and their format, and whether high recall or high precision is preferred.

It is common (though by no means essential) to map out the whole search strategy in advance, including alternatives in the case of inadequate results. The searcher also tries to anticipate any potential problems, and to be ready with tactics to deal with too many or too few citations, which is a frequent result even with a search formulation that is impeccable in subject terms. Other searchers prefer to leave more options open, taking full advantage of the interactive nature of the search system. It is perhaps worth stressing in this context that CD-ROM searchers, freed from the tyranny of connect charges, should not lapse into the attitude that there is less need to prepare a careful and economical search formulation because one can take one's time repairing any deficiencies at the terminal at no extra cost. The principal practical objection to this is that it is inefficient, inasmuch as it ignores the cost of the reference librarian's time. The second objection is that it is also likely to be ineffective: with a computer search it is simply not possible to substitute action for thought, and muddle one's way through. But to many librarians the cardinal objection would be that it is unprofessional and, what is more, would plainly be seen as such, as bluff and blunder at the keyboard is immediately visible on the screen.

There are of course various modes of searching, sometimes picturesquely described, such as the successive facet approach, the building block (or Chinese menu) approach, the citation pearl-growing approach, and various others. Each has certain advantages for particular kinds of question, although the choice is often a matter of personal preference or even individual searching style. For it has been discovered here too that searching is by no means an exact science. Indeed, Christine L. Borgman's view was that 'In many ways, searching is an art rather than a science, and only the basic skills can be taught'. Stephen P. Harter and Anne Rogers Peters also believed that 'At this point in its short history, online information retrieval possesses many of the characteristics of an art . . . there are few specific rules of action or well-defined procedures that are known to apply in all retrieval situations'. According to Jeremy W. Sayles, 'we incorrectly assume a computer search is a "scientific" process because it is executed via a machine. We equate technology, mechanical processes, and mathematical calculations with precision and correctness. But this is not always so, since computer searching, like all other aspects of reference service, is an art – not a science.' Even 'the formulation of good Boolean queries', according to Gerald Salton, 'is an art rather than a science'.

## Computer limitations

It is appropriate at this point to consider some of the more obvious limitations of the computer as it is currently utilized in reference work. As Borgman so well expressed it, 'Information retrieval systems are little more than a set of elaborate matching routines performed very quickly on a high speed computer; the system cannot "think" in the same manner that humans can'. Furthermore, this matching is confined to alphanumeric characters it can recognize: it cannot search for concepts, only words. Neither can it 'interpret the language structure or the logical relationships between concepts, or . . . know the alternative forms of words or synonyms for the phrases given – all of which is done by the human in interpreting such questions'.

As mentioned above, there are obvious limitations as to the ways in which the computer can combine concepts using Boolean logic. Bates is worth quoting again here: 'Online systems . . . are not as sophisticated as clients may assume. Boolean logic is simpler than natural-language syntax – and also rides roughshod over many grammatical distinctions that make a difference in the relevance of a document to a request. Consequently, false drops are endemic in the online industry.' The very basis of the post-coordinate search itself is statistical probability – that the more concepts that are combined, the greater the likelihood that the citations produced are relevant.

The common method of controlling output size by dropping a concept to increase the number of citations, or adding a concept to reduce them, is extraordinarily crude, and quite different to the method used in manual searching in such circumstances. Sayles has explained this further: in selecting citations from printed indexes 'There is a relationship between what is selected and what is rejected; in fact, what is selected is often defined by what is rejected. These relationships, required for an understanding of an inquiry's scope and the setting of limits, cannot be examined on the terminal since citations "discarded" from an output cannot be known.'

For it is the case that much of the time one is searching blind: as Newlin put it, 'a database is completely opaque – you can never see the part that your search strategy leaves untouched'. It was the view of C. P. R. Dubois that 'there must be few systems in other areas where poor performance is so effectively concealed as in online retrieval from bibliographic databases'. Incidentally, it is this invisibility until retrieved on screen that makes evaluation of databases so much more difficult than with print sources.

Some of the limitations arise from the way a particular system has decided to create its machine-readable file, with some fields searchable but not others, some phrase-indexed but not word-indexed, and so on. On a more humdrum level, the parsimonious way in which continuous text has to be scanned on the screen does not begin to measure up in either speed or effectiveness to the method we develop from childhood for the printed page. And of course simultaneous searchers need a terminal each: queuing is already a serious problem in many libraries.

The warning given by Theodore Roszak, a professor of history and a trenchant critic of computers, seems particularly relevant to reference work: 'as with all computer exercises, the mastery comes through adapting to the computer's way of doing things' and he cited 'the great reductive principle: If the computer cannot rise to the level of the subject, then lower the subject to the level of the computer'. Dennis Dillon reported that at a discussion at the University of Texas at Austin on the future of reference service a systems analyst in the audience 'warned that librarians, like everyone else, often approached problems backwards, by looking at the available tools and then trying to force solutions on them. This not only does not solve the problem, but results in bigger headaches that require even more time and money to solve them.'

Peggy Champlin had already observed this reductive principle operating in online searching: 'It is not an uncommon experience in preparing a search strategy, for the searcher to reframe a question so that it can be expressed in the thesaurus terms for a particular database'. She believed this may actually hinder the research process, which should be open-ended by definition. Similarly, because the computer will display nothing until it is specifically asked for, browsing and serendipity – both well recognized as fruitful paths to information – are ruled out.

But no litany of caveats should be allowed to obscure the fact that computer searching has added a major weapon to the reference librarian's arsenal. Machines in the past have extended the power of human muscle and the reach of our senses; the significance of the computer, deriving from its base in microelectronics, is that it extends the power of human logic and memory. This is why it holds such potential for reference librarians: their traditional strengths have been system, memory, persistence, and the mastery of detail, and the computer can immediately be incorporated into their methods of working.

More mundanely, but perhaps even more evident, is the speed and physical ease of searching, sitting down, without the need to handle heavy volumes, or to transcribe the findings by hand.

## Specific skills for computer searching

The *personal* attributes to be desired in the reference librarian were discussed in Chapter 3, where it was noted that the advent of the computer had required little or no change in the specification. So far as concerns the more purely *intellectual* skills, however, it has often been asserted, by Borgman, to quote but one example, that 'some special skills are required for online searching in addition to those required for reference librarianship'. Among the talents most frequently called for in the literature are: abstract reasoning ability, problem-solving skills, an analytical mind, a logical mind, conceptual skills, high verbal skills, ability to devise search strategies, and so on. It has also been argued, by Dolan among others, that 'A good search analyst possesses a certain mind set, or cognitive style . . . no amount of training can develop this method of thinking. In other words, the skills which characterize an exceptional search analyst are inherent.'

One not unexpected rejoinder to inventories of this kind is that from Carol Tenopir: 'One could argue that a person who possesses all of these traits should be good at anything. Certainly an argument can be made that a good reference librarian possesses most of these characteristics, whether or not he/she uses online tools.' Rosemarie Riechel too would settle for 'the skills of an excellent/experienced reference librarian'. Indeed, it is worth quoting at some length the view of Randolph E. Hock, a DIALOG manager:

> 'A reference background is necessary because the purpose of online systems is not for searching as an end in itself. Online systems are rather a way of making use of a large collection of research tools. Online systems can radically increase the usefulness and accessibility of these tools, but in the end it is the research tools, the abstracting and indexing tools, the directories, the statistical collections, which are being accessed. If the searcher does not know what tools exist, what kinds of information are to be found in those tools, and how the tools differ from one another, then these tools cannot be used to their full advantage. It is for this reason, above all, that the skills possessed by a good librarian or information specialist are essential if an organization expects to achieve maximum use of online systems.'

Where there can be no disagreement is on the importance of the issue: because most searching is done by intermediaries it is essential that they should be skilled. Borgman was plainly right to warn that 'It cannot be said too often that an information retrieval system is only as effective as the person who operates it'.

It should perhaps be added that over and above technical competence there is something more, which soon came to be recognized. At a conference at the University of Aston in 1979 there was a discussion on the type of person who made a good online searcher: 'Apart from a natural aptitude, a logical mind, a willingness to use new approaches and imagination the good searcher possessed "IT" – an indefinable quality. No one could find the words to express this quality but all agreed that the good searcher could be distinguished from the indifferent one because he possessed IT.'

137

**End-user searching**

The earliest computer searches were of course batch-processed, normally after the enquirer had gone home, often overnight, and, as has been described in Chapter 3, the advent of interactive searching online was originally hailed by some as a boon to users who could henceforward conduct their own searches. In 1969 for example, Alan M. Rees wrote that 'To the on-line individual interacting with a computer . . . the interposition of an intermediary in the form of a reference librarian may appear to be superfluous'. In 1980 Brian Neilsen warned: 'Both technological and economic factors make it appear likely that there will be a declining role for librarian intermediaries in the future'. Yet an Aslib survey reported in 1987 that 91% of online searches were still carried out by 'library/information professionals'.

Even end-user systems specifically designed as such and targeted at the home user are widely used by librarians. In 1989 Melvon Ankeny reported 'some indication in the literature that the end-user market at which these services aimed are lagging behind expectations. The end-user products have found a home in many libraries.'

In 1990 Chen and Raitt wrote that 'CD-ROM technology has created an unprecedented opportunity for information producers and librarians alike to distribute electronic information to end-users via microcomputers', though, as already mentioned in Chapter 1, they were obliged to report that in both the United States and Europe CD-ROMs were still being used mostly by library staff rather than end-users. A 1989 survey of 656 British libraries of all kinds found 30% using CD-ROMs or other optical discs, 'but mainly by library staff for library purposes'.

Although in absolute terms there has been an increase in end-user database searching, particularly in academic libraries, the number of searches undertaken by intermediaries shows no sign of diminishing and it is worth exploring the reasons.

The more general intellectual skills that are needed have already been discussed. As for the more specific requirements, this is what Stephen P. Harter and Carol H. Fenichel believed to be necessary: 'Online searching is more than simply learning the commands of a language. Effective searching demands a knowledge of system design, file loading practices and their effect on retrieval, the effects of specificity, exhaustivity, stoplists and other indexing practices on retrieval. Boolean logic, ability to read, interpret, and use abstruse database documentation, ability to . . . select appropriate databases and fields for searching, to design a research strategy likely to produce relevant output, to evaluate intermediate output and modify the search strategy accordingly, and much more. None of these are purely technical skills, like typing, for example. They involve intelligence, judgement, and knowledge of principles.' Equally important, once acquired, they need constant practice to keep them from getting rusty, as all professional searchers have discovered.

Similar considerations apply to quick-reference searching too, and it is interesting to note the view expressed in 1986 by Barbara E. Anderson, the manager of DIALOG customer services: 'Using online sources for ready reference requires the same skills as used currently by the traditional reference librarian of an all print collection – a knowledge of what is available in each of several hundred databases. ... Movements to bring online searching to the end user, whether within a library or at home, are not likely to change the traditional role of the reference librarian with regard to ready reference lookups.'

Several surveys have shown that a skilled intermediary can reduce search time by more than half, and of course with online searching time is money. Based on charges as they were in 1979, DIALOG found that 'a very skilled operator can realize significant cost savings over a less-skilled operator (e.g., reduce the average search costs by half) while still achieving the same (or better) search results'.

But cost is not the important issue, and neither is the question as to whether reasonably interested users can learn to carry out computer searches for themselves. There is no doubt that they can: Harter maintained that 'Any competent searcher can teach a moderately intelligent novice to be a *bad* online searcher in 30 minutes', and such a novice can then produce search results with surprising ease. But herein lies the problem: as Justine Roberts and Lydia Jensen explained, 'the marketing of end user searching is strongly influenced by its economic roots, and the message is that – for a price – information is accessible easily, by anyone, anywhere and at any time'. In an experiment at the University of California at San Francisco, where 43 medical questions previously searched by a reference librarian were searched again by a novice, they found 'large differences in skills'. Their conclusion was that 'The buyer may be unaware that the most relevant material was not retrieved'.

Other surveys bear this out: those enquirers who conduct their own searches – often computer devotees already – do indeed become enthusiastic end-users, particularly of the easy-to-use systems, including CD-ROM databases. It has even been noted on many occasions that users, particularly students, will queue to use a CD-ROM database, even though the equivalent printed index is available a few yards away. But their simple searches are not as effective as they might be, and experience has shown that they have particular difficulty in selecting an appropriate database; in analysing the topic and conceptualizing the key facets; with Boolean logic and search formulation, omitting relevant synonyms, for instance, and using truncation incorrectly; and in recognizing and using controlled vocabularies. They rarely search bibliographical databases, and most of them never get beyond the novice stage. They resist printed aids, much preferring on-screen help: this in itself, according to Harter, 'is probably the primary obstacle standing in the way of effective end-user searching'.

More seriously, they appear unaware of the inadequacy of many of their searches. Richard Blood noted in 1983 that 'The fact that a computer has done the work so amazes most users that they do not think to question the completeness or accuracy of the results'. According to some reference librarians, therefore, the issue of the 'quick-and-dirty' end-user search has an ethical dimension, especially in academic libraries. It has been pointed out, however, by Susan McEnally Jackson among others, that 'This misuse of sources is not a new phenomenon as librarians have long recognized that when users search print materials they may choose marginal or inappropriate sources and use poor search tactics [though] optical disc systems will likely compound the problem . . . because of their speed and convenience'. R. J. Hartley and his colleagues offered wise advice in their 1990 text *Online searching*: 'studies show that most of the end-users are happy with most of their searches most of the time, however they must be reminded that if a more up to date and comprehensive search is required this is probably best done by an intermediary'. Some libraries have taken the step of posting notices to similar effect.

The other problem about end-user searching has already been referred to several times in earlier chapters: many users simply do not wish to search for themselves, however capable they might be if they tried. They see it plainly as a task for a professional, especially if they are professionals themselves: this came through most clearly in the survey of City firms by David Nicholas and his colleagues mentioned in Chapter 3. Ethics enters the scene here also: should users be obliged, or even persuaded or encouraged, to search for themselves if they simply do not want to?

It is not to be doubted that there are distinct shortcomings to a delegated search. This of course is why the presence of the user at the search is regarded as so important. Indeed, as one of the rightly praised advantages of computer interrogation is its interactive nature, permitting instant feedback, many librarians insist on having the enquirer by their side at the terminal. On searching United States legal databases for example, the view of Fred M. Greguras, himself an attorney, was that 'The best search results occur when the attorney is present at the terminal, even if someone else actually operates the terminal'. Research findings show an increase in precision, recall, and user satisfaction, though Doris B. Marshall has noted that 'most frequently the cost is at least tripled because the end user wants to discuss the findings while online'.

One difference from manual searches is that the librarian is often at pains to explain exactly what is happening, sometimes by way of what is almost a running commentary. As Anne B. Peters and Claire B. Drinkwater expressed it, 'The intermediary brings to the search bibliographical skills and the end user brings subject knowledge – together they get the best out of the system'. The Aslib survey mentioned earlier found that the user was present with the librarian in half of all searches.

**Computer search aids**
In many instances the search 'terminal' is in fact a microcomputer emulating a terminal, using communications software. In 1983 Sara D. Knapp wrote: 'Microcomputers . . . promise many improvements in online searching. Among these are the ability to store and edit search output; automatic searching; storage of profiles; storage of search aids; automatic dial-up and sign-on; simplified interfaces for the unskilled; translation from one system's commands to another; and simulation systems for training searchers cheaply.' Most of these are now commonplace: the most interesting in the context of reference work are the search aids – so far mainly experimental – designed to take over some of the functions of the reference librarian as described in this volume.

A system that will directly answer questions is still some way in the future, but what we do have are a number of interesting attempts to automate specific parts of the reference process, such as discovering something about the enquirer's background, translating the query into a search statement for online searching, or selecting appropriate databases or reference books to consult. Experimental or prototype systems have been designed consisting of modules to undertake one or more of these tasks.

The term 'expert systems' has been used, in some cases rather loosely, to cover some of these and similar search aids. What a true expert system seeks to do is to embody within a computer the knowledge and decision-making skills of a human expert in a particular 'domain' – a specific field – so that the system can offer intelligent advice or take an intelligent decision about a problem posed to it. It is intended to produce useful results, as human intelligence does, in cases where algorithmic solutions are not possible.

In oversimplified terms, an expert system comprises three components: an interface module to elicit details of the problem from the user; a knowledge base in the form of a set of heuristics or rules that an expert would normally follow; an 'inference engine' in the shape of a software program that specifies how to apply these rules to the data gathered from the enquirer in order to arrive at a solution. It is also regarded as desirable that it should include an explanation capability, a means of describing to the enquirer the line of reasoning it followed in reaching a particular conclusion.

In essence the task facing expert system designers is to extend the role of computers by teaching them heuristic techniques, and the heart of a system is of course the set of heuristics, sometimes called cognitive elements, or rules of thumb, or even more graphically, 'chunks' of knowledge. The problem is that much of an expert's knowledge is derived from personal experience and extensive practice, and is often private, subconscious, unanalysed, and unrecorded. And the scale of the task can be gauged from one estimate that an expert such as the latest Nobel Laureate in chemistry might possess from 50,000 to 100,000 such 'chunks', quite apart from all the *factual* knowledge stored in his memory.

Expert systems have been designed and used with some success in medical diagnosis, mineral prospecting, and biochemical analysis, for example, but it is fair to say that they have been employed more as decision-support tools than as replacements for the practitioner.

It does perhaps need to be explained that an expert system for reference work, unlike some of these other kinds, does not contain within itself the 'answers', any more than a reference librarian's memory does. The expertise it seeks to embody is that of *finding* answers: its function is to substitute for the librarian, not the library. In other words, the fact base, as opposed to the rule base, is outside the system and the objective is to indicate the location of answers in this external store. It is perhaps for this reason that some systems have been described as 'referral' systems.

Perhaps the best way to comprehend such systems is to regard them as located along a spectrum, across the whole of which a computer substitutes to a greater or a lesser extent for a human intermediary. At one end we find relatively simple systems employing on-screen menus to provide direct answers to common or typical administrative or directional enquiries. Some way along are systems that guide the enquirer with a quick-reference question through a sequence of menus of increasing specificity in order to identify the topic of concern, and then give directions to one or more reference books likely to have the answer. More sophisticated are systems which accept a user's direct query, convert it into a search statement, and then run the search on an appropriate online database. At the far extreme – not yet reached – we may one day see a full expert system of the kind specified by Alina Vickery and her colleagues in 1987. The knowledge base of such a system

> 'must embody the understanding and activity of the search intermediary: it must incorporate the procedures by which he interprets, analyses and elaborates an initial user question to formulate an appropriate problem statement; it must be able to translate a problem statement into a search statement acceptable to the retrieval system; it must further have the searcher's ability to evaluate the search output and to modify the search statement as required. In such an expert system, the actual retrieval process becomes just one module of a complex set of interacting functions. The overall system should carry out tasks that, if performed by an intermediary, we should consider intelligent.'

Such systems as have been devised have so far been restricted to quite small domains: the administrative arrangements specific to a particular library, for example, or electrical engineering databases, or quick-reference books on agriculture in a specific library collection, or United States government documents, or a very narrow subject field such as gardening. Particular attention has been focused on natural language interfaces which take the user's query, exactly as expressed in natural language, and translate it into a fully formulated search statement. Briefly, one way this is done is by looking up each word in the question in a specially compiled computer-held dictionary of the subject field concerned, eliminating those that are on a stoplist, stemming the rest (by stripping them of their inflections, prefixes, and suffixes), and adding synonyms, etc. If further details are needed, about words that are not recognized for example, or missing information as measured against a question frame, the system prompts the user for more. A parser is sometimes used to single out the verbs and identify the roles filled by the other parts of speech. The result is then structured, using Boolean logic, truncation, and so on, as required, to produce a search statement.

Another area of research activity is the attempt to build a model of the user by asking questions, usually in the form of menu choices, about educational level, length of experience, expertise in the field, knowledge of computers, or understanding of languages, and a variety of other relevant matters such as number of citations required, geographical coverage, and so on.

But these tasks are very difficult, and so it is not surprising that performance does not yet match that of a skilled intermediary. There are those who doubt that it ever will, because they believe it is impossible for machines to solve problems the way humans do, and that what John Cotton Dana wrote in 1899 is still the case: 'No mechanical devices can take the place of face to face question and answer'. What certainly does remain true, in the words of James Radlow, a professor of computer science, is that 'Human thinking is still the greatest mystery known to science. . . . The human brain is by far – by so huge a margin that the imagination cannot comprehend it – the most complex and the most complicated entity in the universe as we know it.'

### Conduct of the search
A point that the student of the reference process should bear in mind here is that although the interview and the search are clearly quite different and easily distinguished they often appear in practice to fuse into one. Sometimes a tentative search strategy will begin to take shape in the librarian's mind during the course of the reference interview. There are many occasions where the interview continues even after the search has started, and the two stages of the process can be seen to be taking place at the same time. This is especially true with computer searches. It enables the reference process to continue as a mutual relationship, with the enquirer responding and reacting to the progress of the search in a way that enables the librarian further to refine the understanding of the enquirer's problem, and to modify the search strategy to ensure a more precise match between the library's resources

and the enquirer's needs.

We have seen how desirable it is to have the user present at a computer search, but whether or not the enquirer should be invited to accompany the librarian round the shelves during a manual search is a matter to be decided on it merits. Even if the enquirer plays no part in the search, the practice has psychological value in demonstrating in a tangible way that the exercise is a duet in harmony rather than a solo performance. As often as not, especially with material-finding enquiries, the user's presence at the librarian's elbow permits an instantaneous reaction to each item found. This can be invaluable with complex or troublesome searches, either confirming the librarian's search strategy, or providing further input to allow it to be modified or corrected. Not the least of its advantages is its maximum visibility to other library users, perhaps nursing unasked questions of their own.

For the success of any search it is necessary for the actual procedure to be competently executed: searchers must be thoroughly familiar with the library catalogues, in whatever format; they must be expert in the use of indexes, including citation indexes; they must be able to decipher a bibliographical reference, even if it refers to a law report or a government document or a patent specification. At the computer terminal they must be confident without being rash. And so on and so forth. Bates has developed a series of 'search tactics' to be deployed in the course of a search. These are mental devices, or manoeuvres, resorted to at appropriate junctures to move the search on. They are applicable to most kinds of searches in both manual and online systems. Some examples are: 'To watch for and correct spelling and factual errors in one's search topic'; 'When selecting among several ways to search a given query, to choose the option that cuts out, eliminates, the largest part of the search domain at once'; 'To make the search formulation precise by minimizing (or reducing) the number of parallel terms, retaining the more perfectly descriptive terms'; 'To search for the term logically opposite from that describing the desired information'. She has also devised a range of 'idea tactics' to bring into play when 'the searcher is stumped or needs to think of a new way to attack the problem', with the hope of providing 'a flash of insight or inspiration'. These include 'To ask a colleague for suggestions or information in dealing with a search'; 'To break a habitual search pattern, that is, put it aside temporarily, in order to take a search tack more suited to the particular problem in question'; 'To watch for clues that revise one's notions of the nature of the question or of the answering information'.

The titles that she gives to some of these 'idea generation' and 'mental pattern breaking' idea tactics, such as 'Wander', 'Change', 'Skip', remind us that one quite common mode of searching, as mentioned earlier, even for the reference librarian, is to browse an appropriate part of the collection – the books on the shelves, recent issues of a journal, or a vertical file – in the hope that something might turn up. This is by no means as unfruitful as its haphazard nature might suggest, especially if one is not absolutely sure what is wanted, for serendipity is widely recognized as playing an honoured role in discovery.

It is also important, though often omitted, to extend the usual courtesies of civilized behaviour to enquirers. If a search, manual or computer, appears likely to last more than a few minutes, and should the librarian decide not to encourage the enquirer to join in the hunt, good practice requires that the visitor be given something to be going on with and invited to sit down. R. L. Collison's rule was that 'the reader should never be left without material while the librarian goes elsewhere in search of information'.

One failing to which many library managers are prone is to treat the user's time as a variable that can be manipulated with a degree of freedom not permitted with other variables such as opening hours and personnel. One reads, for instance, that one parameter in assessing the maximum period an enquirer can be kept waiting is the 'aggravation quotient'. It is as well to remember that so far as reference work is concerned, the main reason users put questions to librarians is that they know that they can find the answers more quickly. Nor must the librarian forget Ranganathan's Fourth Law: 'Save the time of the reader'. James Benson and Ruth K. Maloney have drawn an important distinction: '*Any* search which locates the desired information is an *effective* search; the *efficient* search, however, is the effective one that locates desired information with a minimum amount of time and effort'. Speaking of the hard world of industrial libraries, M. W. Hill reminded an international conference that 'Speed of response always impresses any client, whereas the service that takes its time, no matter how good the results, rarely does so even though the information may in fact arrive on time. This may seem to purists or those with no experience of industry to be unfair, but unless one accepts this as a fact of life it is no use expecting industrial clients to use one's services.'

It really is distressing to observe in some libraries the casual and perfunctory way in which enquirers are treated as people. That this is not an inevitable consequence of the system is demonstrated by those staff with an obvious and genuine interest in enquirers as fellow human beings as well as the bringers of questions. As any objective observer can see any day of the week, it is possible to make even the most business-like encounter a pleasant human exchange. But sad to relate, neither of the following incidents is untypical, and each was recorded by a trained observer. In the first case (as reported by Marian Barnes) the librarian was aware of the presence of the observer: 'An elderly lady came to the enquiry desk to return a book on mythology which had been retrieved from the stack for her on a previous visit. She was rather hesitant in her approach and stood well back from the desk while talking to the member of staff who was standing, half turned away from the desk, dealing with some documents on the desk. The user remarked that she had quite enjoyed the book she was returning as she found the subject very interesting, but it had been rather difficult for her and what she really wanted was something similar but simpler. Did the librarian know of anything suitable? The librarian's response, made without moving or even turning towards the user, was to indicate the card catalogue and to comment that if the user looked in the catalogue at the catalogue number she would find on the spine of the book she already had, she would find out what other books the library had on the subject. The user looked vaguely in the direction of the catalogue, placed the book on the enquiry desk and moved away.'

In the second example (reported by Peter Hernon and Charles R. McClure) the encounter was observed during an unobtrusive test: 'One of the proxies approached the card catalog desk and waited five minutes while the librarian [whose task it was to deal with questions about the catalogue] helped another patron. Finally the librarian, standing approximately ten feet away from the proxie, looked up from the book that he was holding and shouted "Do you have a question?" The proxie paused for a moment and the librarian becoming impatient said "Well, what is it?" The proxie asked the question [about a government document] and the librarian responded that the card catalog was a comprehensive list of that library's holdings. He then looked back at his book and terminated the reference interview.'

An excuse often given for the deterioration in human-fellow feeling is the increased use of machines instead of people: 'As the atmosphere of automation creeps into the institution it is accompanied by a certain frame of mind. Creation and use of technical innovations become the end of human activity . . . human beings are no longer responsible to other beings for the events which are produced by technical activities.

One is responsible only for seeing that the technical act is done correctly.' Though quoted by a computer reference librarian, this passage did not describe libraries and librarians but hospitals and the nursing profession. It may well be a foretaste of what is to come, but present evidence, as has been noted, suggests the precise opposite: paradoxically, the computer has brought the reference librarian and the enquirer into a much closer human relationship.

## The personal touch
Perhaps surprisingly to some, a librarian's intrinsic personal qualities count for much at the search stage of the reference process also. Of course the more extensive one's acquaintance with the sources of information and the more developed one's skill in their use, the better placed is one to be of service, but without interest in the subject, enthusiasm for the hunt, and a flexible attitude towards materials and methods, mere technical expertise may never have a real chance to deploy itself.

G. K. Chesterton once said 'There is no such thing on earth as an uninteresting subject: the only thing that can exist is an uninterested person'. The best reference librarians never find it necessary to make an effort to kindle their interest in a subject: it is sufficient for them that the topic has been asked about by an enquirer. This impetus stems directly from their commitment to service. David C. Mearns' opinion of this virtue was that 'It is the single circumstance that raises librarianship and specifically reference librarianship from a technique to a mission'.

Over 50 years ago one of the wisest writers on the subject, Margaret Hutchins, gave her opinion as to 'the two leading motives of the true reference librarian'. As might be expected, 'the desire to help other people' was one; but the other was 'the desire to achieve success in the hunt, whatever the cost of patience and perseverance'. In his famous 1948 address already cited in Chapter 3 Mearns echoed this latter motive; and the combination of what he called enthusiasm and persistence furnishes a powerful recipe for success in the search.

Enthusiasm in a searcher, of course, all are agreed on: 'he must delight in the chase for its own sake'. But without the second virtue, persistence, there would be frequent failures. Mearns said 'He must doggedly resist discouragement, and, persuaded of the existence of a truant only temporarily invisible, stubbornly refuse to abandon the hunt'. It is interesting to note that this often underrated virtue is seen as especially necessary in the harsh competitive world of the entrepreneurial librarian. In 1988 Susan E. Feldman described how 'The bulldog aspect of reference work – getting a sticky question and refusing to give up on it – is a major part of information brokering. Clients don't pay for easy-to-find information.'

It is at those critical points in a search when the path has turned into a dead end that reference librarians have the opportunity to display another of those important personal attributes so central to reference work, the one that as noted in Chapter 3 is on everyone's list: imagination. However carefully devised a search strategy may be, good searchers always keep a couple of alternatives up their sleeve: this is doubly valuable with the more formally structured computer searches. And it is the searcher's faculty of imagination that on occasion allows the playing of a distinctly constructive role; as Ervin J. Gaines proclaimed, 'The reference librarian doesn't "look things up" – he imposes shape and form on the great pile of knowledge so that others may use it well'. A search can indeed be a genuine act of creation.

## Ethics
A traditional article of faith in reference work is that no enquiry is unimportant: the circumstances which give rise to the question are of no concern to the librarian, except insofar as they assist in clarifying more precisely what is required to solve the user's problem. But as has often been pointed out, the effort exerted in seeking an answer may vary unconsciously according to the 'importance' of the enquirer. This is easy to observe in one's colleagues, but more difficult to detect in oneself.

The differential response is instinctive. Deliberately to pay less attention to a query because it comes from the mayor of the city, or the chairman of the company, or the vice-chancellor of the university, would betray a perversity foreign to the normal well-adjusted librarian. It is difficult to know what to do about this. In 1910 Dana made no bones about it; indeed he was an early advocate of positive discrimination. He argued that priority should be given to the enquiries of businessmen, city officials, and prospective benefactors of the library. Similar discriminatory attitudes are found today, though sometimes in the reverse direction: Judith Farley, a reference librarian in the Main Reading Room of the Library of Congress, frankly admitted 'I usually offer more help to a poor-looking reader than a prosperous one; to the very old and the very confused rather than to the self-assured'.

Acknowledged bias of this kind is usually positive in intention, though of course for those not so favoured it is negative in effect. But unmistakable negative bias, whether conscious or unconscious, would be much more serious. Reference librarians are understandably less willing to admit to this, and most evidence is anecdotal. It is probably rare. Farley, a self-confessed 'strong union supporter', has told us how she had to grit her teeth in order to help one enquirer seeking strategies and tactics for his employer to use to circumvent the union attempting to organize in his workplace.

Certainly, it is rare to find differential treatment set out as policy, formally or informally, but institutional silence on such matters does have the effect of leaving it in the hands of the individual librarian, thus at least opening the door to discriminatory service. Of course in some cases this differentiation has been institutionalized and is well understood: some university libraries offer a lower level of service to non-members. Debbie Masters and Gail Flatness have explained how this works: 'We try not to be overt but will subtly withdraw from the question [if it extends 'beyond a certain point in time'] or refer the person elsewhere if they turn out to be a non-affiliated user'.

Every student should think about Foskett's words in his stimulating 1962 address to the Library Association Reference, Special and Information Section in Manchester, published as *The creed of a librarian*: 'During reference service, the librarian ought virtually to vanish as an individual person, except in so far as his personality sheds light on the working of the library. He must be the reader's *alter ego*, immersed in his politics, his religion and his morals. He must have the ability to participate in the reader's enthusiasm and to devote himself wholly and wholeheartedly to whatever cause the reader has at the time of the enquiry. He must put himself in the reader's shoes.'

This much-quoted paper used as subtitle a phrase that had been current for a generation and more as a maxim for librarians, 'no politics, no religion, no morals', and his plea for professional objectivity has a long history in the literature of reference work: Samuel Swett Green urged in 1876 'Avoid scrupulously the propagation of any particular set of views on politics, art, history, philosophy, or theology'. He warned sternly: 'The librarian who uses his position to make proselytes prostitutes his calling'. But the student should be aware that others may disagree. Indeed, Rothstein has pointed out that 'reference librarianship provides more and keener instances . . . of ethical concern than . . . most other types of library work'.

This is perhaps an appropriate point to consider whether there may be certain enquiries that the librarian should refuse to answer on ethical grounds. The classic example, quoted by generations of librarians, is the request for information on how to pick locks, but actual up-to-date instances posing similar problems are enquiries seeking details of the manufacture of nerve gas, or hallucinogenic drugs, or poisons used in espionage for assassination purposes. It could be argued that if such information is available in the open literature (as it is) the librarian who assists the enquirer to obtain it can in no way be held responsible, morally or legally, for the use to which such information is put. Indeed, in 1976, a century after Green, in a classic unobtrusive survey of six public libraries and seven academic libraries in the United States, Robert Hauptman found that in no case was the librarian unwilling to provide information on making an explosive device sufficient to blow up a small house. Even where information is sought on activities that are unequivocally illegal, such as (in some countries) the growing of cannabis, or badger-baiting, or computer hacking, there are still those who would insist on the neutral moral nature of information *per se* and the consequent duty of the librarian to supply it when asked, without questioning the purpose to which it may be put. As was mentioned in Chapter 4, this is the traditional stance of the reference librarian, but there is some evidence that many would no longer be able to retain the same detached approach to an enquirer seeking, for instance, information on evicting a tenant, or books on black magic in order to put a spell on a girl-friend, or the most painless way of committing suicide, or evidence for the intellectual inferiority of the black races.

There are two separate issues here. The first arises when personal ethics conflict with professional ethics – when conscience is affronted by the code, as promulgated by Foskett and Green. Hauptman's considered view, a dozen years after his survey, was that the Foskett position 'is usually correct. If the information provider filtered each request through a personal set of criteria, insisting that none of his or her personal beliefs be countered, the result would be professional chaos, since many patrons would be turned away for illegitimate reasons.' Yet Mary Lee Bundy and Paul Wasserman reminded librarians in 1968 that 'Professionals view the freedom to function independently, the exercise of discretion, and the formation of independent judgments in client relations based upon their own standards and ethical views, as essential to professional performance'. One example of this approach can be found embodied in the words of the Bar Council, which maintains that a lawyer

151

'recognizes a higher duty than that of mere compliance with his client's wishes whatever they may be'. Discretion is perhaps the key here: as has been explained more than once in previous chapters, identical questions from different people may require different handling. Not everyone seeking information on an illegal or a socially undesirable or a personally offensive practice has the intention of going out and doing it.

The second issue concerns the professional code itself. Hauptman's view was that 'an *absolute* adherence to the dubious professional commitment of dispensing information is also unacceptable'. It has to be said that neither the Library Association's Code of Professional Conduct nor the American Library Association's Ethics of Service resolve the matter, and the stark question remains: how is the balance to be struck between unfettered service and intellectual freedom on the one hand and social responsibility and regard for the consequences of one's actions on the other? Hauptman concluded that these two positions are so antithetical at times that only the individual can make a choice, but this is not unreasonable, since the foundation of any professional ethical code should be the individual consciences of its members. It is worth noting another comment by Rothstein: 'it is the very existence of numerous and substantial ethical problems that attests to librarians' claims to professionalism'.

*Further reading*

Bates, Marcia J., 'Information search tactics', *Journal of the American Society for Information Science*, **30**, 1979, 205 – 14.

Bates, Marcia J., 'Idea tactics', *Journal of the American Society for Information Science*, **30**, 1979, 280 – 9.

Rothstein, Samuel, 'Where does it hurt? identifying the real concerns in the ethics of reference service', *Reference librarian*, **4**, 1982, 1 – 12.

Swan, John C., 'Ethics at the reference desk: comfortable theories and tricky practices', *Reference librarian*, **4**, 1982, 99 – 116.

Vickery, Alina, and others, 'A reference and referral system using expert system techniques', *Journal of documentation*, **43**, 1987, 1 – 23.

Grogan, Denis J., 'Databases for quick reference', in Armstrong, C. J. and Large, J. A., *Manual of online search strategies*, Aldershot, Gower, 1988, 716 – 40.

McCombs, Gillian M., 'Public and technical services: the hidden dialectic', *RQ*, **28**, 1988, 141 – 5.

Hildreth, Charles R., 'Extending the access and reference service capabilities of the online public access catalog', in Smith, Linda C.,

*Questions and answers: strategies for using the electronic reference collection*, Urbana-Champaign, University of Illinois, 1989, 14 – 23.

Richardson, John, Jr, 'Towards an expert system for reference service: a research agenda for the 1990s', *College and research libraries*, **50**, 1989, 231 – 48.

Hartley, R. J. and others, *Online searching: principles and practice*, London, Bowker-Saur, 1990.

Piternick, Anne B., 'Decision factors favoring the use of online sources for providing information', *RQ*, **29**, 1990, 534 – 44.

# — 6 —

# The response

The concluding stage of the reference process starts with the presentation to the enquirer of the search findings. If the reference interview is the period of analysis, this is the period of synthesis, which may account for its comparative neglect in the research literature until recently. Synthesis is said to have less appeal to the academic mind. William A. Katz believed, however, that 'the librarian is as involved with the answer as in finding the answer; and this concept is badly in need of development. The step after the information is located may be the most important phase of the entire search process, particularly when the librarian is working with a user who has only a vague notion of what is needed.' Indeed, the first thing to note about the response stage is that it does demand a combination of skills and personal qualities somewhat different to those commonly regarded as standard equipment for the compleat reference librarian. For it is at this point that librarians undergo one of their severest tests, not of their professional competence, but of their character. Perhaps surprisingly to some, one of the essential personal attributes of the reference librarian, as of the true scholar, is humility. However knowledgeable or experienced one might be, the temptation to display the fact must be sternly resisted. One should cultivate the habit, in Tennyson's phrase, of 'wearing all that weight of learning lightly like a flower'. More explicitly, as David C. Mearns has explained, 'The reference librarian must always resist an impulse to be glib; he must scourge and throttle his vanity; he must reach a conclusion rather than begin with it. He cannot afford to be profound, or to impress a patron with his instant knowledge, for truth is his stock-in-trade, and although truth is fixed and firm and tangible, men's minds cast different lights and change its form and give it different meanings. The reference librarian must seek not his own truth but the truth of those he serves.'

## Fact-finding responses

In the great majority of instances, particularly if the enquiry is of the fact-finding kind, the response simply takes the form of a straightforward presentation to the enquirer of the specific item or items of information requested. If at all possible this should be in documentary form, or if given orally (over the telephone, for example) should be derived directly from the consultation of a document at the time and should be indicated to the enquirer as such. There are three good reasons for this stern rule. First, the librarian who relies on memory alone will one day make a mistake; as Mearns warned, 'Recollection is treacherous; it is usually too broad or too narrow for another's use; and what is more serious, it is frequently undependable and worn and feeble'. Even more reprehensible than the unsupported recollection is the guess, however well informed. Secondly, although surveys have shown that some users are impressed by staff 'who know the answer without looking it up', the effect on many an enquirer is to make them feel somewhat cheated. Library readers, not surprisingly, do like to see their answers in black and white and they often want to make a note; they are not always flattered to think that their problems are so simple that librarians can produce the answers out of their heads; and they know as well as anyone that reference librarians are not infallible. The third reason is that the production of the source makes clear what the authority of the answer is.

It is true that a lot of information is not available in documentary form, and in some disciplines oral sources are a significant part of the communication system, particularly with regard to recent developments. Robert Fairthorne has claimed, for instance, that 'at any time the bulk of scientific knowledge is not yet recorded'. It is only right to add, however, that in many cases such word-of-mouth converse serves merely as a pointer to documentary sources.

Though it is important to be aware of such informal communication channels, and indeed to study them where appropriate, librarians remain by and large outside them. On those rare occasions where they do find themselves serving as a link in the chain by passing oral information on to an enquirer from a third source, it is a wise procedure to make evident the non-documentary status of the data.

## Material-finding responses

The search product of a material-finding enquiry is not a specific item of fact but an array of information commonly gathered from more than one documentary source. It can also take the form of a listing of the documents as a preliminary to the actual examination of the items by the enquirer later. The student should not lose sight of the fact, however, that it is the content of these documents that is of concern and not the documents themselves, as such. Usually, of course, the relevant materials are produced there and then for the enquirer to look at on the spot.

They may simply be laid before the individual user as they are found, 'dumped in his lap' as one writer put it, but there is no doubt that a more helpful presentation is often appreciated. Probably any reference librarian with a degree of sensitivity will instinctively organize for each enquirer the information that a search throws up, even if no more is involved than presenting first the introductory or basic material, and then offering the advanced or detailed material later.

It needs no stressing that a material-finding search that fails to turn up any material at all is not going to please. What is often forgotten is that a search that produces too much for the enquirer to digest can also cause mental discomfort. Like the young reader who complained to the reference librarian that the *Encylopaedia Britannica* told her more about crocodiles than she wanted to know, most enquirers have a pretty good idea when they have enough for their needs. Of course the perceptive librarian is on the alert for signs of this, but, sad to relate, there are those who will be deterred by nothing short of a loud cry of 'Stop!'. This is a common failing of librarians and can be observed daily: they seem unable to recognize when enough is enough. Roger Horn has told of one who actually complained in print that just as the materials began to pile up nicely the enquirers were in the habit of disappearing. As he rightly commented, '*They* do not love the questions the way we do'. Mearns, too, has warned against 'profligate expenditure of time and effort when the reference librarian's own curiosity is fired to a point where he feels himself impelled to seek personal satisfaction'. Peggy Sullivan tells of a colleague who 'worked so hard on any question that she spent years of her own time coming back to continue unsuccessful searches after her day's work. When she did that, she wore a hat to indicate that she was on her own time and was to be allowed to work without interruption.' She is by no means an isolated example, even in her use of a hat as a signal.

It will occasionally be found that some enquirers may actually prefer an incomplete or partial answer if it can be provided quickly to satisfy an immediate need.

## Explanation

In many instances a degree of explanation is called for to supplement the information supplied. This may be purely technical, such as the elucidation of a bibliographical citation or an abbreviation, but most frequently it is required where the result of the search appears to be not quite what was asked for, even though the librarian may judge that it meets the need. A request for 'a pamphlet on the silver point process', correctly interpreted by the librarian as a plea for no more than a brief account, might well be better satisfied by an article from an encyclopaedia or a chapter from a textbook. In such cases what librarians try to explain are the reasons for their opinion that the proffered findings do indeed solve the enquirer's problem.

Quite a different kind of explanation may be called for where it turns out to be necessary to clear up some misapprehension on the enquirer's part. The businessman who wanted to know how to wish a Chinese colleague a Happy New Year had to be told that although there is a common written Chinese the spoken language comprises eight mutually unintelligible 'dialects'. Some of the enquiries about correct pronunciation are similarly based on a misunderstanding. In many such cases, there is no single 'correct' way, but a number of genuine alternatives: 'hegemony', for example, has at least six acceptable pronunciations.

A whole subcategory of enquiries calling for explanation are the ever-recurring 'popular fallacies'. Some of course are logical fallacies, as can be demonstrated without recourse to documentary evidence, but most are a consequence of consistent misinformation, and may be deeply rooted. The response in such cases is the presentation to the enquirer of the truth of the matter. In practice, however, this may not always be welcome, and it requires a delicate touch.

If asked for a photograph showing the 'Rock of Ages' (associated with the hymn), or details of the ray developed during World War II for use against German planes that would paralyse internal combustion engines, or information about the alligators breeding in New York sewers, after even a brief search the conscientious librarian would be left with little choice but to try to explain to an enquirer who will almost certainly be reluctant to listen, that the story of the hymn being written in the shelter of a rock during a storm in the Mendips is a legend that has been disproved many times; that the engine-stopping ray was a rumour deliberately promoted to worry the Germans; that the tale of alligators in the sewers is perhaps the best-known example of what are

157

called 'urban myths'. Of course in all such cases the librarian needs to have chapter and verse to show to the user on the true facts of the matter. But this too needs tact: it is not kind when asked an apparently serious question to reach immediately and before the enquirer's very eyes for Burnam's *Dictionary of misinformation* or Ackerman's *Popular fallacies*. And the librarian will find that some people prefer to cherish their illusions, perhaps because, as H. L. Mencken once said, 'What ails the truth is that it is mainly uncomfortable, and often dull'.

Librarians also need to be on their guard against misinterpretation – either by themselves or their enquirers – of the information they find. Gerald Jahoda and Judith Schiek Braunagel have warned that this 'can occur when there are several closely related answers presented in the reference source [and] also when the information is not presented exactly according to the requirements of the query', especially in the case of tables, graphs, and charts.

Once they have provided the basic response, a role reference librarians frequently find themselves playing is that of prompter. As Eve Johansson explained, 'The reference staff work constantly with the need to enhance the enquirer's sense of the source to which he has been referred, to pursue and shape his question and to follow it up with "Did you know there was also ... ?", "Had you thought of looking at ... ?". The reference assistance provided thus goes far beyond simple assistance with catalogues and reference works. It demands a considerable intellectual contribution from the staff, in the interpretation of the collections.' If the topic is controversial some maintain that this places on the librarian an ethical responsibility too: John C. Swan has argued that 'a librarian has a duty to present his patron with as clear a view of an issue as he she can, and the more ambiguous the issue, the more complex the responsibility'.

Margaret Monroe, too, would add stimulation as a reference function alongside information, instruction, and guidance, and Louis Shores gave priority to this function of stimulant and wished to redefine reference as 'the promotion of free inquiry'. He argued that 'the library has an obligation to society to *initiate* questions. If society is not asking these questions, the library should initiate them.' This is a lofty claim: one is reminded of what was said by Mandell Creighton, the Bishop of London, who delivered the commencement address at the very first Library Association classes in 1898: 'The one real object of education is to leave a man in the condition of continually asking questions'.

## Unanswerable questions

It does happen from time to time, as was exemplified in Chapter 2, that a question is asked that the librarian knows from experience to be unanswerable in practice, though in theory it may appear quite possible, such as 'Where are the Ten Commandments Stones?', 'When was King Arthur married?', 'I am looking for illustrations of the banners of the 12 tribes of Israel'. Careful explanation is called for here too. Similarly, the librarian will encounter queries where the answer turns out to be unknown or non-existent: for example, 'Who invented the aneroid barometer?' (disputed), 'What is the origin of the saying "Behind every great man there is a woman"?' (unknown), 'What is the address of the Common Cold Research Unit?' (disbanded), 'Where can I buy a live bat?' (illegal). Again, a convincing explanation is necessary, supported where appropriate by search evidence showing why there is no answer.

Students should be careful to distinguish this response from the unadorned negative answer where the librarian has drawn a blank: this is a quite different matter and will be discussed later. The situation described here is where the librarian does indeed give a positive answer, namely that the question is unanswerable. Such a response, sympathetically offered and convincingly supported, should leave the average intelligent enquirer quite satisfied, though not necessarily pleased. By way of contrast, as will be seen later, the completely negative response can scarcely hope to satisfy either librarian or enquirer.

## Unacceptable questions

An even more diplomatic explanation may be called for in those instances where it is necessary to persuade the enquirer that a question is not acceptable. Such is obviously needed with the kind of enquiry that it is library policy not to answer: some academic libraries may refuse to answer queries about sporting records; some public libraries may reject genealogical questions. A similar explanation must be given where the librarian believes as a matter of principle that enquirers should be encouraged to find the answers to their own questions. This is frequently the case in academic institutions where students are given assignments to complete which specifically require them to make their own use of library materials.

Regrettably, perhaps, even in libraries with the most liberal reference policies and with staff fired with determination to answer any question asked, human nature makes it necessary to refuse some requests from time to time. Even the most ardent protagonist of maximum reference service must logically concede that no library should be expected to respond to unreasonable demands. Philosophically, such an enthusiast may require some convincing that library users do in fact make unreasonable requests, but a week in the front line should be enough. And whatever might be the theoretical niceties in deciding what is or is not reasonable, there is rarely any need for subtlety in practice.

Samuel Swett Green knew all about this over a century ago: 'There are obvious limits to the assistance which a librarian can undertake to render. Commonsense will dictate them.' And it usually does. Green would probably agree with most experienced librarians of today that enquiries such as the following go beyond what is reasonable to ask: 'I would like a list of all the Members of Parliament who have been Whips', 'How many locks are there on the Thames between Oxford and Teddington?', 'Can you find a poem about Ireland by Dorothy L. Sayers and read it out to me? [by phone]'.

It is instructive to ask what it is that makes such enquiries unacceptable to a commonsensical librarian. In content they are all very typical, in form they are by no means complex, and they are not difficult to answer. But they would each take a long time to deal with, and it is this combination of an easy question with a long drawn-out search or response that identifies such enquiries as beyond the reasonable call of duty.

As all the great investigators knew, from Sherlock Holmes onwards, solving cases requires a combination of brains and drudgery. But to employ a professional reference librarian on a case where the intellectual content is trifling and the clerical toil exorbitant is as *unreasonable* as to commission the Great Detective to trace a pair of mislaid spectacles. It is the gist of this explanation that the librarian has to try to convey to the enquirer whose question is being declined.

But triviality *per se* is no excuse for refusing an enquiry, despite L. R. McColvin's advice in 1936: 'Discourage trivial enquiries'. Charles Anderson in particular has argued against unnecessary exclusivity here: 'it's very important to keep reminding ourselves that the questions we're asked don't belong to us – they belong to the questioner. We *can't* classify them as stupid – they aren't our questions to classify', and again, 'Answering a question . . . should be our only concern. Whether the question falls into the idle-speculation category or is classified as serious and weighty, the fundamental assumption should be that we will answer the question . . . insofar as time, finances, and resources permit. Of course each library must decide how much time, money, and resources are or can be made available. But this is a policy decision, and once made, should be applied equally to all questions. The worthiness of the question doesn't deserve to be an issue.' But many would disagree vigorously. Will Manley has written that 'My inclination as a reference librarian is to spend more time on serious questions that presumably have more redeeming social value than the mere settling of a barroom argument or the surfeiting of the flight of fancy of some trivia junkie'. It is of course not always possible to put one's finger on triviality in a reference question, as so much depends on the context. Based on 564 interviews with users in business libraries Norman Roberts and his colleagues concluded that 'The apparent triviality of the information act . . . was unrelated to the significance of subsequent consequences'.

Quiz and competition questions provoke particular controversy, but if they are of the kind that are otherwise acceptable it is difficult to see why. In any case, without prior knowledge many are not recognizable as competition questions, appearing to be quite normal quick-reference queries, for example 'What was the price of a pound of butter in 1885?', 'What does the Russian Orthodox church celebrate on January 7th?', 'Who was the Seraphic Doctor?'.

Of course some are easy to spot, because they are obviously not founded on reality, seeming to be free-floating or dangling in some way: it is difficult to imagine anyone being genuinely anxious to know the answers to questions such as 'What is the only English word other than "cushion" to end in shion?' or 'What year followed 54 BC?' or 'Of which are there more: acres in Yorkshire or words in the Bible?'. Others have quite clearly been 'set' by someone who already knows the answer, for example 'Multiplying a certain measurement by 3.7854 converts it to another standard measurement. What are the two measurements?', 'In 1935 a man with the initials RWW built an important invention. What was his full name and what was the invention?', 'What pianist had the first name Wladziu?'.

Nevertheless, provided the resources are available to deal with such questions, and they are of a nature that would otherwise make them acceptable – requiring brains rather than drudgery – it is difficult to see why reference librarians should refuse them. In fact, Samuel Rothstein advised that 'if you want to demonstrate the reference department's existence and usefulness to a great many people very quickly these [contest and similar questions] are the fastest highways to general recognition . . . the Vancouver Public Library cooperated with a local newspaper on a trivia contest and reaped a huge harvest of effective publicity'.

Of course it goes without saying that in all instances of questions that are judged unacceptable, for whatever reason, the librarian's explanation must include instructions to enable the enquirers to search for their own information; or, if appropriate, a suggestion as to where they can obtain the kind of assistance they are seeking.

It is helpful to the student to see this response-explanation stage of the reference process as the counterpart to the question-negotiation stage earlier on, with the same general objective of ensuring the closest possible fit between the need and its suggested answer.

### 'Repackaging'

Another matter of controversy is how far the librarian should go in interpreting the results of the search. By this is meant the extraction of meaning from the information sources discovered, rewording it, perhaps summarizing it, and re-presenting it in a form more easily assimilable by the enquirer. There are those who would argue that the librarian's task is over when the result of a search is presented, and in any case librarians are rarely trained to do more. On the other hand, Katz argued that 'it is not enough just to locate a piece of data, a source, or a document. There should be some kind of subsequent evaluation, interpretation, or clarification on the part of the librarian. This should be as much a professional duty as the interview and the search itself – although always with two considerations: (1) A user who does not want assistance should not have it forced upon him. (2) There are numerous times, as in most ready-reference queries, when the answer speaks for itself.' As for the librarian's competence to undertake this duty, Mearns, in his list of the attributes of the ideal reference librarian, gave first place to literacy, 'an ability to recognize, beyond the combination of letters into words, and the arrangement of words into sentences, the meaning of the author who contrived them'. He did admit, however, that 'this power is unusual, it is a gift which must be cultivated, an accomplishment which can only be acquired by vigorous and steadfast concentration'.

In many industrial and governmental libraries this kind of 'repackaging' is often an absolute requirement of users, who may with certain enquiries expect the librarian to select and digest the raw material for them as a matter of routine. Obviously, in such instances the search findings are normally presented in writing. This has been so for many years. As long ago as 1912 Matthew S. Dudgeon explained that 'the special librarian must select the material so that only the parts wanted are delivered. It must be cut down in bulk by extracting, summarizing, generalizing, and even tabulating. It must be portable, readily transferable, negotiable.' Speaking for the current generation of special librarians, Edwin M. Cortez maintained that it is the provision of this 'digestible information' that 'has made the special librarian indispensable to modern managers and executives who need current, accurate information on which to base decisions'.

In such a demanding context the limitation of the simple bibliography, however fully annotated, is that 'it leaves the enquirer to do all the necessary synthesis before the information can be put to practical use', as P. J. Bordiss explained. Even where the bibliography is the product of a computer search, as he said, 'What the computer cannot do is perform a final sort for usefulness to the enquirer, critically evaluate the items received and turn them into a more coherent account'. What is normally needed in such cases is something more akin to a state-of-the-art review; a report of a patent search or of an investigation into the financial status of a company would typically take this form. Where the computer can assist, of course, at a workstation with appropriate software, is in reformatting data, particularly in the form of graphics such as tables and charts.

M. W. Hill has advised: 'To achieve effective repackaging the service supplier must get to know his clients. This will involve not only finding out their tastes and their intellectual standing (i.e., their capacity to absorb information and their educational background) but also their normal mode of understanding, by which I mean the language, the words and phraseology, which they are used to.' D. J. Foskett wished to go further, 'to re-organize the data, not simply to "re-package" it. Re-packaging implies no more than a re-arrangement of the same material; re-organization means much more. It means imposing a new form or pattern on the material, based on the intended users' real needs.'

Not all enquirers are prepared to allow a librarian to act as an intermediary between them and information in this way, even in the special library context where both are often colleagues, or at least fellow-employees. Some such users are even reluctant to allow the librarian to search for them. It is not that they are unwilling to admit the librarian's superior search skills, but they simply prefer to work with the literature themselves, an attitude well worth respecting. A not uncommon compromise is for this response stage of the process to be undertaken as a joint exercise, with the client deciding which documents are the most significant, and the librarian summarizing the findings on that basis.

Whatever the views of the individual librarian, the extent to which this repackaging can be undertaken is closely related to the ratio of staff to users. In industrial and business libraries, for instance, where such a service is routine, the ratio of information staff to staff served may be as favourable as 1:40. Nevertheless, as Bob McKee has pointed out, 'similar work is done – time permitting – by academic subject librarians or public librarians developing services for a particular client group', and Katz has forecast a dramatic shift in this respect: 'Today the [basic problem of reference service] is finding the fact, the relevant bit of information, the general book or magazine article. ... The reference librarian of the next generation ... is likely to be more concerned with knowledge than information, more involved in assisting the less-than-expert user with determining what bits of data will solve problems.'

## Assessment and selection

When it comes to assessing the quality of the information provided, and even eliminating some material judged to be of less value, many in the profession hold that this is the business of the user. Increasingly insistent, however, are the voices of those who disagree. Katz has pointed out that 'The most common complaint concerning the use of the computer search is that too much irrelevant material is presented'. Users do appear to require help. It was many years ago that James Thurber said that 'So much has been written about everything that it is difficult to find out anything about it', but others have since encountered the same problem. A 1986 survey of 3,835 scholars by the American Council of Learned Societies found that the majority agreed with the statement that 'It is virtually impossible to even minimally keep up with the literature in my field'.

In 1978 Klaus Musmann stressed that 'With such an over-abundance of available information, the discarding of information may become even more important than the retention of information. The intelligent management of this information flow is one of the pressing problems of contemporary society.' Hill's view, expressed in the same year, was that evaluation, together with repackaging, are 'the two features which distinguish an information service from mere document retrieval'. In 1990 Threasa Wesley commented that despite the fact that 'Some theorists argue strongly against this interventionist view of the librarian's role ... the most valuable skill a reference librarian can cultivate is an ability to think critically about the use of information sources. This analytical thought is the one thread that runs through all quality reference services.'

In many instances of course, even in special libraries, staffing ratios do not permit this evaluation, but some at least of the opposition to it has similar roots to the reluctance of some reference librarians to provide answers to users' questions, as discussed in Chapter 1. Robert S. Taylor noted in 1968 that 'Perhaps the most important obstacle to evaluation by the librarian is the sense of puritanism on the part of both librarians and management who believe, for ethical rather than economic reasons, that everyone should do his own work'. In 1989 Mary Biggs was still encountering 'librarians' habitual unease with, avoidance of, any evaluative role'.

Whatever one's views about evaluation, there should be agreement that reference librarians must try to ensure that the information they furnish does meet certain simple criteria. First and foremost it should be readily understandable. Wittgenstein claimed that 'everything that can be said can be said clearly': by careful selection of alternative materials a librarian can often ensure that a response is less obscure than it might have been. It should also be complete, in the sense that it should include all essential information, or as Jahoda and Braunagel put it, 'all possible correct answers'. As they went on to add, 'Currency is also a component of a complete answer. It is sometimes tempting to limit the answer to the scope available in the answer-providing title.' Rochelle Yates has reminded us that 'Certain news items, dates, and statistics change regularly and are of wide popular interest', and the librarian needs to stay constantly alert to the danger of out-of-date information. Any material supplied should also be simple to use: again a judicious choice from a range of possible sources and formats can often be made, with a marked improvement in the quality of the response.

But as Hill admits, 'These are the easy criteria. The difficult ones are accuracy and reliability: accuracy of factual data; reliability of theories and opinions.' There is of course no simple and certain way of assessing these. Apart from a constant and unwavering critical eye on all sources that are used, what can the librarian do? According to Hill, 'The answer is that he must develop a facility for identifying – and discarding – unreliable sources, a habit of cross-checking wherever possible and, most important, keeping in close touch with his client while the information is being used so that, by feed-back from the client, he can quickly learn if the information is not right and take quick corrective action to provide better or additional material'.

But the accuracy and reliability of information sources is one thing; the accuracy and reliability of reference librarians is quite another, and one about which there has been disturbing evidence in recent years. This will be discussed later in this chapter.

## Advice

Circumstances may well arise where a further call still is made upon the librarian's skills. Enquirers may ask for advice on whether the information applies to their own circumstances, or how it should be used. In effect, they ask 'What shall I do?'. Requests for advice are common in the field of community information services, where the problems arise in the context of the increasing complexity of everyday living: reference librarians are asked to express an opinion as to the course of action a client should follow to solve a personal problem, such as noise from a local record shop, or a flooded basement, or dogs running wild in the neighbourhood.

These of course are all too common domestic problems, though none the less important to the enquirer. Other requests for advice librarians find more difficult, for example 'Should I sign this guarantee?', 'Can you recommend a reliable insurance company?', 'Do I need a work permit to get a part-time job in a local shop?' (from a foreign student). Up to this point, the skills they have exercised, in question-negotiation, in the search, in explaining and interpreting, even in evaluating, have depended on education and training, application and experience. Now they enter a different world, where what is required of them is soundness of judgement and reliability of opinion. They are indeed at the outer margin of reference work. In fact, many would say they have already stepped over the edge: received wisdom in the world of reference is 'Never offer a personal opinion'.

Neither conventional library education nor traditional library practice prepares librarians for this task, yet increasingly such demands are made on them. Many resist, making comments such as 'None of us are in a position to advise people of their rights, only to find out what information we can for them' and 'Our staff don't have the training really to answer the very personal questions that people have'. But in fact numbers of public librarians have taken to the work with enthusiasm and commitment, often finding a pragmatic solution by following the practice traditionally adopted with medical and legal queries.

The sound rule that the librarian must not dispense medical or legal advice goes back well over a century, having been clearly prescribed in Green's pioneer paper of 1876, and has been regularly reinforced. In 1914 an anonymous British librarian reported that giving legal advice 'is one of the two things we decline to do . . . the other is to give medical advice. The books we have are available, but the only advice that can be coaxed out of us is to go to a solicitor or a doctor.' And in their 1980 text Jahoda and Braunagel warn: 'As a librarian you should never attempt to provide legal or medical advice to a client, or to interpret the implications of legal or medical statements in reference sources'. That is not to say that librarians should refuse all medical or legal enquiries. There are now large numbers of self-help legal texts, often published by the most respected authorities, and the provision of consumer health information is a substantial industry. Many specific questions differ only in their subject-matter from those asked in other fields and can be treated in just the same way. Requests for specific documents or texts obviously pose no problems: the Artisans' Dwellings Act of 1875, the juror's oath, a full list of protected birds in Britain, the order of succession to an intestate's property, a facsimile of a deed of gift. Similarly uncontroversial are questions to which there is a straightforward answer, even if lengthy: 'When was the driving test introduced?', 'Is it true that prize-fighting is illegal?', 'What is the difference between evidence and proof?'. When enquiries turn more complicated than this, it is still possible for the librarian to respond by producing relevant materials: 'Can a private citizen make an arrest?', 'Can a child of six be held responsible for an accident?', 'How can you avoid legal responsibility when giving someone a testimonial or a reference?'. But any attempt at interpretation or explanation should be avoided; if pressed, recommending the enquirer to consult a qualified practitioner is the only safe course.

Medical queries are, if anything, even more common: while most of us most of the time avoid legal problems, all of us at some time have medical problems, and many of us seek information from libraries. Reference librarians should treat medical questions with equal circumspection, following similar guidelines. Straightforward answers can be provided to questions such as 'What does SLE stand for?', 'What is the pH factor of skin?', 'What are spoon nails?', 'How is sleeping sickness transmitted?', 'What is glue ear?'. Similarly, literature is readily available on tests for colour-blindness, the effects of Drinamyl on the nervous system, salt-free diets, health hazards from VDUs, and the medicinal uses of garlic. But again, this information should be offered, as Dottie Eakin and her colleagues put it, 'without interpretation, without opinion or counselling, and with no attempt to influence the actions or decision making of the individual'. And there are some questions it is probably wise to refuse altogether, for instance 'Can you identify this pill for me?', 'How much barium carbonate can one take without being poisoned?', 'How much water should you drink each day?'.

But the whole issue is far from simple. In 1984 lawyers were publicly critical of out-of-date legal books in British public libraries: in an article headed 'Public misinformation' in the *Solicitors' journal* they complained of 'actually damaging information' and 'information time bombs'. A few years earlier in the United States a bibliography of medical and legal reference works typically found in public library collections was challenged by medical and legal experts as containing titles that were 'deceptive, out-of-date, totally worthless, and even harmful'.

For the reference librarian the basic rule is still valid: referral to the appropriate qualified expert is the best response should it become evident at any stage that what is really needed is medical or legal advice, i.e. whether or not a specific item of information is applicable to a particular case. It is interesting to note that the new breed of entrepreneurial librarians has taken the same traditional stance.

And on the broader issue of advice in general Patricia Ainley spoke good sense: 'It all depends on the definition of advice. The sort of "advice" which we are well able to give is factual and even interpretive but leans towards the information end of the spectrum. The sort of advice we are not able to give is that which is interpretive/supportive and leans towards the counselling end of the spectrum.'

**Referral**

As was mentioned briefly in Chapter 5 this passing on of the enquirer to another agency for the answer to a question is one possible response the librarian can make. Indeed, community information services make extensive referrals as a matter of policy, hence their alternative description as information and referral services; Kriss Taya Ostrom discovered that they 'never wasted time and effort searching their own files for information which could be more quickly and precisely obtained elsewhere'. Of course this is less frequent in normal public and academic library routine, and unobtrusive surveys have shown referral surprisingly little used. In fact, in larger libraries, there are those who regard it as tantamount to an admission of weakness or even defeat. F. W. Lancaster has noted that 'Others may refuse to refer because they adopt a tenacious and proprietary interest in a particular question'. But this is bad practice: good reference librarians have always referred enquirers elsewhere if that was the best solution to their problem, and in some special libraries it is almost as common as in community information services. Any library worthy of the name keeps a file of names and addresses of individuals and organizations able to provide specialist information.

What is important is for referral to be regarded as a regular and usual procedure in appropriate cases, one of the quite legitimate weapons in the librarian's armoury, even though normally held in reserve. Less and less can libraries hope to be self-sufficient: accepting this, the librarian must surely take steps to exploit the possibilities of referral. Patsy J. Hansel hoped that the advent of online databases was helping librarians overcome this 'errant professional pride'. But it is vital that it be approached systematically: a referral should never be merely a last resort, suggested to the enquirer because nothing else comes to mind. Gail Dykstra had two sound pieces of advice: 'one, either librarians must learn how to do referrals the right way or they shouldn't do them at all; and two, a referral that has been handled badly is more lethal than a wrong answer'. It should take the form of a deliberate and positive recommendation, decided on as the best means of reaching the solution to a particular problem. And never should referrals be made 'blind', in speculative fashion. Peggy Sullivan has described this as 'abandonment, not referral'. The librarian must have a good sound reason for choosing the alternative that is recommended; knowledge of extramural sources of information should be an essential part of every reference librarian's equipment.

Few libraries have developed any specific techniques for the referral of enquirers (as opposed to the referral of questions), still less of follow-up: what enquirers do when they leave with the librarian's recommendation is largely unknown. Surveys of referrals made by Citizens' Advice Bureaux indicated that 'the dropout rate of some types of referral may be . . . as high as 50 per cent'. It is known that enquirers do not like being sent elsewhere. In some instances the librarian will in fact make the initial contact with the source referred to, thus preparing the way for the enquirer. This is rare except in community information services and certain special libraries. Attempts have also been made to devise a simple referral form, as described by Patricia Gebhard and others: the form is handed to the enquirer with instructions on it where to go; the reverse is used to report back on the outcome; the numbering of the forms provides an indication as to how many enquirers decide not to bother. Even rarer is the librarian who checks to see what has happened: according to Terence Crowley this 'Follow-up advocacy [is] the most controversial and least practised activity'.

What is indisputable is that the overwhelming majority of the questions that people ask do have an answer somewhere: indeed, as was pointed out in Chapter 1, this is the challenge that committed reference librarians find so stimulating. Even if the resources at their immediate disposal are not sufficient, their professional knowledge and experience should enable them to say almost for sure where the required information can be found.

### Relevance and pertinence

Yet another sound rule laid down by Green in 1876 was the following: 'A librarian should be as unwilling to allow an inquirer to leave the library with his question unanswered as a shop-keeper is to have a customer go out of his store without making a purchase'. He urged, furthermore, 'Hold on to them until they have obtained the information they are seeking'. He was referring specifically to the distinct possibility that some enquirers may leave without what they came for, even though the librarian has dealt with their query. While no sane librarian would deliberately provide an unsatisfactory answer, it does happen from time to time that what enquirers accept as matching their needs at the conclusion of the search turns out on closer examination to be not what was required at all. This is why it is good practice where it seems appropriate to leave them in no doubt that they must ask again if they are not suited, and a little later, like a good restaurant manager, not to be above enquiring whether everything is to their satisfaction.

The central point for the student to grasp is that the 'correctness' or suitability of the answer supplied is not a property of the information itself. There is only one effective test of the success of the search and the satisfactory completion of the reference process, and that is whether it solves the user's problem. And ultimately, the one and only judge must be the enquirer. But of course the information has first to be applied to the problem and it may take some time before it can be seen whether it has provided a solution, and there always lurks the possibility of an undetected mistaken diagnosis of the problem at the outset. So, for practical purposes, the judgement the enquirer makes at this point is whether or not the material supplied meets the need. And as has been seen, the librarian also will have come to an opinion on the product of the search.

Jesse H. Shera and others have distinguished these two sets of judgements as follows: the decision made by the librarian at the end of the search matches the answer against the user's question, and is a judgement of *relevance*; the decision made by the user at the time of the response matches the answer against the need, and is a judgement of *pertinence*. But Charles A. Bunge has pointed out that 'In a system where the patron and the librarian react throughout the reference process, these two types of judgment are not so distinct since the librarian's and the user's judgment can be made together'.

The ideal to seek is to make relevance and pertinence coincide: the enquirer's need should have been ascertained so precisely at the interview that anything the librarian finds relevant should also turn out to be pertinent. Gerald Salton has offered some excellent advice on how to achieve this: 'One of the most fruitful ways of upgrading retrieval performance consists in using multiple searches based on user feedback information furnished during the search process'.

### The unsuccessful search

The great majority of library searches are successful in the sense that they produce material on the topic asked about that appears relevant to the librarian; and it would seem that a majority of these particular searches are also successful as measured by their pertinence to the enquirer's need.

But there are also those that are not successful. In some the information supplied turns out not to be pertinent to the enquirer's need, even though judged relevant to the question by the librarian. This is far from uncommon, but it is normally simple to cure. The cause is less frequently a misunderstanding of the subject of the enquiry; more often it can be traced to inadequate specification of the response at the interview stage, in terms of amount and level and form, as described in Chapter 4. But whatever the reason, here is seen the value of Salton's advice about using feedback from the user to modify the actual course of the search, and the suggestions made in Chapter 5 about mutual interaction in a jointly conducted search. One potential source of dissatisfaction – the over-generous response – also makes its presence felt as a rule during the search, as was discussed earlier in this chapter.

It must be said too that the judgements as to pertinence may be made by the enquirer at less than objective levels. The well-known resistance to materials in microform, although perfectly legitimate (and often shared by the librarian) is of this kind, as is the occasional reluctance to accept as conclusive any evidence that is unwelcome. Searches may be judged unsuccessful by enquirers if they only produce citations already known to them. Sometimes the issue may well be a matter of opinion: for example, whether the item provided really is the 'introductory account' of the topic that was asked for, or is as 'up to date' as the enquirer had in mind. In one study Brenda Dervin found that in 20% of the cases where enquirers at first felt their problem had been solved they had changed their minds 45 minutes later. Caroline E. Hieber found that many users have some unconscious expectation of the format of the answer, but if this remains unexpressed at the interview stage it is unlikely to be satisfied at the response stage. In practice it is not uncommon for the librarian to be obliged to persuade the enquirer to accept an answer in a form that the library can supply. On the other side of the coin, there is ample evidence that many users are inclined to say they are satisfied when they are not, either for fear of giving offence, or because they are grateful to be given any help at all.

More difficult to explain to the enquirer are those searches where no relevant material has been traced whatsoever, even after employing every possible alternative strategy. The student will remember to distinguish such negative findings from those cases where positive evidence is produced that the question is unanswerable. This is the time to heed James Benson's advice: 'Systematic failure analysis reaps not only immediate results regarding the search in question, but is also vital in developing one's future searching knowledge and capabilities'. There is almost always a reason for lack of success: Jan Kemp and Dennis Dillon have published a flow chart of the reference process indicating 13 points at which failure may occur. These fall into four categories: 'problems with the reference interview, problems caused by inadequate knowledge of sources, problems caused by library system failure, and problems due to the inescapably fallible nature of human beings'. Commonly encountered reasons are that the source that actually contains the answer lacks an index, or that the appropriate reference tool is not sufficiently up to date, or that the information is not yet published, or that time does not permit the extensive search necessary. And so on. The computer searcher in particular should be suspicious of a negative result in the shape of zero postings. As Stephen P. Harter warned, 'It may mean the database had nothing of interest on the topic to be searched, but more usually, it reflects an error by the searcher'. David Isaacson has reminded us that 'Sometimes the librarian's most sophisticated service may be . . . the discovery that the patron does not have an answerable question. Deciphering the question may be more important than finding an answer.' Finally, it is not unknown for failure to be the result of an individual librarian's stubbornness in refusing to consult someone else, or a lack of experience, or ignorance, or incompetence.

Obviously, some of these are beyond the control of the individual, but others are not. Reference librarians must assure themselves that they have eliminated every possibility that lies within their power before concluding that they have indeed drawn a blank. Mention was made in Chapter 5 of the valuable information resource represented by the collective experience and accumulated knowledge of a good library staff. Constance Winchell's instructions in the reference department's staff manual at Columbia University were quite firm on this matter: an enquiry is 'not to be finished in the *negative* until the assistant who has undertaken the question refers it to one of the administrative members of the Reference staff for advice or decision as to whether the negative report is justified'. Similarly, Clara Stanton Jones' rule in her book on *Public library information and referral service* was that 'no one is *ever* to respond to an enquiry by saying "I'm sorry, but the library does not have that information"'.

Even if after all this, the 'answer' is still technically a negative, an excellent maxim to remember is Nathan A. Josel's '"No" is never an answer'. What is being suggested here is that even though the search product is nil, the response to the enquirer can still be made helpful and positive. For one thing, the librarian's failure analysis exercise should normally enable a suggestion to be made why there is no answer: this often softens the blow. The policy rule at Vancouver Public Library Business and Economics Division was 'Do not give a negative answer until you are sure you know the reason for there being no satisfactory answer'. Some writers advise that where the response has to be negative, a referral should always be suggested. Josel's view was that 'If reference has to go from information to referral, then for the patron at least, that is better than nothing at all'. This needs to be weighed carefully. As the student has been warned, referral must never be used as a forlorn hope.

It must not be forgotten that there are searches where a negative result is what the enquirer hopes for: the most obvious example is a patent search for novelty, but many other searches at the start of a research project are of this kind. Roger W. Christian reported that 'A full thirty percent of the [computer searches at the Massachusetts Institute of Technology] yield nothing at all, and the researchers are delighted. It reassures them that the line of enquiry they have in mind has not been pre-empted.'

## Therapy

Sometimes an answer may have to be counted as 'unsuccessful' even though the pertinence judgement of the enquirer can be clearly seen to be irrational. Judith Farley has described how one enquirer in the Library of Congress Main Reading Room persisted in her wish to see photographs of the Iron Curtain.

No one can spend any considerable time in the service of library users without becoming aware that some of them are not as others are. This is a universal finding of experienced librarians in all types of library: a public librarian's naïve assertion at a professional conference that of course special libraries did not have the problem of eccentric users provoked an amused chorus of denials from the many industrial, learned society, and government librarians in the audience. And the academic library is the natural habitat of the absent-minded professor.

Nevertheless, it is undeniable that the ripest crop of unrecognized great inventors, vexatious litigants, pyramidologists, long-lost heirs to dormant peerages, and assorted harmless drudges is to be gathered in the public reference libraries of our great cities. And it is not only librarians who have noticed this. The novelist John Cooper Powys found that libraries attract 'bad mixers, odd fish, misfits, queer ones of every wounded sort of wing, who take refuge there in regions unknown to their neighbours'. Thomas Carlyle wrote of what is perhaps the world's most renowned library: 'I believe that there are several people in a state of imbecility who come to read in the British Museum. I have been informed that there are several in that state who are sent there by their friends to pass away the time.' Louis Macneice too spoke in his poem 'The British Museum Reading Room' of 'Cranks, hacks, poverty stricken scholars . . . cherishing their hobby or their doom'. Any reference librarian soon has to learn how best to provide for the needs of such users. Answering their questions – where answers are indeed possible – may not always suffice, and a special combination of tact, patience, and humanity are needed to serve them satisfactorily. From time to time other skills may also be needed. One Superintendent of the BM Reading Room defined the ideal holder of his post as a 'combination of scholar, a gentleman, a police-constable and a boatswain's mate'.

But we should not forget the advice of G. W. Horner, the fruit of many years' experience in Westminster Reference Library in the heart of London: 'There is some evidence that . . . the public reference or reading room, crowded, anonymous, purposeful, and pacific, is a setting of therapeutic value'. A point that always needs to be borne in mind in any service profession is that the actual demand for a specific form of assistance, in this case a request for information, may cloak another form of need entirely, often emotional. In practice this sometimes means for the librarian that in a certain sense it is not the actual question that matters, provided that the response satisfies the enquirer's need. As Barron Holland has rightly said, these 'are really pleas for understanding and personal involvement . . . and may or may not involve reference to information sources as well'. Of course, here we are at the outer edge of reference work as such, but librarians should at least be aware that people frequently find counsel and support and encouragement more effective than the supply of specific information to solve their problems.

## Evaluation of reference work
Surveys of the opinions of users who have actually asked questions have consistently shown a very high level of satisfaction with the response they get: percentage scores in the high 80s and in the 90s are commonplace. Rothstein's conclusion in 1964 was that 'the results could hardly have been bettered by paying for testimonials'. Many others besides Rothstein suspected the truth of these figures for years, despite their derivation from the users themselves, and gradually the truth has emerged. As Sydney Pierce explained, 'client satisfaction is a highly questionable indicator of the quality of service. . . . Though the users may be the best judges of the librarian's skills in interpersonal interaction (even here, question negotiation skills are problematic), they are notoriously poor judges of the quality of information received.' It is possible to argue that if they were in a position to assess the accuracy or completeness of an answer to a question, they probably would not have needed to ask it in the first place. Even more significantly, in Douglas L. Zweizig's words, 'experience with such measures of "user satisfaction" shows that what is being measured by such questions ["Did you find the service helpful?"] is not the quality of service but the desire of users to be polite'. This was perfectly illustrated in Herbert Goldhor's

survey of reference questions in the Urbana (Illinois) Public Library: 'The 100 patrons were also asked if they were satisfied with the answer they got. . . . The predominant impression received from the answers . . . include gratitude for the service rendered, frequent expressions of appreciation for the lengths to which staff would go, and a desire to make clear that any unfavorable experience was more the fault of the patron (and his/her question) than that of the library.' Many other studies have borne this out: indeed instances are to be found where users have expressed their satisfaction with answers that, unknown to them, are actually wrong.

If reliance cannot be placed on evaluation by the users, why not seek the opinion of the other party to the reference transaction, the reference librarians, who, according to Edward B. Reeves and his colleagues in 1977, 'are in a position to make the most insightful appraisal of reference activities'? The obstacle here too is the inherently improbable results in the reported surveys of librarians' self-evaluation: again Rothstein reported that 'The percentage of questions to which reference librarians claim to have found satisfactory answers . . . is consistently very high'. Scores were found of 96%, 91%, 88%, 97%, and in 1950 the Los Angeles Public Library staff reported a success rate of 99.71%.

As a matter of fact, it has been suggested over many years that perhaps reference work cannot be evaluated: 'Reference service is so greatly a matter of variables and intangibles that attempts to evaluate . . . are rather baffling' (Joseph L. Wheeler and Herbert Goldhor, 1962); 'Measuring the immeasurable' (Ruth White, 1972); 'The imposition of any measure on reference service is an unnatural act' (Zweizig, 1984). While it is probably true that the rule will never be laid on what Mary W. George has called its 'infinite, unpredictable variety . . . unlimited creativity . . . one-to-one idiosyncratic nature', the pressures of accountability over the last decade or so have reinforced Rothstein's 1964 warning: 'reference librarians, in failing to provide the means for accurate judgment on their place and contribution in library service, run the serious risk of having their work undervalued or ignored. . . . A harsh fact of library life seems to be that if it cannot be counted, it does not count.'

But if the totality of the process cannot be assessed, are there parts of it that can, such as the correctness of the response, or the librarian's negotiation skills, or attitudes towards the user? And if measures of user satisfaction are dubious and librarians' self-evaluation scores are implausible, could a third party undertake the task? The use of an independent assessor to observe actual reference service was suggested as long ago as 1945 by Lowell A. Martin, but this is very time consuming: each response has to be scrutinized individually for accuracy, completeness, etc., and there is a very high dross rate, that is to say a high proportion of what is observed is irrelevant for the purpose of evaluation. Indeed, most investigators agree with Lancaster: 'On the whole, then, the best way to evaluate question-answering services is through some form of simulation'.

This means asking test questions. But if reference librarians know they are being tested, they might change their behaviour, and thus achieve test scores that would not be typical. Many would try harder, search rather more carefully than usual, take somewhat longer, give up less easily. Some, on the other hand, may be so nervous that they would perform worse than normal. In either case, the overt artificiality could contaminate the test results. While a number of such studies have been undertaken, it is to overcome some of these problems that investigators over the last 25 years or so have developed the alternative strategy of asking questions without letting the librarians know that they were being tested: a team of anonymous 'proxies', very often library school students, pose as genuine enquirers and visit libraries or telephone them to ask the test questions. Because this does not obtrude on the normal reference process, it is known as 'unobtrusive' testing, a technique borrowed from the social scientists, where it has been used for many years, for example by consumer groups to test services in shops, banks, garages, etc. Indeed, in some of the earliest library tests the proxies were described as 'anonymous shoppers'. They were described in different terms by some of the reference librarians once they found out: 'snoop groups' was one of the politest.

It would not be an overstatement to say that when the results of the earliest unobtrusive surveys were published, they sent a shock wave through the profession. Terence Crowley and Thomas A. Childers were the first to apply the method in their doctoral dissertations of 1968 and 1970 (published in 1971): they discovered – and survey after survey in the United States and elsewhere was to replicate their results – that reference librarians were providing correct answers to only about half the questions asked. Over 40 such investigations have now been completed, usually in public and academic libraries and mostly in the United States, but also in England, Australia, Canada, New Zealand, and Germany. Lancaster has summed up the sober findings: 'all the studies have something important in common: they show that the user

177

of a library faces a surprisingly low probability that his factual question will be answered accurately. Overall, the studies tend to support a probability in the range of 50 to 60%, with some libraries or groups of libraries doing much worse than this, and a few doing rather better.' Others have not been so judicious, with charges of 'Half-right reference', and the formulation of the '55% rule'. It is perhaps worth noting at this point Kenneth D. Crews' comment in 1988 that the results from similar *obtrusive* studies reveal 'only slightly higher accuracy rates even when librarians know that the questions are part of a research study'.

As Lancaster was careful to say, these results relate (in the main) to answers given in response to fact-finding questions, where a correct and complete answer can be unequivocally specified. Examples include the boiling point of pure ethyl alcohol, the word that means 'irrational fear of noise', the author of the poem 'The revolt of Islam', the date when Gaddafi took over Libya, the derivation of the name of the Gallup poll, the meaning of Lex Talionis, the date when the first working steam engine was patented, the number of divorces in the UK in 1983, the name of the Secretary of State for Transport, the name of the currency of Poland. While questions such as these are certainly common in all types of libraries, they by no means represent the whole of reference work, and thus the results of many unobtrusive tests have been challenged, for example by Ian Douglas: 'I would argue that the uniformity of the results is as much an artifact of the methodology as the quality of reference services offered by libraries. . . . I am not satisfied that any of the sets of queries can be considered an acceptable sample of queries actually asked of reference services.' It also has to be said that the query samples are usually small: 10 would be a typical number, but many surveys have used fewer, occasionally only one or two. But considerable care is taken to ensure that the queries are typical of those that might be asked any day of the week in the libraries under scrutiny – usually they are actual queries, taken from library records – and are indeed answerable from their collections.

It is probably as inevitable in the field of reference work as in any other comparable service that you start by measuring those things that are easiest to measure, even though they are not necessarily the most important things: the very earliest such attempts were no more than simple counts of the number of questions asked. In 1977 Ellen Hoffmann warned that 'The constant danger is that we will evaluate what's visible and quantifiable rather than what's essential'. Some investigators have in fact gone beyond simple fact-finding and have tried material-finding enquiries: the first survey in England, by David E. House in 1974, asked for 'all available information on David Shepherd, the artist known for his paintings of African wild life'. But the scores were even lower: 'Twelve libraries out of the twenty . . . were able to produce no information at all'. Others have followed, but in the absence with such questions of a simple measure of 'correctness', more elaborate methods of scoring have had to be devised, such as the five-point scale used by Janine Schmidt, ranging from 'Fully correct answer. Several sources or types of sources used. All aspects of the question have been covered in the answer' to 'No sources consulted. No suggestions made'.

Even more ambitious have been the attempts to use unobtrusive testing to evaluate the negotiating skills of librarians and their attitudes to users. Marilyn Von Seggern has written at some length of 'the difficulty of studying the reference desk interview, which is usually brief and conducted without an appointment, in a public setting and while moving freely within an area. Moreover, an attempt to evaluate an entity as variable and complex as the reference interview, practised in numerous styles and approaches by reference librarians of all levels of expertise, risks all the criticisms of qualitative evaluation. Yet, because it is at the very heart of the contact between patron and librarian, the interview bears scrutiny if consistently high-quality reference service is of concern.'

One method tried with some success is to use test questions that are incomplete in some way and therefore need to be negotiated. Childers used such 'escalator' questions in 1978 and 1980 and he found that irrespective of how general the initial question was, in 67% of the cases no attempt was made to probe further, and in only 20% of instances did the librarian reach the final negotiation step. As already quoted in Chapter 4, in the 1983 survey of Maryland public libraries 12 of the 40 test questions asked in 60 libraries (i.e., 720 out of 2,400) were of this kind. Analysis by Ralph Gers and Lillie J. Seward showed plainly: 'The behaviour most strongly associated with correctness of answers received is questioning the user to discover *specifically* what his/her question is'. In only 49% of the cases was the user's question probed in this way; the survey found that 'there was no instance of a user receiving a correct answer when the librarian failed to elicit the specific question'.

Though a *sine qua non*, getting the answer right is not the whole of reference work: what might be recorded as a 'success' should perhaps be judged a failure if, for example, the user is made to feel a nuisance.

It is now well known, as has been noted in Chapter 4, that the attitude of the librarian plays a key role when users come to assess the service they receive; indeed, there is evidence that some pay it more heed than the intellectual response. Library school students unobtrusively observing 266 reference interviews were found by Joan C. Durrance in 1989 to be 'far more forgiving when library staff members had weak interviewing skills or gave inaccurate answers than they were if the staff member made them feel uncomfortable, showed no interest, or appeared to be judgmental about the question'. From Martin's pioneer survey of Chicago Public Library in 1969 right up to the present, a number of investigators have attempted to take into account the librarian's personal approach to users, perhaps by asking the observers to note whether the response was polite/impolite, friendly/unfriendly, helpful/unhelpful, interested/not interested, and sometimes to add their own comments. A 1979 survey of five United States academic libraries gave a positive rating for 61.7% of the respondents and a negative rating for 38.3%. A 1980 survey of 100 public library service points in Kent found that while almost all replies were polite, only a quarter were polite and friendly and helpful. Obviously, findings of this kind are highly subjective, but the technique does reveal some extraordinary responses, now recorded for posterity in the literature: 'I'm too busy to answer questions like that'; 'This is going to take a hell of a lot of time and we may not be able to find it'; 'We've had this question before and we've spent a lot of time trying to answer it and couldn't't'; 'I have no idea and I can't think of any books in the library that would cover it'; 'There's nothing in the catalogue. If you don't know an author, it's like looking for a needle in a haystack'; 'Come and look at an encyclopaedia'; 'We don't do research like that'; 'College libraries only do reference work that takes a minute or two'; 'You've got the wrong number, this is a public library'.

Such conspicuous disclosure of what some librarians undoubtedly regard as private conversations raises an ethical question that troubles many, quite apart from the issue of injured pride. More generally, the surreptitious nature of unobtrusive testing inevitably requires a degree of deception, with the questioners not only pretending to be genuine enquirers, but usually coming equipped with a 'rationale' – more bluntly, a cover story, obviously false – in case they are questioned further. Evelyn H. Daniel has put the other side of the case: 'Surely any professional operating in the public arena can have no objection to being observed or even tested if it does not interfere with the

180

performance of primary tasks. ... As a researcher, I believe that any technique that causes no harm to human subjects and that has a high probability of securing reliable and valid data is a suitable technique.' And in any case, as Childers pointed out very early, the results are used to evaluate institutions not individuals; indeed, individuals are never identified.

Lancaster has long argued for microevaluation, looking more closely into the reasons for the results: 'the greatest value of these types of analyses . . . lies in their diagnostic possibilities . . . to identify weaknesses and sources of failure and to lead to corrective actions designed to improve future performance'. The techniques of failure analysis have already been mentioned; the other main approach is statistical. It has often been suggested, for example, that lack of time is one of the reasons for the poor showing of librarians, particularly in cases where probing of the question is necessary. But statistical analysis of the research findings does not support this: as Crews has summarized, 'These studies show that librarians needed only five minutes or so per question – whether successfully answered or not. Within those few minutes, librarians can negotiate, deliver information, and ask a follow-up question to confirm the patron's satisfaction.'

Another statistical approach is to try to relate success rates to institutional variables such as the size of the reference collection or the materials budget or the qualifications of the reference staff – in other words to compare outputs with inputs. There had been a fairly widespread assumption that, in the words of Ronald R. Powell, one of the first actually to put it to the test in his 1976 PhD dissertation, 'the quality of a library's service is strongly related to the quantifiable resources of that same library'. In a survey of 60 Illinois public libraries he found support for his main hypothesis that 'the greater the number of volumes in a library's reference collection the greater the percentage of reference questions that the library's reference staff would be able to answer correctly'. Some later studies have confirmed this, and some have not. Vaughan P. Birbeck's 1986 survey of 24 English public libraries found that 'size tends to be the factor affecting the number of correct answers a library gives – the large libraries answer more questions correctly than smaller libraries'. But he found the results inconclusive for other independent variables he studied: the number of professional posts, total bookstock, expenditure on books, and total expenditure. The most detailed statistical analysis so far is that following the Maryland survey, when 11 variables were compared. Gers and

Seward reported that 'The amount of resources has only a very slight association with the accuracy of answers. ... The variables that appear to make a difference in performance are *behaviors that are within the control of the individual librarian* providing the service.' As noted above, the behaviour most strongly associated with correctness of answers is probing the question, but others include showing interest in the user's question, being comfortable with the question, and following up by enquiring 'Does this answer your question?'. Drawing on these findings, they went on to develop a 'training package for the purpose of increasing the level of correct responses' incorporating 'model reference behaviors'. After attending a three-day intensive workshop, staff from two of the libraries improved their performance from 42.5% to 97.5% and from 70% to 92.5%.

It has to be said, however, that practical applications such as this are rare. A 1984 citation study by Alvin M. Schrader, who attempted to measure the impact of unobtrusive testing, found that it had 'not yet become a component of the standard methods for evaluating library and information service performance' but had 'remained in the realm of methodological tools for research'. In 1990 Peter Hernon and Charles R. McClure, joint authors of the most detailed study of unobtrusive testing, wrote that 'Our experience suggests that while there is much discussion about the evaluation of reference services, *actual* formal evaluation (regardless of type of evaluation), overall, occurs much less frequently'.

Very early Crowley remarked in his 1968 dissertation that 'There is probably little doubt that for many inquiries the respondent is the key element'. Twenty years on and 40 surveys later Hernon and McClure had reached a similar conclusion: 'Performance on a question is obviously related to individual interests and ability to resolve information needs'.

**The art of reference work**
Despite the increasing systematization of the field and the advance of information technology, there is still widespread agreement among its practitioners that in virtually all its aspects reference work remains an art. Attentive readers of this book will have been left in no doubt on the matter. Bunge has cited a *Reader's digest* quotation to the effect that 'the difference between art and science is that science is what we understand well enough to explain to a computer, and art is everything else'. If, as Jahoda told us, 'we do not really know how reference

librarians perform their task', then he was right to conclude that 'Reference work is still largely an art'. And if Barbara M. Robinson was correct when she said that 'There are no simple formulae which standardize the level of reference resources and effort required to address the multitude of questions received from a wide variety of clientele', then she was also accurate in her verdict that 'Reference is really an art, not a science'.

## Discipline and theory

Reference work is likely to remain an art for at least as long as one of its central elements, human communication, resists complete systematization. But it has long been a hope of reference librarians that with the application of sufficient thought, based on experience and close observation in the field, their work and their art may emerge as a worthy discipline, or branch of learning.

As S. D. Neill has explained, 'A theory of reference will answer the question "Why is the reference process the way it is?"'. This is no easy task and the profession has been ill-served in the past by its expositors and would-be theoreticians: its extensive literature of thousands of papers and books is swollen by a mass of the trite, the transient and the trivial. It is often asserted, for instance, that there is no theory of reference work. Such declarations are usually to be found somewhere in the first few paragraphs of the dozens of papers that then go on to propound yet another new theory of reference work. As Louis Shores pointed out with some feeling, 'The most that dissenters should say is that the theory is bad'. And Neill would add that 'even a weak theory . . . is useful'. More seriously to be regarded are those who argue that no theory is necessary, that reference work is merely a practical skill – of a high-grade kind, to be sure – but a mere dexterity, a mental facility, acquired by practice. Such a stance appears to ignore the many warnings to the effect that theory without practice may be sterile, but practice without theory is blind. And, as Kurt Lewin the social psychologist once said, there is nothing so practical as a good theory.

The root of the problem is the same as it was in 1942 when McColvin wrote 'The nature of the various types of reference work has not yet been understood'. By 1958 Foskett had found little change to report: 'The truth is that we have not arrived at the basic principles of reference service, though many librarians and scientists have written about the procedures they use themselves'. All that John W. Berry could add by 1985 was that 'One fact emerges from all reference services studies in recent years – we simply do not yet know enough about the reference process to fully understand its subtleties and complexities'. Neill has recently spelled out the difficulty: 'Because much of the reference process is subjective, the patterns are hard to find, and much is hidden, as it is mental work which does not always show clearly in verbal and non-verbal behavior'.

The essentials of a good, i.e. valid, theory or organizing principle of reference work are that it should be comprehensive, in the sense that all the parts are described and every last element of the process accounted for, and that it should also form a coherent whole, unifying the field of learning. It should be drawn from the philosophy developed in the discipline over the years and should embody universal principles, i.e. generalizations applicable to every reference encounter, which will, in effect, allow predictions to be made. It should elucidate actual practice, of both the reference librarian and the enquirer. It must be couched in terms that pertain to the discipline of library and information science, and not some other subject field. It should not only reflect the present but should also have the capacity to stimulate new concepts and theories and suggest further lines of research or investigation – in other words, express what ought to be as well as what is.

Perhaps the immediate way forward is to develop not one universal model but a series of partial context-dependent models mirroring different aspects of the process, looking at it in different lights and from different angles. It may well be the case that human behaviour is too complex to reduce to universal laws, but research studies over the last decade or so, particularly from the United States and Canada, give grounds for cautious optimism. Neill is surely right to hope that 'There will come a time when we are so sure we know the what and how of reference that we can concentrate on an overall comprehensive theory'. The impact of vigorous new minds on this venerable craft continues to leave a clear mark on the way the profession regards this most personal of the librarian's roles. Investigation, study and reflection have confirmed for even the most experienced practitioners that their skills are indeed firmly rooted in those humane and theoretic principles underpinning their discipline of which they were always instinctively aware. Such recognition and acknowledgement cannot but illuminate and improve the practice of the art, which in its turn will lead to the more effective solution of the information problems of individual enquirers, which, it must never be forgotten, is the sole aim of practical reference work.

*Further reading*

Birbeck, Vaughan P. and Whittaker, Kenneth A., 'Room for improve
ment: an unobtrusive testing of British public library reference
service', *Public library journal*, **2**, 1987, 55 – 60.

Hernon, Peter and McClure, Charles R., *Unobtrusive testing and library
reference services*, Norwood, NJ, Ablex Publishing Co., 1987.

Neill, S. D., 'Can there be a theory of reference?', *Reference librarian*,
**18**, 1987, 7 – 19.

Williams, Roy, 'An unobtrusive survey of academic library reference
services', *Library and information research news*, **10** (37 & 38), 1987,
12 – 40.

Douglas, Ian, 'Reducing failures in reference service', *RQ,* **28**, 1988,
94 – 101.

Kemp, Jan and Dillon, Dennis, 'Collaboration and the accuracy
imperative: improving reference service now', *RQ,* **29**, 1989, 62 – 70.

Von Seggern, Marilyn, 'Evaluating the interview', *RQ,* **29**, 1989,
260 – 5.

Burton, Paul F., 'Accuracy of information provision', *Journal of
librarianship*, **22**, 1990, 201 – 15.

# Books on reference work

The following brief list of recommended books with a substantial reference work content is arranged in chronological order. The scope of some of them is wider than reference work as strictly defined in this volume, but in each the subject is treated at some length. Even the earliest contain much that the student will still find useful.

Wyer, James I., *Reference work: a textbook for students of library work and librarians*, Chicago, American Library Association, 1930.

Butler, Pierce (ed.), *The reference function of the library*, Chicago, University of Chicago, 1943.

Hutchins, Margaret, *Introduction to reference work*, Chicago, American Library Association, 1944.

Ranganathan, S. R., *Reference service*, 2nd ed., London, Asia, 1961 (1st ed. 1940).

Galvin, Thomas J., *Problems in reference service: case studies in method and policy*, New York, Bowker, 1965.

Grogan, Denis J., *Case studies in reference work*, London, Bingley, 1967.

Linderman, Winifred B. (ed.), *The present status and future prospects of reference/information service*, Chicago, American Library Association, 1967.

Galvin, Thomas J., *Current problems in reference service*, New York, Bowker, 1971.

Grogan, Denis J., *More case studies in reference work*, London, Bingley, 1972.

Kumar, Suseela, *The changing concepts of reference service*, Delhi, Vikas, 1974.

Grogan, Denis J., *Practical reference work*, London, Bingley, 1979.

Davinson, Donald, *Reference service*, London, Bingley, 1980.

Jahoda, Gerald and Braunagel, Judith Schiek, *The librarian and reference queries: a systematic approach*, New York, Academic Press, 1980.

Thomas, Diana M. and others, *The effective reference librarian*, London, Academic Press, 1981.

Murfin, Marjorie E. and Wynar, Lubomyr R., *Reference service: an annotated bibliographical guide*, Littleton, CO, Libraries Unlimited, 1977. *Supplement, 1976 – 1982*, 1984.

Grogan, Denis J., *Grogan's case studies in reference work*, London, Bingley, 1987, 6 vols.

Katz, William A., *Introduction to reference work: volume II Reference services and reference processes*, 5th ed., New York, McGraw-Hill, 1987. (1st ed. 1969, 2nd ed. 1974, 3rd ed. 1978, 4th ed. 1982). (The five editions of this work differ considerably, and many chapters of the first four editions are by no means superseded by the fifth.)

Bopp, Richard E. and Smith, Linda C. (eds.), *Reference and information services: an introduction*, Englewood, CO, Libraries Unlimited, 1991.

# Index

This is an index to subjects treated and authors mentioned in the text and the introduction.

Dolan, Donna R.   68, 129, 137
Donovan, William   99
Douglas, Ian   178, 185
Drinkwater, Claire B.   141
Dubois, C. P. R.   135
Duckett, Bob   61, 62, 67
Dudgeon, Matthew S.   163
Duncan, C. B.   2
Dunn, Elizabeth Bramm   20, 132
Durrant, Joan C.   73, 95, 98,
    99, 180
Dwyer, James R.   121
Dykstra, Gail   169

Eadie, Tom   21, 35
education of reference librarians
    33, 59, 61, 62, 67, 88,
    99, 107, 116, 166, 182
education of users see bibliographic
    instruction
Edwards, Edward   25
Eichman, Thomas Lee   72 – 3
Einstein, Albert   64
electronic mail, enquiries by   47
end-user searching   19, 57 – 8,
    58 – 9, 138 – 40
enquirers see users
enquiries   34, 52 – 3, 56, 63
  categories of   36 – 45, 47
  competition, puzzle, quiz
    14, 161 – 2
  context of   79 – 80, 82
  genealogical   14, 42 – 3, 159
  incomplete   65, 71 – 5
  legal and medical   167 – 8
  length of   100 – 1
  second-hand   82 – 3
  sporting   159
  telephone   14, 15, 21, 47, 83,
    94, 121, 125, 155, 160
  to newspapers, radio stations
    93 – 4
  trivial   160 – 2
  unacceptable   14, 151, 159 – 62
  unanswerable   43 – 5, 159, 173
  unanswered   125, 159
  unasked   92 – 4

unreasonable   160
ethics   14, 15 – 16, 79, 91, 140,
    149 – 52, 158, 165, 180 – 1
Euster, Joan R.   20
evaluation of reference work   3,
    64, 89 – 90, 95, 98, 166,
    169, 175 – 82, 185 see also
    user satisfaction
evaluation by librarian of
    responses   54, 162 – 6
experience, importance of   1 – 2,
    110, 111, 114, 124, 127,
    170, 173
expert systems   3, 142 – 4, 152,
    153
explanation of responses   157 – 8,
    162, 167 – 8
external sources of information
    125, 169, 170

facet analysis   116 – 17
fact-finding enquiries   38 – 9,
    41, 42, 45, 110, 111, 130,
    131, 178
  responses to   155
failure analysis   56, 64, 172 – 3,
    181
Fairthorne, Robert   155
Falk, Stephen   12
fallacies, popular   157 – 8
family history enquiries   14,
    42 – 3, 159
Farley, Judith   149, 150, 174
fax enquiries   47
Fazle Kabir, A. F. M.   19
Feldman, Susan E.   149
Feldman, Tony   132
Felicetti, Barbara White   68
Fenichel, Carol H.   138
Ferguson, Charles   34
Fastinger, Leon   77
Fisher, David P.   5, 12
Fitt, Stephen D.   106, 108
Flatness, Gail   150
Fleming, Hugh   17
flow charts   11, 55, 172
Forster, Margaret   91

192

Foskett, Douglas J. 30, 76, 114, 116, 119, 128, 150, 151, 163, 183
Foster, W. E. 60, 93
Francillon, Mary 8
free-lance librarians *see* information brokers
Freeman, Marilla Waite 83
Friend, Linda 59

Gaines, Ervin J. 149
Galsworthy, John 12
Galvin, Thomas J. 186
Gebhard, Patricia 169
genealogical enquiries 14, 42 – 3, 159
generalization of enquiries by users 71 – 3
geographical constraints 83 – 4, 133
George, Mary W. 114, 176
Gers, Ralph 64, 179, 181 – 2
Gibbs, Sally E. 96
Gillis, Trisha 99
Gloag, John 29
Goffman, Erving 73
Goldhor, Herbert 23, 36, 175 – 6, 176
Gore, Daniel 16
government libraries 48, 118, 162
Gray, Richard A. 119
Green, Samuel Swett 24, 27, 33, 70, 99, 150, 151, 160, 167, 170
Greguras, Fred M. 141
Grogan, Denis J. 152, 186, 187
Guild, Reuben A. 24 – 5

Hansel, Patsy J. 169
Harris, Roma M. 105
Harrison, Robert 25
Harter, Stephen P. 134, 138, 139, 140, 172
Hartley, R. J. 140, 153
Hatchard, Desmond B. 90
Hauptman, Robert 34, 66, 151, 152

Hayes, Robert M. 19
Hernon, Peter 147, 182, 185
heuristics 110, 114, 142
Hewart, Gordon, *Lord* 23
Hieber, Caroline E. 172
Hildreth, Charles R. 121, 152
Hill, M. W. 146, 163, 164, 165 – 6
Hinckley, Ann T. 34, 36, 124
history of reference work 1, 4, 23 – 8, 49
Hitchingham, Eileen 130
Hock, Randolph E. 137
Hodges, Julia E. 5
Hoffman, Ellen 178
holdings transactions 9, 37 – 8
Holland, Barron 175
Holland, Maurita Peterson 131
Holler, Frederick 10
Holmes, Oliver Wendell 78
Hoover, Ryan E. 84
Hopkins, Frances L. 18, 35
Horn, Roger 49, 156
Horner, George W. 78, 83, 175
House, David E. 179
Housman, A. E. 112
human element in reference work 2, 3, 22 – 3, 33, 39, 51, 56, 60, 64 – 5, 172 *see also* interpersonal communication; personal attributes of the reference librarian
Hurych, Jitka 57
Hutchins, Margaret 5, 61, 99, 112, 148, 186
Huxley, T. H. 38 – 9

identification, bibliographical 38, 131
image of the librarian 11 – 13, 35, 97
inarticulate users 63, 74
incomplete enquiries from users 65, 71 – 5
index entries in searching 9, 112, 115 – 17, 133 *see also* wording of enquiries

repackaging of responses in 164
staff information files in 125
therapeutic role of 175
unacceptable enquiries in 14, 159
unobtrusive tests in 177, 179, 180, 181
*see also* community information services
puzzle enquiries 14, 161 – 2

queries *see* enquiries
question analysis and taxonomy 3, 45 – 9, 65, 74, 75, 127
questions by reference librarian 71, 80 – 2, 106, 108
questions from users *see* enquiries
quick-reference computer searching 85, 130 – 2, 139, 152
quick-reference enquiries 38 – 9
Quint, Barbara 59 – 60
quiz enquiries 14, 161 – 2

Radford, Marie L. 102 – 3, 109
Radford, Neil A. 17, 20, 35
radio stations, enquiries made to 93
Radlow, James 144
Raitt, David I. 19, 132, 138
Ranganathan, S. R. 8, 21, 23, 28, 33, 116, 146, 186
Rast, Elaine K. 120
reaction against psychology in reference work 106 – 8
readers *see* users
readers' advisory service 2
ready-reference computer searching 85, 130 – 2, 139, 152
ready-reference enquiries 38 – 9
Rees, Alan M. 50, 138
Reeves, Edward B. 176
'reference librarian' (term) 27
reference materials 10, 28 – 9, 65, 110, 118, 120, 158
categories of 122 – 3, 127
history of 26 – 7
inadequacies of 172

indexes to 115
searching 88
*see also* bibliographies
'reference process' (term) 50
'reference service' (term) 2
'reference work' (term) 1, 2, 28 – 33, 50
referral 48, 125, 143, 162, 168, 168 – 70, 173
Reilly, Jane A. 20
relevance of responses 170 – 1
reluctant users 15, 90, 95
repackaging of responses 162 – 4
requests *see* enquiries
research enquiries 42 – 3
residual enquiries 43
responses 54, 55
categories of 154 – 85
negative 14, 43 – 5, 125, 151, 159 – 62, 173 – 4
specification of required 82 – 4, 171
speed of 83, 146
Rettig, James 21, 51
Richardson, John, *Jr.* 153
Riechel, Rosemarie 60, 61, 137
Robbins, Jane 97
Roberts, Justine 139
Roberts, Norman 161
Robinson, Barbara M. 46, 49, 79, 183
Robinson, Otis Hall 15, 16, 24, 70
Rogers, Will 70
Roose, Tina 85
Rosenblum, Joseph 107
Ross, Catherine Sheldrick 79, 87, 102, 108
Roszak, Theodore 135 – 6
Rothstein, Samuel 7, 13, 16, 23, 24, 98, 107, 121, 150, 152, 161, 175, 176
Rouse, Sandra H. 23
Rouse, William B. 23
Rubacher, Richard 98
Rugh, Archie J. 30, 107
Russell, Bertrand 23

200